Hot Springs and Hot Pools of the U.S.

Hot Springs and Hot Pools of the U.S.

Jayson Loam
David Bybee
Marjorie Gersh

AQUA THERMAL ACCESS

Hot Springs and Hot Pools of the U.S.

Copyright 1990 by Jayson Loam

First edition 1990

Cartography, design, layout and production by Jayson Loam

ISBN 0-9624830-0-1

Manufactured in the United States of America

Published by: Aqua Thermal Access
        3100 Erin Lane
        Santa Cruz, CA 95065

Grateful acknowledgements to:

Don Haaga for his original art direction and continuing influence; Tom Winnett, for his patience and cooperation; Evie Litton, who escorted Dave Bybee through the wilds of Idaho and shared her detailed manuscript on hiking trails to hot springs in the Pacific Northwest; Roger Phillips for sharing the distilled wisdom in back issues of the *Hot Springs Gazette*: Jayson's children, Gary, Mel, Randy and Melanie, who assisted again and again on the field research and in the production of photographs; Writer's Connection for computer production services; Jan Stiles for meticulous editing; the Santa Cruz firms of Lasersmith for print-outs, Graphic Services for photostats, Bay Photo for film processing, and Dancing Man Imagery, for PMT's; Lincoln Graphics of Santa Clara for separating and composing the color cover; Publishers Group West for assistance on the design of the overall project; everyone who has ever offered new information about any hot spring; and all of the subjects who so graciously consented to be photographed.

Photo Credits:

Marjorie Gersh, 6L, 7TR, 61R. Kathy Thurmond (Esalen Institute), 7BR, 206T. Gary Sohler, 12TL, 228, 232T, 232B, 256B, 257L 258L, 258R, 261, 265, 269, 270, 271. Arlington Hotel, 15L, 274L. Harrison Hotel, 15B. Hot Springs Hilton, 16CL, 274R. The Greenbrier, 17TR, 280L. Hot Springs Health Spa, 19TR, 272, 273TR, 272BL, 273BR. Sycamore Hot Springs, 19BR, 205TR. Ten Thousand Waves, 20CL, 259TL 259TR. Hot Tub Fever, 20BL. Jasper National Park, 28T, 29T. Nakusp Hot Springs, 35T. British Columbia Ministry of Forests, 41. David Bybee, 45, 57L, 61Bl, 67T, 83B, 85T, 86R, 111B, 112TR, 118, 120B, 122R, 169, 170L, 179L, 179BR, 183B, 184B, 185T, 187CL, 187BL, 190TR, 190BL, 191TL, 191TR, 191BR, 194L, 194R, 195L, 195R, 196T, 196B, 199T, 199BR, 202L, 203B, 206B, 236L, 246L, 251TL. Town Tubs and Massage, 46B, Wellspring, 46T. Robert Jacoby, 47R. Doe Bay Village Resort, 51T, 51R, 51L. J Bar L Ranch, 54T. Jerry Brown, 54B. Howard Holliday, 55B. Peter Moore, 70T. M. Vogel, 70B. Phil Wilcox, 121. Granite Creek Hot Springs, 138B. Desert Reef Beach Club, 152L. Box Canyon Motel, 157. Orvis Hot Springs, 158T, 158B, 159T, 158B. White Sulphur Springs, 174. Vichy Springs, 180L. Mono Hot Springs, 193L. California Hot Springs, 201. Wheeler Hot Springs, 202R. Different Soaks, 207. Lupin Naturist Resort, 208B. Realax/C.A.L.M., 210. Murietta Hot Springs Resort, 221R. Family Hot Tubs, 233L. Elysium Institute, 233R. "Skip" Hill, 237. Kachina Spa, 243. Splash, 259BR. Elms Resort, 275. East Heaven Tub Co., 277L, 277R. Gideon Putnam Hotel, 278T. Crystal Spa, 278B. Berkeley Hot Springs, 279TL, 279BL, 279TR. The Homestead, 280TR, 280BR. Jayson Loam, all others.

Front Cover:	Back Cover:	
Travertine Hot Springs Page 186	TL Glenwood Springs	Page 146
Photo by David Bybee	TC Valley View Springs	Page 152
	TR Indian Springs	Page 145
	BL Cedar Springs	Page 37
	Photos by Jayson Loam	

Dedication:
To the spirit that created All That Is,
especially hot springs.

Table Of Contents

Introductions / 6

Introduction

This is a book for people to use, not an academic discussion of geothermal phenomena. For me there is a special joy and contentment which comes from soaking in a sandy-bottom pool of flowing natural mineral water, accompanied by good friends and surrounded by the peaceful quiet of a remote, primitive setting. At such an idyllic moment it is hard to get overly concerned about geology, chemistry or history. In this book it is my intent to be of service to others who also like to soak in peace and who could use some help finding just the right place.

The cataclysmic folding and faulting of the earth's crust over millions of years is a fascinating subject, especially where geologic sources have combined just the right amount of underground water with just the right amount of earth core magma to produce a hot surface flow that goes on for centuries. It would probably be fun to research and write about all that, including new data on geothermal power installations, but that is not what this book is about.

Many hot springs have long histories of special status with Indian tribes which revered the healing and peace-making powers of the magic waters. Those histories often include bloody battles with "white men" over hotspring ownership, and there are colorful legends about Indian curses that had dire effects for decades on a whole series of ill-fated owners who tried to deny Indians their traditional access to a sacred tribal spring. That, too, would be an interesting theme for a book someday, but not this book.

In the 19th century it was legal, and often quite profitable, to claim that mineral water from a famous spa had the ability to cure an impressive list of ailments. Such advertising is no longer legal, and modern medicine does not include mineral water soaks, or drinks, in its list of approved treatments. Nevertheless, quite a few people still have an intuitive feeling that, somehow, spending time soaking in natural mineral water is beneficial. I agree with the conclusion that it is "good for you," but it would take an entire book to explore all the scientific and anecdotal material which would be needed to explain why. Someone else will have to write that book.

This book simply accepts the facts that hot springs do exist, that they have a history, and that soaking the human body in geothermal water does indeed contribute to a feeling of well-being. That still leaves several substantial, practical questions. "Where can I go to legally put my body in hot water, how do I get there, and what will I find when I arrive?" The purpose of this book is to answer those questions.

When I began to design the book, I had to decide which geothermal springs should be left out because they were not "hot." Based on my own experience, I picked 85º as the cut-off point and ignored any hot springs or hot wells below that level, unless a commercial operator at the location was using gas or steam to bump up the temperature of the mineral water.

The second decision I had to make was whether or not to include geothermal springs on property which was fenced and posted or otherwise not accessible to the public. There are a few hot spring enthusiasts who get an extra thrill out of penetrating such fences and soaking in "forbidden" mineral water. It was my conclusion that I would be doing my readers a major disservice if I guided them into a situation where they might get arrested or shot. Therefore, I do not provide a listing for such hot springs, but I do at least mention the names of many such well-known locations in the index, with the notation NUBP, meaning "not usable by the public."

And then there were several more pleasant

Skookumchuck Hot Springs: Volunteers piped in hot and cold water to this tank. Page 40.

Valley View Hot Springs: A natural hot spring which is close to ideal. Page 152.

decisions, such as whether or not to include drilled hot wells. Technically, they are not natural hot springs, but real geothermal water does flow out of them, so I chose to include them.

Within the last 30 years the radical idea of communal soaking in a California redwood hot tub filled with gas-heated tap water has grown into a multi-million dollar business. Thousands of residential tubs are installed every year, all the larger motels and hotels have at least one, and there are now dozens of urban establishments which offer private- space hot-tub rentals by the hour. I chose to include the rent-a-tub locations, which is why the book title is Hot Springs and Hot Pools of the U.S.

I have a personal prejudice against taking a shower with my socks on and against wearing clothes when I soak in a natural hot spring, or any hot pool, for that matter. At the same time, I am aware that a substantial portion of the population has an equally strong prejudice in favor of laws and regulations which require textile concealment in every social situation. It has been my experience that most "skinnydippers" do not intend to offend and therefore try to join others in safe places where they can be barefoot all over, while the "respectables" understandably try to avoid those places where "bares" might be encountered. For the benefit of both elements in the population, I chose to include information on the clothing requirements or customs at each location, insofar as those could be determined. For the special benefit of skinnydippers such as myself, I have included a selection of nudist parks and clothing-optional naturist resorts which have a hot pool. Most of them specifically prohibit the wearing of clothes in their pools.

Early on I realized that there is no such thing as a "typical" hot spring, and that there is no such thing as

a "typical" hot spring enthusiast. Some readers will have a whole summer vacation to trek from one remote, primitive hot spring to another. Others will be trying to make the most of a two week vacation, a long weekend, a Saturday, or a few hours after a hard day's work. Some readers will have a self-contained RV, while others will have only a family automobile; and still others must depend on air travel and airport transportation connections. Some readers will want to find skinnydippers, while other readers will want to avoid skinnydippers.

Whatever your schedule, transportation and modesty needs, this book is intended to help you make an informed choice and then get to the locations you have chosen.

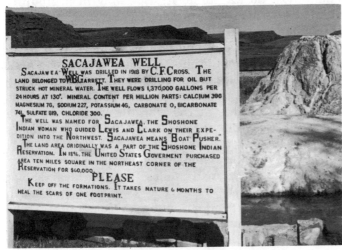

Fountain Of Youth: This hot well mineral formation looks like a hot spring. Page 133.

Esalen Institute: Ocean surf can be heard in these cliffside soaking pools. Page 206.

When I first discovered hot springs, my old and new values were waging an internal war. Therefore, I was fascinated by the Indian tradition of declaring a hot spring to be a neutral zone, devoted to peace and healing rather than conflict, and decided to follow their lead. How wonderful it is to immerse my body in a hot spring, or even in an urban hot tub, and declare it to be my personal neutral zone.

Gathering factual information for a book about hot springs required two summers and over 15,000 miles of travel through the western states and Canada. In the process it became my personal challenge to also make a subjective evaluation of which ones "felt the best", and to observe my mental impressions of the different kinds of people who frequent the springs.

At first, I applauded almost any type of geothermal soaking pool as being a gem of natural magic. As I

▲ "Big Hot" Warm Springs is a super combination of a gorgeous view and fun people. Page 23.

visited more and different springs I gradually acquired a strong preference for rustic hikes to primitive pools fed by flowing springs, and a strong prejudice against crowded commercial resorts and chlorinated pools. I noticed that some traditional resorts advertise the unique mineral analysis of their geothermal water, but I am more interested in the water being clean, comfortably warm and free of "rotten egg" odors. I especially enjoy those natural soaking pools located next to a creek where it is possible to adjust the water temperature by moving a few rocks.

During my travels I developed a theory about why natural non-commercial hot springs pools felt so much more relaxing than commercial resort pools. At the natural pools there is no need to "maintain an image," and almost no way to do it, especially in a group of skinnydippers. It always amazed me that sitting in the same pool might be a lawyer and his wife who had driven up from town in a Cadillac; a family touring in a motorhome; and a group traveling around the area on their motorcycles. Some of us were "barefoot all the way," others had on bathing suits. The diversity was complete. Yet, here in the warmth of the water we were all soaking together in peace. Everyone's harmonious presence complemented the quiet beauty of the remote natural hot-spring pools.

Although I live many miles from the nearest hot spring, I have the benefit of two local rent-a-tub facilities which offer outdoor communal tubs surrounded by trees, grass and flowers. Such an arrangement is indeed almost as good as the real thing. If you can't be at the pool you love, love the pool you're at.

Information

to you

Idaho has more non-commercial, difficult to reach, wilderness hot springs than any other state in the U.S. For those dippers who equally enjoy hiking and backpacking, we suggest that you look for a copy of Evie Litton's book, *HOT SPRINGS FOR HIKERS IN THE PACIFIC NORTHWEST,* which further details hot springs listed herein, plus others so remotely located that they are beyond the scope of this book. Send inquiries to:

Falcon Press
P.O. Box 1718
Helena, MT 59601

•••

The *Hot Springs Gazette* is a pioneering hot spring periodical. created ten years ago as an irreverent and irregular quarterly by Eric Irving. It features personal accounts of hot spring adventures sent in by subscribers, as well as colorful prose from Eric and from Roger Phillips, the current editor/publisher. Subscriptions, single copies and back issues are available. Send inquiries to:

Silvertip Publishing Co.
12 South Benton Ave.
Helena, MT 59601

•••

The **American Sunbathing Association** is a 50-year-old national nudist organization which is the U.S. representative in the International Naturist Federation.
The A.S.A. annually publishes a *Nudist Park Guide,* containing complete information about nudism and all of the local clubs and parks. The A.S.A. also publishes informational pamphlets which are free for the asking. Send your inquiry to:

A.S.A. Dept HS
1703 North Main St.
Kissimmee, FL 32743

•••

The Naturist Society, which was started as a free beach movement, has expanded its goals to include the legalization of nude swimming and sunbathing on designated public land, including parks and forests as well as beaches. It offers individual membership and publishes a quarterly journal about clothing-optional opportunities. If you would like to know more, address your inquiry to:

The Naturist Society, Dept. HS
P.O. Box 132
Oshkosh, WI 54902

•••

from you

We are satisfied that the information we have gathered into this guidebook is as complete and correct as possible at press time. However, we have learned that it is possible for us to make improvements with the cooperation of our readers. You can help in three ways:

1. Corrections: Despite repeated checking and proofreading, some errors do slip by into print. If you spot a mistake, please let us know so that we may correct it in the first reprint run.

2. Deletions and Additions: Most hot springs have a history of flowing consistently for centuries, but the ownership, and public access to, any one specific location may change several times in less than a decade. If you discover that a commercial hot spring location, or rent-a-tub establishment, described in this book is no longer open for business, let us know so that we can delete the entry from the next reprint run. If you find out that a closed location is reopening, or that a new business is starting up, send us the news so we can include it in the earliest revised edition. And if you know of a location which you believe should have been included in the book, but wasn't, tell us about it so we can check it out.

3. Revisions: Any successful business must continually reassess public demand and revise policies and facilities to accommodate changes. This is especially true in the merchandising of pools of mineral water and tubs of hot tap water. Therefore, it is inevitable that some of the descriptive information for some of the locations in this book will become at least partially obsolete. Sometimes, but not always, the owner of the location lets us know about such changes. If you notice that any of our descriptions needs to be revised to reflect changes at any specific location, please drop us a note to that effect.

We thank you in advance for your interest and cooperation. Such support from all readers will enable us to constantly improve future editions for the benefit of all readers. Send your information to:

ATA Directory Editor
Box 91
Soquel, CA 95073

1. Hot Springs Belong To Everyone

Jerry Johnson Hot Springs: A one-mile trail leads to this ideal hot spring. Page 77.

Long before "the white man" arrived to "discover" hot springs, the Indians believed that the Great Spirit resided in the center of the earth and that "Big Medicine" fountains were a special gift from the creator. Even during tribal battles over camping areas or stolen horses, it was customary for the sacred "smoking waters" to be a neutral zone where all could freely go to be healed of their wounds. Way back then, hot springs did indeed belong to everyone, and, understandably, we would like to believe that nothing has changed.

Most of us also have a mental picture of an ideal hot spring. It will have crystal clear water, of course, with the most beneficial combination of minerals, but with no slimy algae or rotten egg smells. Water temperature will be "just right" when you first step in, as well as after you have soaked for a while. It will occupy a picturesque rock-rimmed pool with a soft sandy bottom, divided into a shallow section for lie-down soaks and a deeper section for sit-up-and-talk soaks. Naturally, it will have gorgeous natural surroundings with grass, flowers and trees, plus an inspiring view of snow-capped mountains. The location will be so remote that you have the place to yourself, and can skinnydip if you choose, but not so remote that you might get too tired from a long hike. Finally, if you like to camp out, there will be a lovely campground with rest rooms conveniently nearby or, if you prefer more service, a superior motel/restaurant just a short drive down the road.

Oh yes, this ideal spring will also be located on public land and therefore belong to everyone, just like all of the other hot springs. That leaves only the problem of finding that ideal spring or, better yet, lots of them.

The "good book" for hot spring seekers is the Thermal Springs List of the United States, published by the National Oceanic and Atmospheric Administration and available through the NOAA Environmental and Data Service office in Boulder, Colorado. This publication contains nearly 1,500 entries, nearly all of them in the western states. For each hot spring entry, latitude, longitude, water temperature, and the name of the applicable USGS quadrangle map are specified. The list is accompanied by a nice big map, sprinkled with colorful location dots.

This impressive package of official information has prompted more than one desk-bound writer to reproduce or recommend this list, implying that there is a publicly-owned, freely available, idyllic, primitive hot spring under every dot; just pick your spot, buy your USGS map and go for it. Unfortunately, the real world of geothermal water is not quite that magical.

From that starting figure of 1,500, it is necessary to subtract the following (in round numbers): 500 which are not hot enough (less than 85º), 100 in Alaska and Hawaii (beyond the scope of this book) 150 in Yellowstone Park (not usable by the public), and 450 on non-commercial private property or otherwise not open to the public. That leaves 300, of which 200 are privately-owned commercial enterprises and only 100 are on public land, accessible without charge. The state of Idaho has more than half of that 100.

Space does not permit reporting all of the reasons why various springs on the NOAA list are NUBP (not usable by the public). In some cases the NOAA data is 50 or 100 years old, and the spring has simply ceased to flow due to earthquake or heavy irrigation pumping. Some springs have been capped and fed into municipal water systems or drowned by the construction of a water reservoir. The Yellowstone Park rules prohibit any entry into geothermal springs and even forbid entry into the runoff from a geothermal spring until after it has joined with a surface stream.

The largest single group of NUBP springs are those on private property. Under our public liability laws, a hot spring's owner is practically forced to either operate a commercial establishment or post the property with NO TRESPASSING signs. An owner who had graciously permitted free public use of a spring for years had a user hurt himself on the property, file suit against the owner and collect damages. An owner's only defense against such suits is to fence and post the property, then show that the injured person was trespassing and therefore not legally entitled to blame the owner for anything.

Owners whose hot spring property adjoins national forest land have an additional risk. If a fire starts on that property and spreads into the national forest, the property owner can be sued by the Forest Service for the total cost of fighting that fire. A cattle rancher with an attractive hot spring on his property also faces extra risks if he permits public access; he can expect to lose some livestock when thoughtless users leave gates open.

All of which adds up to the fact that only seven percent of the springs on that original list of 1,500 are publicly owned and freely usable. Fortunately, that final 100 includes a few wilderness beauties, as well as some forlorn ditches on barren slopes.

▲ *Firehole River at Midway Bridge*: Yellowstone Rangers banned public use in 1979. Page 141.

▲ *Leonards Hot Spring*: A typical volunteer-built rock-and-sand soaking pool. Page 169.

11

McCauley Hot Spring: The mineral water flow from this National Forest hot spring is collected into a large pond by a dam built by the CCC more than 50 years ago. Page 257.

Hot Tub Hot Spring: Volunteers built this soaking pool several yards from the 110º source spring. A gravity-flow hose is used to add more hot water whenever needed.

Olympic Hot Springs: This pond in Olympic National Park is the last remnant of a resort which burned decades ago. Page 49.

● Non-commercial Mineral Water Locations

On the key maps in this book and in each hot spring listing, a solid round dot ● is used to indicate a non-commercial hot spring, or hot well, where no fee is required. At a few remote locations, you may be asked for a donation to help the work of a non-profit organization which has a contract with the Forest Service to protect and maintain the spring.

The first paragraph of each listing is intended to convey the general appearance, atmosphere, and surroundings of the location, including the altitude, which can greatly affect the weather conditions. The phrase "open all year " does not mean that all roads and trails are kept open regardless of snowfalls or fire seasons. Rather, it means that there are no seasonally closed gates or doors, as at some commercial resorts.

The second paragraph describes the source and temperature of the mineral water and then conveys the manner in which that water is transported or guided to a usable soaking pool. "Volunteer-built pool" usually implies some crude combination of at-hand material such as logs, rocks and sand. If the situation requires that the water temperature be controlled, the method for such control is described. River-edge and creek-edge pools are vulnerable to complete washouts during high runoff months, so some volunteers have to start over from scratch every year.

The third paragraph identifies the overnight facilities available on the premises, or nearby, and states the approximate distance to a motel, RV park, restaurant, store, service station and all other services.

If needed, there is a final paragraph of directions, which should be used in connection with a standard state highway map and with any local area map which may be provided on the page near the listing.

Bonneville Hot Springs: Much of this warning applies to all hot springs. Page 112.

> **CAUTION**
> # NATURAL HOT SPRINGS
> - Water temperatures vary by site, ranging from warm to very hot . . . 180°F.
> - Prolonged immersion may be hazardous to your health and result in hyperthermia (high body temperature).
> - Footing around hot springs is often poor. Watch out for broken glass. Don't go barefoot and don't go alone. Please don't litter.
> - Elderly persons and those with a history of heart disease, diabetes, high or low blood pressure, or who are pregnant should consult their physician prior to use.
> - Never enter hot springs while under the influence of: alcohol, anti-coagulants, antihistamines, vasodilators, hypnotics, narcotics, stimulants, tranquilizers, vasoconstrictors, anti-ulcer or anti-Parkinsonian medicines. Undesirable side effects such as extreme drowsiness may occur.
> - Hot springs are naturally occurring phenomena and as such are neither improved nor maintained by the Forest Service.

To Bare Or Not To Bare

With regard to skinnydipping, you had best start with the hard fact that any private property owner, county administration, park superintendent or forest supervisor has the authority to prohibit "public nudity" in a specific area or in a whole forest or park. Whenever a ranger station has to deal with repeated complaints about nude bathers at a specific hot spring, it is likely that the area will be posted with NO NUDE BATHING signs, and you could get a citation without warning by ignoring them. In a few places the National Forest rangers may be tolerant of clothing-optional preferences, but the local county sheriff, especially one running for re-election, may decide to enforce a county ban on public nudity. Such county laws apply even within a National Forest.

The absence of NO NUDE BATHING signs does not necessarily imply an official clothing-optional policy. Posted signs may have been torn down, or a forest-wide ban on public nudity may have been adopted but never posted. In any case, the absence of a sign will at least give you the opportunity to explain that you had no desire to offend and that you are quite willing to comply with the rule, now that you know it exists.

At any unposted hot spring it is unlikely that you will be hassled for skinnydipping unless the officer is responding to a complaint. Therefore, your most important goal should be to make sure that there is no complaint. This means a high degree of consideration for other people, no matter who happened to get there first. You may be pleasantly surprised at the number of people who are willing to agree to a policy of clothing optional if, in a friendly manner, you offer them an opportunity to say yes.

If you are skinnydipping when other people arrive on the scene, do not wait for them to express their approval or disapproval. State your preference for a policy of clothing optional, which lets each person decide what to wear. If that is not acceptable to the newcomers, gracefully accept your need to wear clothing for as long as they remain. If you arrive on the scene and find clothed people in the pool, do not just strip and jump in. State your preference for a policy of clothing optional and ask for their agreement. If they choose not to agree, accept gracefully your need to remain clothed for as long as they are present.

The description of each remote hot spring includes a reference to the local bathing suit customs, insofar as they could be determined. Our purpose is to help both skinnydippers and suit-wearers to find like-minded friends. Our hope is that if both groups happen to occupy an unposted primitive hot spring simultaneously, they will make a sincere effort to accommodate each other. It would be a shame to spoil the quiet of natural beauty by invoking the harsh voice of the law.

 Big Caliente Hot Spring: To keep a permanent sign the Forest Service had to make it from metal and set it in concrete. Page 203.

Spence Hot Spring: Bare hippies and dressed townfolk clashed here in the 60s. This was a wise Forest Supervisor's solution. Page 256.

13

2. The Merchandising Of Mineral Water

Montezuma Hot Springs: The Victorian main building of this historic resort looms over dormitories and bathhouse ruins. Now under United World College ownership, some of the bathhouses are being restored and made available for use to the public. Page 259.

The Indian tradition of free access to hot springs was initially imitated by pioneering palefaces. However, as soon as mineral water was perceived to have some commercial value, the new settler's private property laws were invoked at most of the hot springs locations, and the Indians were herded off to reservations. After many fierce legal battles, and a few gun battles, some ambitious settlers were able to establish clear legal titles to the properties. Then it was up to the new owners to figure out how to turn their geothermal flow into cash flow.

Pioneering settlers dismissed as superstition the Indian's spiritual explanation of the healing power of a hot spring. However, those settlers did know from experience that it was beneficial to soak their bodies in mineral water, even if they didn't know why or how it worked. Commercial exploitation began when the legal owner of a hot spring first started charging admission, ending centuries of free access. Today, extracting a fee from the customer for the priviledge of bathing in hot mineral water is still the fundamental transaction in the business, but the fee you pay will seldom buy you an Indian-style soak, in a natural, free-flowing, sand-bottom hot spring in the wide open spaces. You are more likely to be offered a Victorian-style soak, in a one-person cast-iron tub in a small room in a men's or women's bathhouse, using mineral water piped in from a capped spring.

The shift from outdoor soaks to indoor soaks began when proper Victorian customers demanded privacy, which required the erection of canvas enclosures around the bathers in the outdoor spring. Then city dwellers, as they became accustomed to indoor plumbing and modern sanitation, were no longer willing to risk immersion in a muddy-edged squishy-bottom mineral spring, even if they believed that such bathing would be good for their health. Furthermore, they learned to like like their urban indoor comforts too much to trek to an outdoor spring in all kinds of weather. Instead, they wanted a civilized method for "taking the waters," and the great spas of Europe provided just the right model for American railroad tycoons and land barons to follow, and to surpass.

Around the turn of the century, American hot spring resorts fully satisfied the combined demands of Victorian prudery, modern sanitation, and indoor comfort by offering separate men's and women's bathhouses, with private porcelain tubs, marble shower rooms and central heating. A scientific mineral analysis of the geothermal water was part of

Glenwood Hot Springs Lodge: This successful resort met changing public demands by adding a new wing with hydropools, fitness centers, gift shops and a patio restaurant. Page 146.

Arlington Resort Hotel: This century-old landmark on Hot Springs Row continues to offer traditional bathhouse services, plus this new communal hydrojet pool . Page 274.

Harrison Hot Springs: A golf course and a lake with boat rentals supplement the indoor and outdoor mineral water pools, fitness centers, restaurants and shops offered by this famous Canadian resort. Page 38.

Carson Hot Springs (WA): Look for these traditional claw-footed bathtubs. Page 47.

The Arkansas *Hot Springs Hilton* offers modern tubs in its two bathhouses. Page 274.

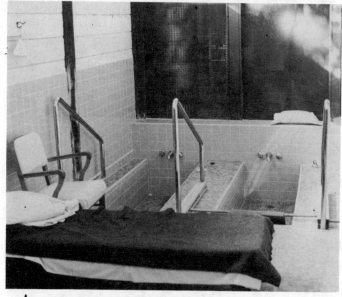

KAH-NEE-TA Vacation Resort installed tiled roman tubs in its bathhouses. Page 69.

every resort merchanidsing program, which included flamboyant claims of miraculous cures and glowing testimonial letters from medical doctors. Their promotion material also featured additional social amenities, such as luxurious suites, sumptuous restaurants, and grand ballrooms.

In recent decades, patronage of these resorts has declined and many have closed down because the traditional medical claims were outlawed and modern medical plans refuse to consider a soak in hot mineral water to be a valid treatment. A few of the larger resorts have managed to survive by adding new facilities such as golf courses, conference and exhibition spaces, fitness centers and beauty salons. The smaller hot spring establishments have responded to modern demand by installing larger (six persons or more) communal soaking tubs, and family-size soaking pools in private spaces for rent by the hour. Most locations continue to offer men's and women's bathhouse facilities in addition to the new communal pools, but some have totally discontinued the use of traditional one-person cast-iron tubs.

In addition to the privately-owned hot spring facilities, there are several dozen locations which are owned by federal, state, county or city agencies. In Canada, the National Parks System owns and staffs their geothermal installations. In the United States, the Parks Departments of states, counties and cities generally follow the same policy. However, installations in U.S. National Forests and National Parks are usually operated under contract by privately-owned companies. The nature and quality of the hot mineral water facilities offered at these publicly-owned, but commercially-operated, hot spring locations varies widely.

If some form of fee is charged, the location is designated as being commercial, regardless of who owns the property.

Carson Hot Springs (NV): These roman-style tubs are large enough for a group. Page 241.

■ Commercial Mineral Water Locations

On the key map in this book and in the hot spring listing, a solid square ■ is used to indicate a natural mineral water commercial location. A phone number and mailing address are provided for the purpose of obtaining current rates, additional information and reservations.

The first paragraph of each listing is intended to convey the general appearance, atmosphere and surroundings of the location, including the altitude. "Open all year" does not imply that the facility is open 24 hours of every day, only that it does not have a "closed" season.

This book is about hot springs and hot pools where you can legally put your body in hot water. Therefore, the second paragraph of each listing focuses on the water and the pools available at the location. It describes the origin and temperature of the mineral water; the means of transporting that water; the quantity, type and location of tubs and pools; the control of soaking water temperatures, and the chemical treatment used, if any. The listing for each hot spring does not include a scientific chemical analysis of the mineral water. Today, most hot spring soakers are more concerned about the amount of chlorine added to the water than about the minerals in the water as it comes out of the ground.

There actually are a few commercial locations where rare geothermal conditions make it possible for a customer, or several, to soak in a natural sand-bottom hot spring open to the sky. On the other hand, there are many commercial locations which still offer soaks only in the traditional one-person cast iron tubs in separate men's and women's bathhouses. Most commercial locations fall in between those two extremes, and offer a wide range of soaking

▲ In West Virginia, *The Greenbrier* has a two-hundred year history of tasteful facilities. This indoor pool has colorful tile, Grecian columns and decorator drapes. Page 280.

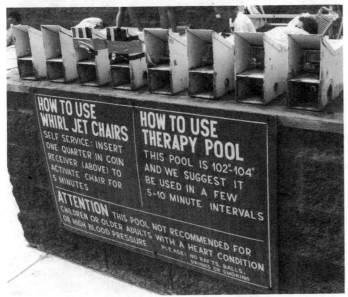

▲ At *Glenwood Hot Springs* a coin-operated machine sells bubbles in the pool. Page 146.

▲ *Downata Hot Springs*: This commercial spot is a typical community plunge. Page 97.

17

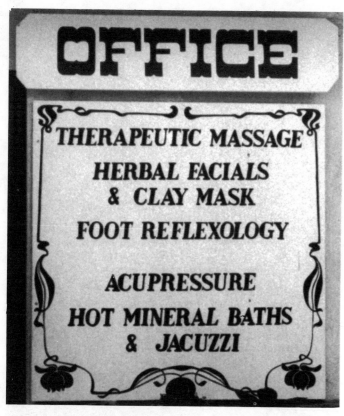

Roman Spa: Recently new therapies have been added to the traditional mineral baths offered by Calistoga resorts. Page 177.

Fountain of Youth Spa: This is the largest of several trailer parks built around hot wells. They all have winter sun and multiple mineral-water soaking pools. Page 217.

opportunities. Source hot springs are usually covered and the water carried away in pipes, so customers seldom get to see a real spring, much less soak in one. Instead, the water is piped to health-department-approved swimming pools, soaking pools and hydrojet pools, usually outdoors and available for communal coed use. At a few large resorts the swimming and soaking pools may be located indoors, and some locations offer hydropools in private spaces for rent by the hour. In the last decade several resorts have also constructed special motel suites, each containing its own hydrojet pool.

In all states, health department standards require a minimum treatment of public pool water with chlorine, bromine or the equivalent. A few fortunate locations are able to meet these standards by operating their smaller pools on a continuous mineral water flow-through basis, thereby eliminating the need for chemical treatment. Many other locations meet these standards by draining and refilling tubs and pools after each use or after the end of each business day.

At those hot springs resorts which are being run as a business, bathing suits are normally required in public places. There are a few locations, usually operated by small special-interest groups, which have a policy of clothing optional in the pools and sometimes everywhere on the grounds. If you are in doubt about the implications of such a policy, use the telephone to get answers to all of your questions.

The third paragraph of a commercial hot springs listing briefly mentions the principal facilities and

This popular waterslide at *Star Plunge* has warm water in the pick-up pool. Page 135.

services offered, plus approximate distances to nearby services and the names of credit cards accepted, if any. This information is intended to advise you if overnight accomodations, RV hookups, restaurants, health clubs, beauty salons, etc., are available on the premises, but it does not attempt to assign any form of quality rating to those amenities. There is no such thing as a typical hot spring resort and no such thing as typical accommodations at such a resort. Don't make assumptions; phone and ask questions.

For the quick-reference convenience of our readers, we include some code letters in the heading of each listing:

PR = Tubs or pools for rent by hour, day or treatment.

MH = Rooms, cabins or dormitory spaces for rent by day, week or month.

CRV = Camping or vehicle parking spaces, some with hookups, for rent by day, week, month or year.

The PR code obviously applies to rent-a-tub establishments, and it is also used for those hot springs resorts that admit the public to their pools on a day-rate basis.

The MH code covers every kind of overnight sleeping accomodation for rent, including tents and trailers as well as motel and hotel rooms, cabins and dormitories.

The CRV code is very general, indicating that there is some kind of outdoor space in which some kind of overnight stay is possible. Some locations permit tents, most do not. Some have full hookups for RV's, most do not.

Hot Springs Health Spa: Coed tubs and medicare-approved physical therapy meet new public demands at this facility. Page 273.

Outdoor mineral water hot tubs for rent by the hour and motel rooms with private hot tubs on the balcony were pioneered by *Sycamore Mineral Springs.* Page 205.

Sol Duc Hot Springs: A superb contract-resort in Olympic National Park. Page 50.

19

3. Almost As Good As The Real Thing

Sweetwater Gardens: One of the first No. California hot-tub rental spots. Page 181.

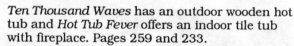

Ten Thousand Waves has an outdoor wooden hot tub and *Hot Tub Fever* offers an indoor tile tub with fireplace. Pages 259 and 233.

According to California legend, the historic redwood hot tub was invented by a Santa Barbara group which often visited Big Caliente Hot Springs, in the nearby mountains at the end of a Forest Service gravel road. One evening a member of the group wished out loud that they could have their delicious outdoor soaks without having to endure the long dusty trips to and from the springs. Another member of the group suggested that a large redwood wine tub might be used as a group soaking pool in the city, but it would not be the real thing because it would be filled with tap water instead of mineral water. After a very short debate, it was unanimously agreed that convenience was more important than authenticity, so the search was on for a used redwood tank to be purchased and assembled in the backyard of the member who first spoke up.

Over time, the pioneering group discovered that their backyard redwood pool needed more than just a gas-fired water heater. It also needed a circulation pump and a filter and chlorine treatments and seats for the people. Before long, other refugees from the long Big Caliente drive began to build their own group soaking pools, and the communal hot tub era was born.

For many years, the very idea of men and women bathing together in the same tub, especially if they didn't wear proper suits, was perceived as major moral decadence and was denounced accordingly. However, as the installation of residential hot tubs gradually became a major industry nationwide, public disdain turned into public acceptance and then became public demand. Health clubs, hotels, motels and destination resorts responded by installing communal hot pools, indoors and outdoors, complete with modern skimmers, hydrojets and decorative tile. The construction plans of many large new motels also include several special suites, each of which has its own hydrojet pool.

Thanks to the continued proliferation of motel and residential hydropools, each year has seen an increasing number of people who get their first opportunity to experience communal hot pool soaking. Many of these enthusiastic first-timers could not then install a hydropool in their apartment, nor could they afford to register into a motel each time they wanted a soak. What they needed was a place in the city where they could pay by the hour for a soak in a hot pool. To serve this newly created market, urban rent-a-tub facilities began to appear. The earliest ones, in California, offered rustic authenticity in the form of private space outdoor redwood tubs and showers on weathered wood tree-shaded decks. Some even offered a large communal pool with a policy of clothing optional.

Unfortunately, not all of the rent-a-tub customers were enthusiastic about an outdoor soak in a cold rain, and an empty tub is not good for business. Then county health departments began to ban wooden hot tubs in new construction for public use because wood is too difficult to keep clean. As a result, the new urban authenticity has become a tiled fiberglass pool in a private room with a stereo sound system and sometimes even a TV set with VCR. However, it is still possible to find some establishments which offer outdoor tubs and/or wooden tubs.

❏ Tubs Using Gas-heated Tap Or Well Water

In this book the listings of rent-a-tub locations begin with an overall impression of the premises and the general location, usually within a city area. This is followed by a description of their private spaces, tubs, water treatment method, and water temperature policies. Generally, clothing is optional in private spaces and required elsewhere. Clothing-optional policies, if any, are stated. Facilities and services available on the premises are described, and credit cards accepted, if any, are listed. Nearly all locations require reservations, especially during the busy evening hours, and most employees are experienced at giving directions.

Nudist/naturist resorts are included as a special service to those who prefer to soak in the buff. It is true that nudist/naturist resorts are not open to the public for drop-in visits, but we wanted to give skinnydippers at least a few alternatives to all of the conventional motels/hotels/resorts which require bathing suits in all their pools. Most of the nudist/naturist locations specifically prohibit bathing suits in their pools and have a policy of clothing optional elsewhere on the grounds. The nudist/naturist resorts are difficult to find because they are seldom known by travel agents and they appear in very few yellow pages. You will have to obtain an invitation before driving in the gate, but a confirmed skinnydipper will consider that to be less of a bother than walking around in wet clothing.

 A small admission fee is charged to these municipal *Emerald Park* pools. Page 65. *Waterhole #1* is a unique Idaho tavern which offers hot tubs with a view. Page 122.

4. Outdoor Tips For City Slickers

This is an enthusiastic testimonial and an invitation to join us in supporting the work of the U.S. Forest Service, the National Park Service and the Canadian National and Provincial Park Services.

At Forest Service offices and ranger stations, we have always received prompt, courteous service, even when the staff was also busy handling the complex administration of " The Land Of Many Uses." Beyond that initial courtesy we also received the benefit of alert interest in what we were trying to do, and the kind of help we needed. There was a willingness to phone another ranger station if necessary to put us in touch with the ranger or supervisor who could best respond to our requests for information. This cheerful, efficient cooperation was evident at all Forest Service offices in the eleven western states.

National Park personnel also get high marks for courtesy, but only Olympic National Park permits the public to soak in easily accessible hot spring water. The official attitude at other popular parks is that geothermal water is "holy," to be seen but not touched, to be preserved but not used. Hopefully, they will eventually realize that the appropriate "natural state" of a hot spring is when it is providing healing warmth to human bodies.

Parks Canada has built large and beautiful public facilities at Radium Hot Springs, at Banff, and at Miette. The Provincial Park Service of British Columbia was very responsive to our need to identify and locate those primitive springs which could be legally used by the public.

Nearly all usable primitive hot springs are in national forests, and many commercial hot spring resorts are surrounded by a national forest. Even if you will not be camping in one of their excellent campgrounds, we recommend that you obtain official Forest Service maps for all areas through which you will be traveling.

Maps may be purchased from the Forest Service Regional Offices listed below. To order by mail, phone or write for an order form:

Pacific Northwest Region
Washington and Oregon
(503) 221-2877
319 SW Pine St.
Portland, OR 97208

Northern Region
Montana and Northern Idaho
(406) 329-3511
200 East Broadway St.
Missoula, MT 59807

Rocky Mountain Region
Colorado and Eastern Wyoming
(303) 236-9431
11177 West Eighth Ave.
Lakewood, CO 80225

Intermountain Region
Southern Idaho, Utah, Nevada and Western Wyoming
(801) 625-5354
324 25th St.
Ogden, UT 84401

Pacific Southwest Region
California
(415) 705-2874
630 Sansome St.
San Francisco, CA 94111

Southwestern Region
Arizona and New Mexico
(505) 842-3292
517 Gold Avenue SW
Albuquerque, NM 87102

When you arrive in a national forest, head for the nearest ranger station and let them know what you would like to do in addition to putting your body in hot mineral water. If you plan to ride a mountain bike, request information about trails where such vehicles are permitted. If you plan to stay in a wilderness area overnight, request information about the procedure for obtaining wilderness permits. Discuss your understanding of the dangers of water pollution, including giardia (back country dysentery) with the Forest Service staff. They are good friends as well as competent public servants.

The following material is adapted from a brochure issued by the Forest Service - Southwestern Region, U.S. Department of Agriculture. Please do your part to take care of natural beauty while you visit, to show your appreciation for those who have taken care of it all year in order that you may have a place worth visiting.

DO NOT WASH IN STREAMS OR SPRINGS

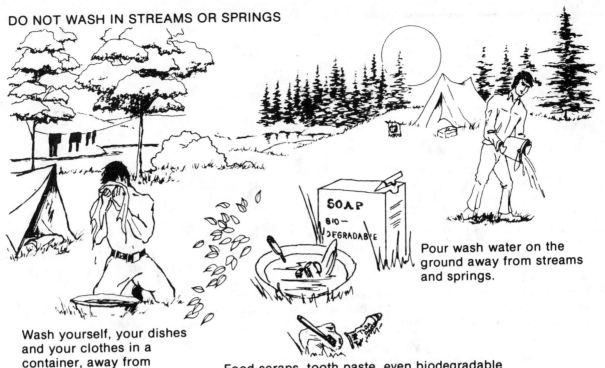

Pour wash water on the ground away from streams and springs.

Wash yourself, your dishes and your clothes in a container, away from water sources.

Food scraps, tooth paste, even biodegradable soap will pollute streams and springs. Remember, it's your drinking water, too!

PACK IT IN — PACK IT OUT

Don't pick flowers, dig up plants or cut branches from live trees. Leave them for others to see and enjoy.

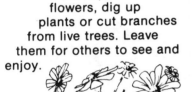

Bring trash bags to carry out all trash that cannot be completely burned.

Try to pack out trash left by others. Your good example may catch on!

Aluminum foil and aluminum lined packages won't burn up in your fire. Compact it and put it in your trash bag.

DON'T BURY TRASH!

Animals dig it up.

DON'T SHORT CUT TRAILS.

Trails are designed and maintained to prevent erosion.

Cutting across switchbacks and trampling meadows can create a confusing maze of unsightly trails.

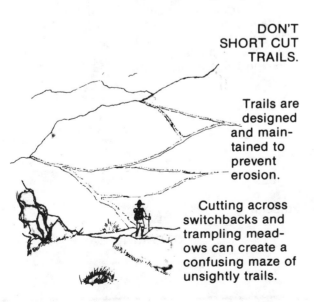

BURY HUMAN WASTE

When nature calls, select a suitable spot at least 100 feet from open water, campsites and trails. Dig a hole 4 to 6 inches deep. Try to keep the sod intact.

After use, fill in the hole completely burying waste and TP; then tramp in the sod.

Backcountry Ethics

U.S. DEPARTMENT OF AGRICULTURE
FOREST SERVICE
SOUTHWESTERN REGION

Times are changing. More and more people are taking to the trails. Poor camping practices can destroy the natural character of the backcountry. We must all learn to use the backcountry wisely, or be faced with more restrictions if heavy use and resource damage increases.

When planning and starting your backcountry trip:
- Check at a Forest Service office for wilderness permit, if necessary; weather, fire and water conditions; size of group; camping locations; maps; and other useful information.
- Keep your party small. Group size may be limited.
- Take a gas stove to help conserve firewood.
- Bring sacks to carry out your trash.
- Take a light shovel or trowel to help with personal sanitation.
- Carry a light basin or collapsible bucket for washing.
- If you take horses or mules, pack plenty of processed feed for them.

SETTING UP CAMP

Avoid camping in meadows; you'll trample the grass.

Pick a campsite where you won't need to clear away vegetation or level a tent site. Do not trench around tents.

Use an existing campsite, if available.

Camp 300 feet from streams, springs, or trails. State law prohibits camping within ¼ mile of an only available water source (for wildlife and livestock).

Do not cut trees, limbs or brush to make camp improvements. Carry your own tent poles.

Before leaving camp, naturalize the area. Replace rocks and wood used; scatter needles, leaves and twigs on the campsite.

Scout the area to be sure you've left nothing behind. Everything you packed into your camp should be packed out. Try to make it appear as if no one had been there.

BREAKING CAMP

CAMPFIRES   Use gas stoves when possible to conserve dwindliing supplies of firewood.

Use only fallen timber for firewood. Even standing dead trees are part of the beauty of wilderness, and are important to wildlife.

If you need to build a fire, use an existing campfire site if available.

Clear a circle of all burnable materials.

Dig a shallow pit for the fire.

Keep the sod intact.

If you need to clear a new fire site, select a safe spot away from rock ledges that would be blackened by smoke; away from meadows where it would destroy grass and leave a scar; away from dense brush, trees and duff where it would be a fire hazard. Keep fires small.

Never leave a fire unattended.

Put your fire COLD OUT before leaving, by mixing the coals with dirt & water. Feel it with your hand. If it's cold out, cover the ashes in the pit with dirt, replace the sod, and naturalize the disturbed area. Rockfire rings, if needed or used, should be scattered before leaving.

PACK AND SADDLE STOCK
   can seriously damage soil and vegetation if not properly cared for.
Camp in areas with enough space to picket your stock away from established campsites and water sources.

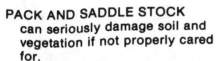

Use light, compact equipment and food to reduce the number of pack stock needed.

Forage is scarce at most campsites in the Southwest backcountry. Avoid grazing your stock or turning them loose at night.
   Instead: string a pack rope between two trees, away from water sources.

DON'T TIE STOCK TO TREES!

One or several animals can be tied to this hitch-line, spaced far enough apart not to become entangled, and tied short enough not to wrap a leg in the lead rope.

Stock tied to trees and brush for extended periods may paw up roots or strip the bark by gnawing and fighting the rope. This can kill brush and trees.

Pack in a good supply of processed feed. Complete ration pellets are excellent. Rolled grains are good, but lack sufficient roughage. Don't use whole grains, which sprout if spilled and compete with natural vegetation.

MAP AND DIRECTORY SYMBOLS

● Non-commercial mineral water pool

■ Commercial (fee) mineral water pool

□ Gas-heated tap or well water pool

〜 Paved highway

--- Unpaved road

···· Hiking route

PR = Tubs or pools for rent by hour, day or treatment

MH = Rooms, cabins or dormitory spaces for rent by day, week or month

CRV = Camping or vehicle parking spaces, some with hookups,
for rent by day, week, month or year

Canada

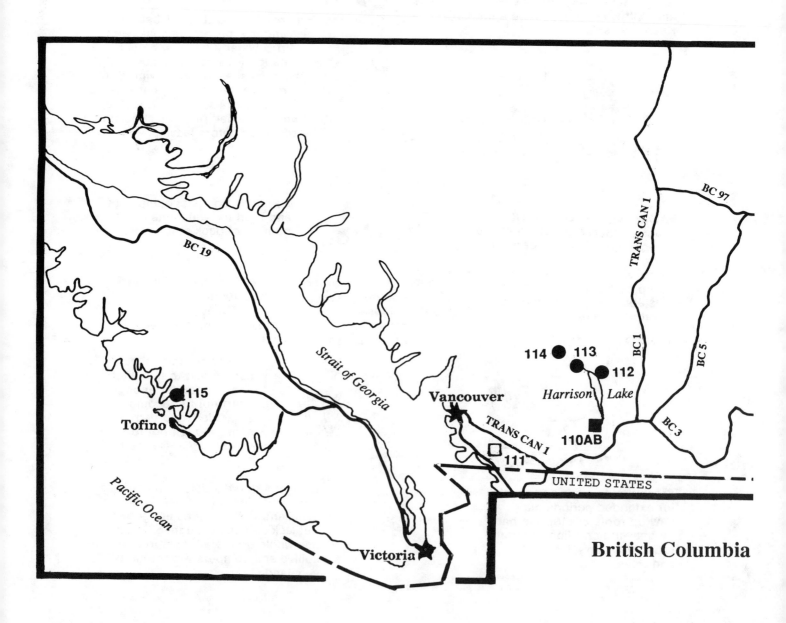

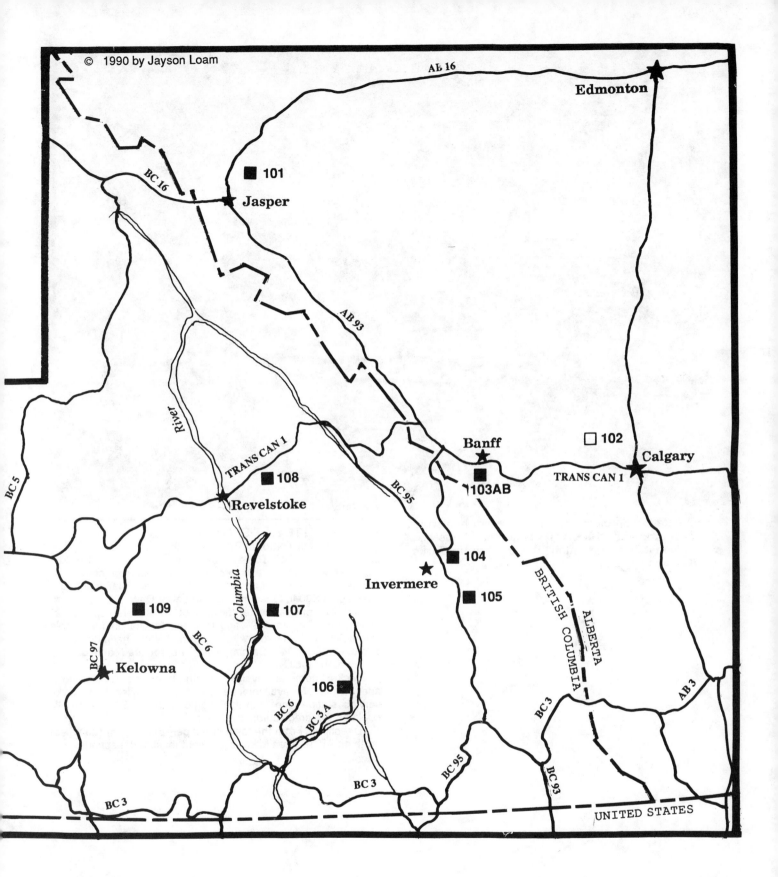

© 1990 by Jayson Loam

AB 16

Edmonton

BC 16

■ 101

Jasper

AB 93

River

Banff ★

□ 102

Calgary

TRANS CAN 1

■ 103AB

TRANS CAN 1

BC 5

■ 108

Revelstoke

BC 95

Columbia

■ 104

Invermere ★

■ 105

BC 97

■ 109

■ 107

BRITISH COLUMBIA

ALBERTA

Kelowna ★

BC 6

106 ■

BC 6

BC 3 A

BC 3

AB 3

BC 3

BC 95

BC 93

BC 3

UNITED STATES

and Alberta.

Miette Hot Springs: Thanks to a recent modernization program, with new pools and bathhouses, this installation is among the finest in the Parks Canada system.

101   MIETTE HOT SPRINGS
Jasper National Park Box 10
Jasper, AB T0E 1E0 Canada   **PR+MH**

A modern, clean and proper, Parks Canada communal plunge in a remote part of beautiful Jasper National Park. Elevation 4,500 ft. Open mid-May to Labor Day.

. Natural mineral water flows out of several springs at temperatures up to 129˚ and is piped to two outdoor pools where it is treated with chlorine and maintained at approximately 104˚. Bathing suits are required and can be rented at the facility.

Locker rooms are available on the premises. A cafe, motel and cabins are available nearby. It is 11 miles to a store, service station and overnight camping and 15 miles to RV hookups. No credit cards are accepted.

Directions: From the town of Jasper, drive 42km (26 miles) north on AB 16, then follow signs southeast to the springs.

One of the many attractions at *Miette Hot Springs* is that smoking is prohibited in the pool area and related buildings.

Sunny Chinooks Family Nudist Recreational Park: This hydropool is indoors as protection from Canadian weather, but a bank of growing plants gives it an outdoor feel.

102 SUNNY CHINOOKS FAMILY NUDIST RECREATIONAL PARK

P.O. Box 486   (403) 932-6633
Cochrane, AB T0L 8W0   PR+MH+CRV

Rustic and secluded nudist park on 40 wooded acres, an hour's drive from Calgary. Elevation 4,500 ft. Open May through September.

Gas-heated well water is used in an indoor hydropool maintained at 102-104° and treated with chlorine. Gas-heated well water is also used in an outdoor swimming pool maintained at 80° and treated with chlorine. Clothing is always prohibited in the pools and, weather permitting, prohibited everywhere on the grounds.

A cafe, convenience store, cabin and trailer rentals, overnight camping and RV hookups are available on the premises. It is 17 miles to a service station. No credit cards are accepted.

Note: This is a membership organization not open to the public for drop-in visits, but prospective members may be issued a guest pass by prior arrangement. Telephone or write for information and directions.

29

Upper Hot Spring: During the summer the water
in this very large soaking pool maintains a temperature which averages 105°.

103A UPPER HOT SPRING

Banff National Park Box 900
Banff, AB T0L 0C0   PR

A modern, clean and proper, Parks Canada communal plunge surrounded by the beautiful scenery of Banff National Park. Elevation 4,200 ft. Open all year.

Natural mineral water flows out of a spring at temperatures ranging from 90-108°, depending on snow run-off conditions, and is piped to an outdoor swimming pool where it is treated with chlorine. Water temperature in the swimming pool is slightly lower than the current spring output temperature. Bathing suits are required.

Locker rooms are available on the premises. It is one mile to a cafe, store, service station and motel, and two miles to overnight camping and RV hookups. No credit cards are accepted.

Directions: From the south end of Banff Avenue, follow signs to the spring.

103B CAVE AND BASIN HOT SPRING

Banff National Park Box 900
Banff, AB, T0L 0C0   PR

A modern, clean and proper, Parks Canada communal plunge within the Cave and Basin Centennial Centre, surrounded by the beautiful mountain scenery of Banff National Park. Elevation 4,200 ft. Pool open June through August. Exhibits open all year.

Natural mineral water flows out of a cave at 85° into a large outdoor swimming pool, which maintains a temperature of approximately 80°. The public may enter and observe the cave through a short tunnel, but bathing in the cave is prohibited. The swimming pool, which is treated with chlorine, is available for public use. Bathing suits are required and available for rent. A separate spring flows into a natural rock basin, which is not available for bathing.

Locker rooms and a restaurant are available on the premises. It is one mile to a store, service station and hotel rooms, and two miles to overnight camping and RV hookups. No credit cards are accepted.

Directions: From the south end of Banff Avenue, follow signs to the spring.

Cave and Basin Hot Spring: A decorative fieldstone wall with windows is used to let the scenery in while keeping the wind out.

There are many bilingual geothermal displays in the *Cave and Basin Centennial Centre*, which includes the famous hot-spring cave.

31

◄ *Radium Hot Springs*: This popular Parks Canada installation has a convenient cafe with observation deck for the non-swimmers.

► Some of the rooms in the nearby Lodge also have a view of the beautifully landscaped pools at *Radium Hot Springs*.

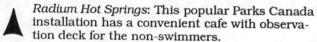

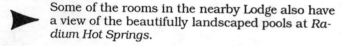

104 RADIUM HOT SPRINGS

P.O. Box 220   (604) 347-9485
■ **Radium Hot Springs, BC V0A 1M0**   PR+MH+CRV

A modern, clean and proper, Parks Canada communal plunge with adjoining commercial services, surrounded by the beautiful mountain scenery of Kootenay National Park. Elevation 2,800 ft. Open all year.

Natural mineral water flows out of five springs at a combined temperature of 117° and is piped to two outdoor pools where it is treated with chlorine. The swimming pool is maintained at a temperature of 82-83°, and the soaking pool is maintained at a temperature of 98-103°. Bathing suits are required.

Locker rooms and a cafe are available on the premises, with rooms, overnight camping and RV hookups available nearby. It is two miles to a store and service station. No credit cards are accepted.

Directions: Follow signs one mile east from the West Gate of Kootenay National Park.

▲ *Fairmont Hot Springs Resort*: These pools, bathhouses and parking areas are in a special section for day-use customers.

▼ Adjoining the lodge at *Fairmont Hot Springs Resort* is this smaller and quieter pool, reserved for registered guests.

105   FAIRMONT HOT SPRINGS RESORT

P.O. Box 10   (604) 345-6311
Fairmont Hot Springs, BC V0B 1L0   PR+MH+CRV

Famous, large, destination resort and communal plunge, beautifully landscaped and surrounded by the forested mountains of the Invermere Valley. Elevation 2,100 ft. Open all year.

Natural mineral water flows out of three springs at temperatures of 108°, 112°, and 116° and is piped to the resort pools where it is treated with chlorine and cooled with creek water as needed. The outdoor public plunge area includes a swimming pool maintained at 87°, a soaking pool maintained at a temperature of 102-104°, an indoor soaking pool maintained at 108-112°, and a cold plunge maintained at 60°. The lodge also has two co-ed saunas. Bathing suits are required.

Locker rooms, massage, cafe, store, service station, hotel rooms, overnight camping (no tents), RV hookups, saddle horses, tennis, golf and skiing are available on the premises. Visa, MasterCard and American Express are accepted.

Location: On BC 93, 64 miles north of Cranbrook and 100 miles south of Banff.

CAVES

Recommended maximum time in caves 10 to 15 minutes

Children must be accompanied by an adult ll times

▲ *Ainsworth Hot Springs*: Here you can give your pores a workout, starting in the caves with the 110° water and the 100% humidity.

► Then you can treat yourself to a stimulating dunk in this 50° *Ainsworth* waterfall which is supplied by pipe from a nearby creek.

▼ In between those extremes at *Ainsworth* you can have a normal soak in a hydrojet pool, and then loll by the hour in the large pool.

106 AINSWORTH HOT SPRINGS
P.O. Box 1268   **(604) 229-4248**
■ **Ainsworth Hot Springs BC V0G 1A0**   **PR+MH**

Modern, all-year destination resort with a multi-pool plunge and geothermal caves, overlooking beautiful Kootenay Lake. Elevation 1,900 ft. Open all year.

Natural mineral water flows out of five springs at temperatures ranging from 110-117°. The outdoor swimming pool and connected hydrojet pool are maintained at 85-95°. The water in the caves ranges from 106-110° and is circulated to the connected outdoor soaking pool, where it ranges from 104-106°. There is a ledge in the cave which may be used as a steambath. There is also an outdoor cold pool containing creek water ranging from 40-60°. All pools are treated with chlorine. Bathing suits are required.

Facilities include hotel rooms, lounge, dining room, banquet rooms, meeting rooms and dressing rooms. Massage, by appointment, is available on the premises. It is three miles to overnight camping and nine miles to a store and service station. MasterCard, Visa and Diners Club are accepted.

Location: On BC 31, 12 miles south of Kaslo and 29 miles from Nelson.

107 NAKUSP HOT SPRINGS
P.O. Box 280   **(604) 352-4033**
■ **Nakusp, BC V0G 1R0**   **PR+MH+CRV**

Modern, clean, city-owned plunge, with creekside camping spaces surrounded by beautiful mountain scenery. Elevation 2,200 ft. Open all year.

Natural mineral water flows out of springs at 135° and is piped to two outdoor pools where it is treated with chlorine. The swimming pool is maintained at 100° and the soaking pool at 110°. Bathing suits are required.

Locker rooms, cabins and overnight camping are available on the premises. It is eight miles to a cafe, store, service station and RV hookups. Visa cards are accepted.

Directions: From a junction on BC 23 one mile north of Nakusp, follow signs eight miles east to the plunge.

▲ *Nakusp Hot Springs*: These town-owned pools are for relaxed social soaking. There is no deep end for diving and swimming.

▼ The lovely rustic cabins and campground at *Nakusp Hot Springs* are rented out to support this fine plunge for day use by residents.

Cedar Springs: This facility combines some of the best features of urban rent-a-tub places with the benefits of outdoor scenery, fresh air and natural mineral water.

Canyon Hot Springs: Even the small commercial hot springs resorts in this area have the benefit of snow-capped mountains.

108 CANYON HOT SPRINGS
P.O. Box 2400   **(604) 837-2420**
Revelstoke, BC V0E 2S0   **PR+CRV**

Well-kept commercial plunge with creekside camping spaces, surrounded by the beautiful scenery below Glacier National Park. Elevation 3,000 ft. Open May 15 to September 15.

Natural mineral water flows out of a spring at 85° and is gas-heated as needed, as well as being treated with chlorine. The outdoor swimming pool is maintained at 85° and the outdoor soaking pool at 105°. Bathing suits are required.

Locker rooms, cafe, store, RV hookups and overnight camping are available on the premises. It is 21 miles to a service station and motel. Visa, MasterCard and American Express are accepted.

Location: 21 miles east of Revelstoke on Canada 1.

109 CEDAR SPRINGS
RR 3   **(604) 542-5477**
Vernon, BC V1T 6L6   **PR**

Recreation-oriented plunge with large wood decks, cedar pools and a private tub on a tree-covered hillside near a ski area. Elevation 4,000 ft. Open all year.

Natural mineral water flows out of a spring at 50°, is heated with natural gas as needed, and is treated with chlorine. The outdoor swimming pool is maintained at 75° in the summer and 80-95° in the winter. The large, cedar outdoor hydrojet pool is maintained at 103°, and the outdoor soaking pool is maintained at 108°. The indoor private-space cedar pool is maintained at 102°. Bathing suits are required except in the private space.

Locker room, juice bar, and Clearly Canadian mineral water by the glass, bottle or case are available on the premises. Overnight camping, RV hookups, cross-country skiing and ice-skating are available nearby. It is six miles to a cafe, store, service station and motel. No credit cards are accepted.

Directions: From 27th Street (BC 97) in Vernon, go north on 48th Avenue (Silver Star Road) five miles to Tillicum Valley Road. Turn right and follow signs one mile to plunge.

 The Harrison Hotel: This full-service resort hotel provides a buffet lunch and bar service at the central patio swimming pool.

 Convivial sing-a-longs make the rafters ring in this hot-pool building, adjoining the main pool area at *The Harrison Hotel.*

110A   THE HARRISON HOTEL

■ **Harrison Hot Springs, BC V0M 1K0**   **(604) 521-8888**
                                            PR+MH

Attractive, large, destination resort located on the south shore of beautiful Lake Harrison. This well-managed facility offers an unusually wide range of recreation activities. Elevation 47 ft. Open all year.

Natural mineral water flows out of a spring at 140° and is piped to cooling tanks before being treated with chlorine. The Olympic-size outdoor swimming pool is maintained at 82°, the indoor swimming pool at 94°, and the indoor soaking pool at 104°. The men's and women's sections of the health pavilion each contain a Roman bath in which the temperature is controllable. Health pavilion services are available to the public, but all other facilities are reserved for registered guests only. Bathing suits are required.

Future development plans include four large outdoor soaking pools with connecting waterfalls and temperatures ranging from 110° down to 85°, two outdoor chlorine-treated fresh water swimming pools ranging in temperature from 78-82°, and a swimway connecting the indoor swimming pool with the outdoor swimming pool. Plans for the health pavilion include mud baths, weight rooms, herbal wraps, facials, manicures, etc. Phone ahead to determine the status of construction.

A restaurant, bungalows, rooms, children's programs, pickle ball, boat cruises and boat rentals are available on the premises. It is three blocks to a store, service station, overnight camping and RV hookups. Visa, MasterCard, American Express, Carte Blanche, Enroute and Diners Club are accepted.

Location: 65 miles east of Vancouver at the south end of Lake Harrison. Phone for rates, reservations and additional directions.

 Harrison Hot Springs Public Pool: The same spring which supplies the hotel two blocks away also supplies this well-kept plunge.

110B HARRISON HOT SPRINGS PUBLIC POOL
c/o Harrison Hotel
■ **Harrison Hot Springs, BC V0M 1K0**　　　　**PR**

Large, modern, indoor communal plunge owned and operated by the hotel, available to the public. Elevation 47 ft. Open all year.

Natural mineral water is drawn from the same spring that supplies the hotel. It is treated with chlorine and maintained at 100° in the swimming pool. Bathing suits are required.

Locker rooms are available on the premises. All other services are within three blocks. Visa and MasterCard are accepted.

Location: On the main intersection at the beach in Harrison Hot Springs.

---

111 SUNNY TRAILS CLUB
Box 1 9900 162A St.　　　　　　(604) 859-1341
❑ Surrey, BC V3R 4B6　　　　　　PR+CRV

An ideal northwest nudist park with 30 secluded wooded acres of trees and grass, a small running stream and many residences, conveniently located within ah hour of downtown Vancouver. Elevation 700 ft. Open all year.

Gas-heated tap water is used in an enclosed fiberglass hydropool which is maintained at 104º, and in an outdoor, unheated swimming pool, both of which are treated with chlorine. Bathing suits are prohibited in the pools. There is no requirement of full nudity regardless of weather conditions, but individual dress is expected to conform to that of the majority at any given time.

Facilities include a wood-fired sauna, cafe, overnight camping and RV hookups. It is three miles to a store and service station and five miles to a motel. No credit cards are accepted.

Note: This is a membership organization not open to the public for drop-in visits, but prospective members may pay a day's ground fee. Telephone or write for information and directions.

Sunny Trails Club: From the deck of their cabin, these residents have a view of the swimming pool and the hot pool in a roofed patio at the end of an adjoining building.

39

Most hot spring visitors patronize those convenient and comfortable establishments which offer tiled pools, hot showers, a restaurant and a souvenir shop, with nearby overnight accomodations. However, a hardy minority make a point of seeking out those remote and primitive hot springs which are inconvenient and, at times, inaccessible.

Many of them are on or near logging roads, which means that quite often public access is prohibited between 6 a.m. and 6 p.m. during logging season, and that the road could be closed by slides, washouts, snow, high fire danger, and actual forest fires. In other words, access to remote and primitive hot springs is a sometimes thing.

Therefore, the best first step toward reaching any specific hot springs is to contact the Provincial Ministry of Forests District Office for the area and inquire about current conditions. Then, if access is possible, you can obtain an area map and first hand directions at a Forest Service office. The office hours are 8:30 to 4:30, Monday through Friday only.

Future Note: There are a few primitive hot springs which could not be included in this edition because of special restrictions, which might be lifted at any time. When you inquire at a District Office about any of the following locations, also ask for information on any additional locations which may have become available to the public.

---

112   SKOOKUMCHUCK HOT SPRINGS (LILLOOET)
(St. Agnes Well)
● **South of the town of Pemberton, BC**

Two large, fiberglass soaking tubs in a small clearing near a logging road along the Lillooet River. Elevation 100 ft. Open all year; however, the road is not plowed in winter.

Natural mineral water flows out of a spring at 129°. Volunteers have mounted the two halves of a fiberglass storage tank near the springs, using long pieces of PVC pipe to bring a gravity flow of hot mineral water. Other pieces of PVC pipe are used to carry a gravity flow from a cold-water spring. Water temperature within each tub is controlled by mixing the hot and cold water. One of the tubs is in the open; the other is under a crude A-frame shelter. In the absence of posted rules, the use of bathing suits is determined by the consent of those present.

There are no services available, but there are numerous nearby self-maintained camping areas along the logging road and at the site itself.

Directions: From the town of Mt. Currie, go approximately 34 miles on a rough logging road along the Lillooet River. At BC Hydro tower #682, turn right onto a camping-area access road and go 1/4 mile to spring. Caution: this dirt road may require a 4-wheel-drive vehicle when wet.

The hot springs are located on private property, and use is permissible without the consent of the property owner. Please respect the hot springs and adjacent property. Pack out all garbage.

113   SLOQUET CREEK HOT SPRINGS
● **Near the north end of Harrison Lake, BC**

Several springs seep from the rocks about Sloquet Creek and flow along the ground before dropping over a short waterfall and forming a small pool which is too hot for bathing. Several other springs percolate from the ground, and volunteers have constructed small, natural-rock pools for bathing along the creek. The hot springs are located about 62 miles south of Mt. Currie, near the Lillooet River and just NW of Harrison Lake. Elevation approximately 1000 ft. Water temperature varies between 135° and 155°.

Few services are available in the area, though there is a logging camp at Port Douglas, at the head of Harrison Lake. Walk-in camping is possible near the springs.

Directions: From the town of Mt. Currie, go about 57 miles south on the logging road along the Lillooet River to a bridge that crosses the river to the west side. Turn left, cross Fire Creek, and go south two miles to a second creek, where you go right. Follow this creek (Sloquet) for about 3.4 miles on an old logging road that takes you to a bridge across North Sloquet Creek. The bridge is washed out and you must cross the creek on foot via a large log. Follow the logging road until you reach an obvious clearing, which can be used for camping. There is a trail leading downhill from the clearing to the creek and the hot springs. It will take two to three hours to drive from Mt. Currie and an additional 45 minutes to walk the remainder of the logging road to the hot springs. There are no posted rules or regulations for use of the site, but anything packed in should be packed out, including garbage.

114 CLEAR CREEK HOT SPRINGS
Along the northeast
side of Harrison Lake, BC

Two small wooden tubs and two old porcelain bathtubs are located near a log cabin along Clear Creek, approximately 35 miles up the east side of Harrison Lake from Harris Hot Springs, and six miles east of the lake up Clear Creek. Elevation approximately 2,200 ft. Hot springs open all year; however, road passable only in summer and only to 4x4's. A spring percolates from the ground at 95°, and volunteers have constructed two wooden tubs connected to the springs with long lengths of PVC pipe. There are two conventional bathtubs which can also be used for soaking.

There are few amenities available in the area other than the log cabin and an outhouse nearby. The springs are located on an active mineral claim which was initially prospected by a woman who built the cabin and an Olympic-sized swimming pool about 15 years ago. The pool is largely filled with algae and silt and not used by bathers any longer.

Directions: From the town of Harrison Hot Springs head up the east side of Harrison Lake for about 33 miles to the logging camp at Big Silver Creek. Stay on the main logging road for another five miles and look for a narrow road going off to the right. This is the old mining road up Clear Creek, and it is extremely rough in places. It is driveable with a narrow 4x4 for most of the six miles to the hot springs and cabin, which are located on the right side of the creek. It will take two-to-three hours to drive from Harrison Hot Springs to the Clear Creek road, and considerably longer if you walk up the road. There are no posted rules or restrictions for use of the site, but anything packed in should be packed out, including garbage.

Clear Creek Hot Springs: Canadian volunteers insist on building their soaking pools of wood and iron rather than rock-and-sand.

115 HOT SPRINGS COVE

Northwest of the town of Tofino, on Vancouver Island

Unique confluence of geothermal run-off and ocean waves, located in Maquinna Regional Park on a rocky peninsula reachable only by boat or floatplane. Elevation 40 ft. Open all year.

Natural mineral water flows out of the main spring at 122° and tumbles over a waterfall as it runs through a rocky channel into three bathtub-size tidal pools. The incoming tide and wave action intermittently flood these pools, thereby reducing the combined water temperature to more comfortable levels. The apparent local custom is clothing optional.

There are no facilities or services on the premises. It is one mile on a boarded walk to an abandoned fish cannery, which is the docking point for boats and floatplanes. During fishing season there may be coffee and fish for sale at the cannery. Overnight camping near the springs, or in the cannery building, is not prohibited.

The remoteness of this location does not assure you of privacy. During summer weekends, you will have plenty of company, which insures a maximum of excitement when the icy waves swirl into the tubs.

The most convenient access, weather permitting, is by boat or floatplane out of Tofino, 23 miles south of the spring.

41

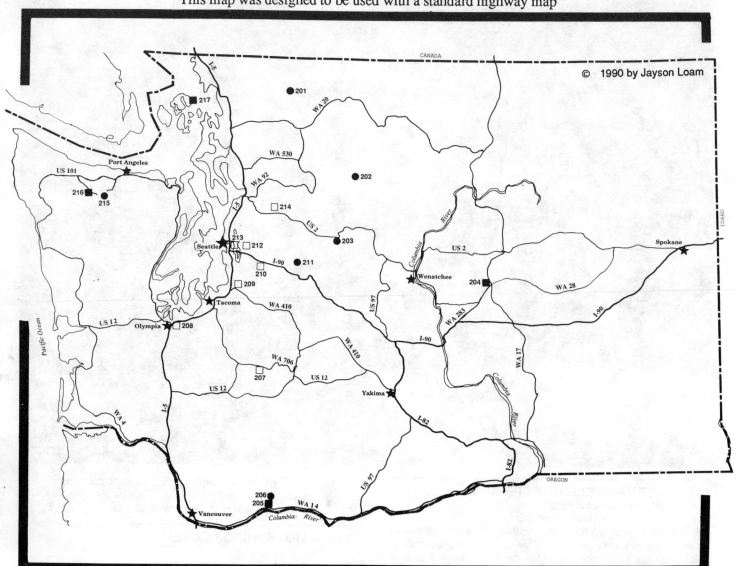

Washington

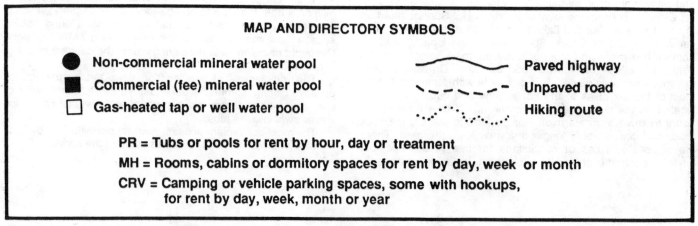

MAP AND DIRECTORY SYMBOLS

● Non-commercial mineral water pool

■ Commercial (fee) mineral water pool

□ Gas-heated tap or well water pool

⎯⎯⎯ Paved highway

⎯ ⎯ ⎯ Unpaved road

······ Hiking route

PR = Tubs or pools for rent by hour, day or treatment

MH = Rooms, cabins or dormitory spaces for rent by day, week or month

CRV = Camping or vehicle parking spaces, some with hookups, for rent by day, week, month or year

201   BAKER HOT SPRINGS

● **North of the town of Concrete**

Charming, primitive spring located at the end of an easy 600-yard path through the lush, green timber of Mt. Baker National Forest. Elevation 2,000 ft. Open all year.

Natural mineral water bubbles up into the bottom of a large, round, volunteer-built pool at 109°. Water temperature in this sandy-bottom pool is controlled by admitting or diverting the water from a small, adjacent cold stream. The apparent local custom is clothing optional. Conscientious visitors have kept the area litter free. Please help to maintain this standard.

There are no facilities on the premises, and no overnight camping is permitted. However, there is a Forest Service campground within three miles. All other services are located 20 miles away, in Concrete.

Directions: From WA 20, five miles east of Hamilton, turn north on Grandy Creek Road toward Baker Lake. Just beyond Park Creek Campground, near the head of the lake, go left on FS 1144, and after 3.2 miles, watch for an unusually large parking area on both sides of the gravel road. (If you reach a U-turn to the left with a branch road going off to the right, you have gone too far.) An unmarked trail to the hot springs starts with wood steps which are visible at the north end of the parking area on your left. Follow the easy trail west to the spring.

Source map: *Mt. Baker-Snoqualmie National Forest* (hot spring not shown).

 Baker Hot Springs: On any ranking of ideal primitive hot springs, this location would have to rate well within the top 10%.

202   KENNEDY HOT SPRING

● **Southeast of the town of Darrington**

A popular scenic hot spring, five miles in on a trail that connects with the Pacific Crest Trail one mile father on. Located in a rugged canyon of the White Chuck River in the Glacier Peak Wilderness. Elevation 3,300 ft. Open all year.

Natural mineral water flows out of a spring at 96° directly into a four-foot by five-foot cedar-plank soaking pool. Even though this spring is a five-mile hike from the nearest road, there is no assurance of quiet privacy during the busy summer months, especially on weekends. There are no posted clothing requirements, which leaves it up to the mutual consent of those present.

Directions: From the town of Darrington, take FS 20 southeast approximately eight miles to the intersection with FS 23. Drive to the end of FS 23, which is the trailhead for Trail 643 up White Chuck Canyon. Consult with the Ranger Station in Darrington regarding weather and trail conditions before starting this trip.

Source map: *Mt. Baker-Snoqualmie National Forest*.

43

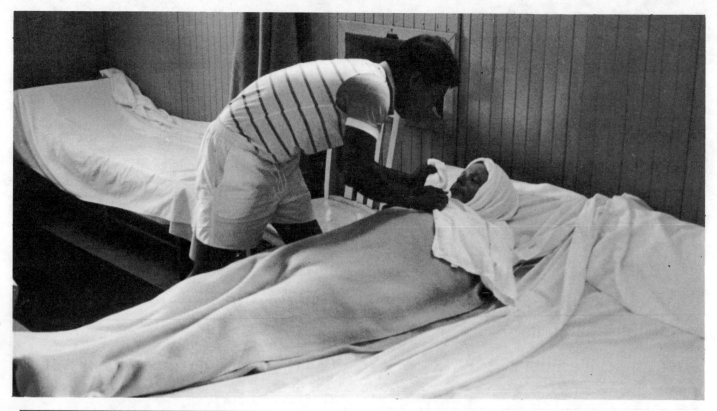

 Carson Hot Mineral Spring Resort: After each soak, a bathhouse patron receives the traditional sweat wrap from an attendant.

203 SCENIC HOT SPRINGS

● **East of the town of Skyhomish**

Wooden soaking box located on a steep hillside above the Tye River in the Mt. Baker-Snoqualmie National Forest. Elevation 3,500 ft. Open all year.

Natural mineral water emerges from several springs at 122˚ and flows through a hose to a four-foot by six-foot soaking box The temperature. of the water in the pool can be cooled by removing the hose. The apparant local custom is clothing optional.

There are no services at the spring and it is 20 miles to all services in Skyhomish.

Directions: From Skyhomish on US 2 go ten miles east to the town of Scenic. Drive across the highway bridge spanning the Burlington-Northern Railrod tracks, turn right (south) onto a primitive powerline road, and park as soon as possible. Walk east and start counting towers. Between the fourth and fifth towers there will be an unmarked path on the right climbing steeply south up the hill to the springs. This is a rugged two-mile hike.

Source map: *Mt. Baker-Snoqualmie National Forest* (hot springs not shown).

204 NOTARAS LODGE
■ 242 Main St. E.   (509) 246-0462
Soap Lake, WA 98851   PR+MH

Large, new, western-style log-construction motel with in-room jet tubs and a public bathhouse. Open all year.

Natural mineral water is obtained from the city water system through an extra pipe which supplies Soap Lake water at temperatures up to 95˚. Five of the motel units are equipped with in-room jet tubs built for two. All rooms have an extra spigot over the bathtub to supply hot mineral water whenever desired. There is also a bathhouse building, using fresh water only, containing a sauna and two private-space, old-fashioned, single bathtubs, plus a hydrojet pool maintained at 95-100˚. The bathhouse facilities are available to the public as well as to registered guests.

Massage and motel rooms are available on the premises. All other services are within five blocks. Visa and MasterCard are accepted.

Location: On WA 17 in the town of Notaras.

205 CARSON HOT MINERAL SPRINGS RESORT

P.O. Box 370   (509) 427-8292
Carson, WA 98610   PR+MH+CRV

Picturesque, historic resort which prides itself on having used "the same bath methods for over 100 years." Elevation 300 ft. Open all year.

Natural mineral water flows out of a spring at 126° and is piped to men's and women's bathhouses. There are eight claw-footed enamel tubs in the men's bathhouse, and six in the women's. Temperature is controllable in each tub, which is drained and filled after each use, requiring no chemical treatment. An attendant, who is with you at all times, applies a sweat wrap after the soak. Bathing suits are not required in the bathhouses, which are available to the public as well as to registered guests.

Television, radio, newspapers and telephones are not available on the premises. Massage, restaurant, hotel rooms, cabins, overnight camping and RV hookups are available. A store and service station are within two miles. Hiking and fishing are nearby. Visa and MasterCard are accepted.

Directions: From the intersection of WA 14 and Bridge of the Gods over the Columbia River, go east on WA 14 and watch for signs. Phone for rates, reservations and further directions if necessary.

206 ST. MARTINS ON THE WIND

● **On the property of Carson Hot Springs Resort PR**

Shallow, rock, soaking pools with a waterfall view on the edge of the Wind River at the end of a twenty-minute boulder scramble along the east bank. (A small fee is charged for use of the pools.) Elevation 150 ft. Open all year.

Natural mineral water flows out of several seeps at 107° into three sandy-bottom pools at the river's edge. If desired, cooling is achieved by moving rocks to divert river water into a pool. The apparent local custom is clothing optional.

There are no services available on the premises, but overnight parking is not prohibited at the parking area. A restaurant, rooms and bathhouses are available within one mile at the Carson Hot Springs Resort. It is eight miles to campgrounds in the Gifford Pinchot National Forest and 15 miles to all other services in Hood River.

Directions: From the WA 14 highway bridge over the Wind River, go 3/4 mile east and turn north on a paved street signed *Berge Rd*. Drive 3/4 mile up this curving road to an intersection with two dirt roads on the left, marked by a sign on the right, *Indian Cabin Rd*. Take the hard left road 1/2 mile to a flat deadend parking area under a power line. A posted sign gives instruction for hiking from there to the springs and for paying the required fee.

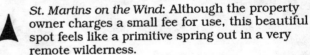

▲ *St. Martins on the Wind:* Although the property owner charges a small fee for use, this beautiful spot feels like a primitive spring out in a very remote wilderness.

▼ *Town Tubs and Massage:* When natural hot springs are too far away, an acrylic tub in a convenient location is almost as good.

▲ *Wellspring:* A roof protects this cedar hot tub from the rain, but the surroundings have a delightful out-in-the-woods feeling.

---

207 WELLSPRING

☐ Star Route   (206) 569-2514
Ashford, WA 98304   PR

A charming, small, rustic spa located in the woods just outside the southwest entrance to Mt. Rainier National Park.

Private-space hot tubs are for rent to the public, using propane-heated spring water treated with chlorine. There are two cedar hot tubs, one in a lush forest setting overlooking a pond and one in a private greenhouse courtyard full of flowers. Water temperatures are maintained at 104-106°.

Facilities include wood-fired cedar saunas. Massage therapy is available on the premises. No credit cards are accepted. Phone for rates, reservations and directions.

---

208 TOWN TUBS AND MASSAGE

☐ 115 E. Olympia Ave.   (206) 943-2200
Olympia, WA 98501   PR

Modern rent-a-tub establishment in downtown Olympia, two blocks from Percival Landing on Puget Sound.

Private-space hot pools with cedar decks are for rent to the public, using gas-heated tap water treated with chlorine. There are six indoor acrylic pools with water temperature adjustable from 95-104º. Each unit has a personal sound system.

Rolfing and therapeutic massage are available on the premises. Visa and MasterCard are accepted. Phone for rates, reservations and directions.

209 GRAND CENTRAL SAUNA & HOT TUB CO.

32510 Pacific Highway South   (206) 952-6154
Federal Way, WA 98003

One of a chain of urban locations established by Grand Central, a pioneer in the private rent-a-tub business. Open all year.

Private-space hot pools using chlorine-treated tap water are for rent to the public by the hour. 19 indoor tubs are maintained at temperatures from 102-104˚. Each unit contains a sauna.

No credit cards are accepted. Phone for rates, reservations and directions.

210 FRATERNITY SNOQUALMIE

P.O. Box 985   (206) 392-NUDE
Seattle, WA 98111   PR+CRV

Long-established nudist park occupying a hillside fruit orchard surrounded by evergreens. Elevation 500 ft. Open to members all year; open to guests from May through September.

The outdoor hydrojet pool is maintained at 104˚ all year. The outdoor swimming pool is solar heated, ranging from 80˚ in the summer to 50˚ in the winter. The wading pool is filled only in the summer. All pools use well water treated with chlorine. There is also a wood-fired sauna.

Clothing is not permitted in the pools or sauna.

Overnight camping and RV hookups are available on the premises. It is four miles to a cafe, store, service station and motel. Visa and MasterCard are accepted.

Note: This is a membership organization not open to the public for drop-in visits, but prospective members may be issued a guest pass by prior arrangement. Telephone or write for information and directions.

▲ *Fraternity Snoqualmie:* The pool may not have natural mineral water, but the absence of swim suits is a plus to a skinnydipper.

211 GOLDMYER HOTSPRINGS

202 N. 85th St. #106   (206) 789-5631
Seattle, WA 98103   PR+C

Very remote and beautiful mountain hot springs being preserved by a nonprofit volunteer organization. Prior reservations are required. (A $10 daily contribution is requested for each adult.) Elevation 1,800 ft. Open all year.

Natural mineral water flows into an old horizontal mine shaft at temperatures up to 120˚. A dam has been built across the mouth of the shaft, creating a combination steam bath and soaking pool with water temperatures ranging up to 109˚. The mineral water also falls into several nearby rock and cement soaking pools where the temperature is cooler in each lower pool. Clothing policy is determined by the caretaker based on the wishes of those present.

The springs are a 1/2 mile hike from the nearest parking, and overnight camping is available on the premises. It is 28 miles to all other services. Access roads vary in quality from Forest Service Class A to Class D, not suitable for trailers, motor homes and low-clearance vehicles. Ask for a current report on weather and road conditions when phoning for reservations and directions.

You can support the work of this organization by sending tax-deductible contributions to Goldmyer Hotsprings/Northwest Wilderness Programs, 202 N. 85th, #106, Seattle, WA 98103.

▲ *Goldmyer Hotsprings:* This stairstep-falls arrangement makes it possible to start soaking in the hottest water and then move to the cooler pools when you feel like it.

212 TUBS BELLEVUE

11023 N.E. 8th (206) 462-TUBS
Bellevue, WA 98004 PR

Large, modern, pool-rental facility located in downtown Bellevue, a few miles east of Seattle.

Private-space hot pools are for rent to the public, using gas-heated tap water treated with chlorine. There are seventeen indoor acrylic pools with water temperature maintained at 102°. Each room also includes a dry sauna, music system, intercom and modern decor.

A juice bar is available on the premises. Visa, MasterCard and American Express are accepted. Phone for rates, reservations and directions. A membership at TUBS gains reservation privileges and discounts.

213 TUBS SEATTLE

4750 Roosevelt Way N.E. (206) 527-TUBS
Seattle, WA 98105 PR

Large, modern, pool-rental facility located in the University district of Seattle.

Private, luxurious hot pools for rent to the public, using gas-heated tap water treated with chlorine. There are 12 indoor acrylic spas with water temperature maintained at 102-104°.

Each private suite also includes a dry heate sauna, stereo system, intercom, shower, and modern decor. An eleven-bed Sun Salon and a juice bar are also available. TUBS CLUB memberships gain members reservation privileges and discounts. Visa, MasterCard and American Express are accepted. Phone for rates and directions.

214 LAKE BRONSON CLUB

P.O. Box 1135 (206) 793-0286
Sultan, WA 98294 PR+MH+CRV

Unusually spacious nudist park with its own 7 1/2-acre lake, waterfall and evergreen forest. Elevation 800 ft. Open all year.

One large, outdoor hydrojet pool using chlorine-treated artesian well water is maintained at 104°. The spring-fed lake warms to 80° in the summer and freezes over in the winter. There is also an electrically heated sauna. Clothing is prohibited in pool, sauna and lake and is optional elsewhere.

Rental trailers, laundry facilities, overnight camping and RV hookups are available on the premises. It is six miles to a cafe, store, service station and motel. No credit cards are accepted.

Note: This is a membership organization not open to the public for drop-in visits, but interested visitors may be issued a guest pass by prior arrangement. Telephone or write for information and directions.

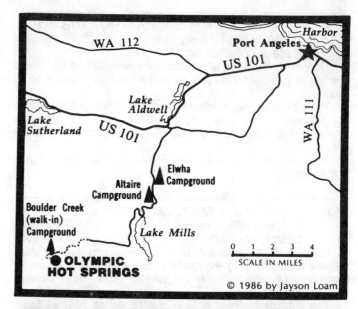

© 1986 by Jayson Loam

 Wise visitors to *Olympic Hot Springs* check water temperatures before plunging in. This pool on a summer day is nearly 110°.

48

 Olympic Hot Springs: Some of the volunteer-built primitive pools have temperatures which are just right for a family frolic.

 The largest of the *Olympic Hot Springs* pools is this last vestige of an old commercial resort which burned down long ago.

---

215   OLYMPIC HOT SPRINGS   (see map)

● **South of Port Angeles**

Several user-friendly, primitive springs surrounded by a lush rain forest at the end of an easy two-mile hike in Olympic National Park. Elevation 1,600 ft. Open all year.

Natural mineral water flows out of several springs at temperatures ranging from 100-112˚. Volunteers have built a series of rock-and-sand soaking pools which permit the water to cool down to comfortable soaking temperatures. Official notices prohibiting nudity are posted often and promptly torn down, resulting in considerable uncertainty. Rangers have been observed issuing a citation after someone complained or after bathers didn't heed orders to dress. However, rangers have not made special trips to the area for the purpose of harassment.

Conscientious visitors have kept the area litter-free. Please do your part to maintain this standard.

There are no services on the premises, but there is a walk-in campground within 200 yards. It is eight miles to a cafe, store and service station, seven miles to a campground, and 20 miles to a motel and RV hookups.

Directions: From the city of Port Angeles, go ten miles west on US 101, turn south and follow signs to Elwha Valley. Continue south on paved road as it winds up Boulder Creek Canyon to where the road is closed due to slide damage. Park and walk the remaining two miles on the damaged paved road to the old end-of-road parking area. At the west end of that parking area is an unmarked, unmaintained path which crosses Boulder Creek and then leads into the hot-springs area. Most, but not all, paths indicate the presence of a nearby spring.

Source map: NPS *Olympic National Park* (hot springs not shown). 10-18-92

216 SOL DUC HOT SPRINGS RESORT

P.O. Box 2169   (206) 327-3583
Port Angeles, WA 98362   **PR+MH+CRV**

Extensively modernized, historic resort surrounded by the evergreen forest of Olympic National Park. Elevation 1,600 ft. Open early May through October.

Natural mineral water flows out of a spring at 128° and is piped to a heat exchanger, where it heats the shower water and chlorine-treated creek water in the swimming pool. The cooled mineral water is then piped to three large outdoor soaking pools, which are maintained at 101-105° on a flow-through basis, requiring no chemical treatment of the water. These pools are equipped with access ramps for the convenience of handicapped persons. All pools are available to the public as well as to registered guests. Bathing suits are required.

Locker rooms, a full-service restaurant, poolside snack bar, gift shop, cabins and RV hookups are available on the premises. It is 1/4 mile to a National Park campground and 15 miles to a service station. MasterCard and Visa are accepted.

Directions: From US 101, two miles west of Fairholm, take Soleduc River Road 12 miles south to resort.

Sol Duc Hot Springs Resort: A recent modernization program improved the old swimming pool and added several shallow tiled pools for less strenuous family fun.

217 DOE BAY VILLAGE RESORT

Orcas Island Star Route 86   (206) 376-2291
Olga, WA 98279   **PR+MH+CRV**

Fantastic combination of running streams, waterfalls, ocean views, hot mineral-water pools, cabins, RV spaces, youth hostel, vegetarian restaurant and a general clothing-optional policy. Ideal for a casual, natural retreat. Elevation sea level. Open all year.

Natural mineral water is pumped out of a well at 105° and is piped to two outdoor pools where it is treated with chlorine. Each pool is large enough for a dozen people, and one of them has hydrojets. Both are maintained at 104-106°, and a small cold pool is maintained at 70-80°. There is also a wood-fired sauna large enough for 20 people. The pools and sauna are available to the public as well as to registered guests. Bathing suits are optional.

Massage, vegetarian meals, cabins, guided kayak trips, overnight camping, RV hookups and a youth hostel are available on the premises. It is seven miles to a store and service station. Visa, MasterCard and American Express are accepted.

Directions: Take the Anacortes Ferry to the San Juan Islands and get off at Orcas Island. Go north on Horseshoe Highway through Eastsound to the resort at the east end of the island.

 Doe Bay Village Resort: This hot-pool deck, overlooking Rosario Strait and the lush greenery of the San Juan Islands, gives the illusion of being up in a tree house.

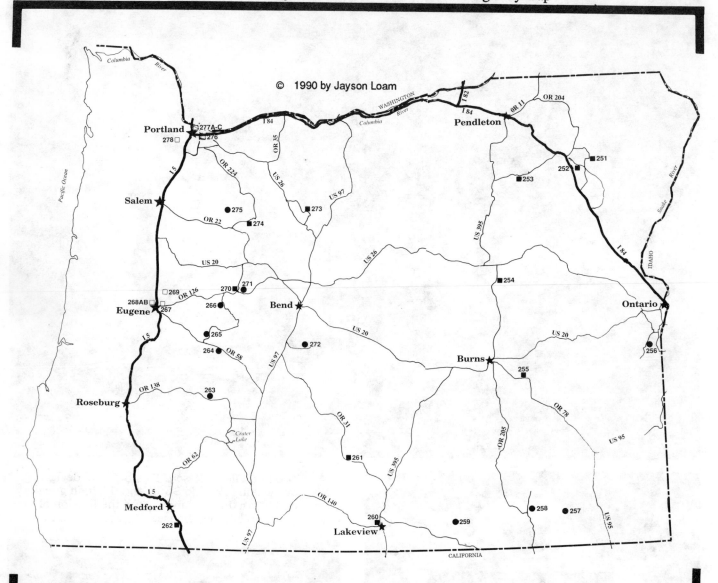

© 1990 by Jayson Loam

Oregon

MAP AND DIRECTORY SYMBOLS

● Non-commercial mineral water pool

■ Commercial (fee) mineral water pool

□ Gas-heated tap or well water pool

〜〜 Paved highway

- - - Unpaved road

⋯⋯ Hiking route

PR = Tubs or pools for rent by hour, day or treatment

MH = Rooms, cabins or dormitory spaces for rent by day, week or month

CRV = Camping or vehicle parking spaces, some with hookups, for rent by day, week, month or year

▲ After being closed for some years *Lehman Hot Springs* has rebuilt and is expanding.

▼ *Cove Swimming Pool* is content to remain a community plunge and picnic grounds.

251   COVE SWIMMING POOL
Rte. 1, Box 36   (503) 586-4890
■ Cove, OR 97824   PR+CRV

Rural community plunge and picnic grounds in the foothills of the Wallowa Mountains. Elevation 3,200 ft. Open May 1 through Labor Day.

Natural mineral water flows out of a spring at 86° directly into and through an outdoor swimming pool. No chlorine is added. Bathing suits are required.

Picnic grounds, snack bar and overnight parking are available on the premises. It is two blocks to a cafe, store, service station and RV hookups, and 15 miles to a motel. No credit cards are accepted.

Directions: From I-84 in La Grandee, take OR 82 exit and go east to OR 237, then south to the town of Cove.

252   HOT LAKE MINERAL SPRINGS
P.O. Box 1601   (503) 963-5587
■ La Grande, OR 97850   PR+CRV

Large RV park and restored bathhouse portion of an historic resort which was a favorite stop along the old Oregon Trail. Elevation 3,000 ft. Open all year.

Mineral water flows out of a spring at 186° and is piped to a coed bathhouse containing six cast iron bathtubs. Water temperature within each tub is regulated by mixing with water piped from a cold spring. Tubs are drained and filled after each use so that no chemical treatment is necessary. A coed steam sauna is continuously operated by spraying the hot mineral water onto one wall. Mineral water is also piped to a hydropool (102°) and swimming pool (89°) in the adjoining RV park. Both operate on a flow-through basis so that no chemical treatment is necessary. Bathing suits are required, except when bathing in either of the two bathhouse tubs, which are curtained.

Facilities include RV hookups, laundromat, convenience store and nature trails. Massage and sweat wraps are available on the premises. Visa and MasterCard are accepted only at the RV park. It is eight miles to central La Grande and all other services. Phone for rates, reservations and directions.

253   LEHMAN HOT SPRINGS
P.O. Box 247   (503) 427-3015
■ Ukiah, OR 97880   PR+CRV

Historic, major hot spring being developed into a large destination resort nestled in a timbered setting of the beautiful Blue Mountains. Elevation 4,300 ft. Open all year.

Natural mineral water flows out of several springs at temperatures up to 167° and is mixed with cold creek water before being piped to a series of outdoor pools. The first pool ranges from 112-115°, the second pool ranges from 107-110°, and the swimming pool ranges from 85-90° in the summer and from 90-96° in the winter. All pools operate on a flow-through basis so that no chemical treatment is necessary. The pools are available to the public as well as to registered guests. Bathing suits are required.

Locker rooms, cafe, camping and RV hookups are available on the premises. Saddle horses, hiking trails, fishing, hunting, cross country skiing and snowmobiling are available nearby. A store, service station and motel are within 18 miles. Visa and MasterCard are accepted.

Developments in the future include plans for a large RV Park, therapy pools, massage, store, garden, golf, motel, lodge, stables and restaurant. Phone for status of construction.

Directions: From Ukiah on OR 224, go 18 miles east. Watch for signs and go one mile south to resort.

J Bar L Guest Ranch: After a day of hiking in the adjoining Wilderness Area, guests are ready for a soak in warm mineral water.

Crystal Crane Hot Springs: Active children can keep warm battling over innertubes in cold water ponds, but adults prefer a leisurely float in a warm water pond.

254 J BAR L GUEST RANCH

I Z Route
Canyon City, OR 97820

(503) 575-2517
PR+MH+CRV

Renovated guest ranch with hot spring, adjoining Strawberry Mountain Wilderness. Elevation 3,800 ft. Open April 15 to November 15.

Natural mineral water flows out of several springs with temperatures ranging up to 120° and is piped to an outdoor swimming pool which ranges from 70-90° depending on weather conditions. Swimming pool is open to registered guests only. Bathing suits are required.

Phone for status of renovation and to make reservations.

Picnic area, cabins, overnight camping and RV hookups are available on the premises. Hiking trails, fishing and hunting are available nearby. A cafe, store and service station are located within ten miles. Visa and MasterCard are accepted.

Directions: Drive ten miles south of John Day on US 395. Turn left on FS 15 and then turn left again immediately into ranch.

255 CRYSTAL CRANE HOT SPRINGS

Route 1, Box 50-A
Burns, OR 97720

(503) 493-2312

A health-oriented resort with private pools, an 80-foot pond for soaking, and a greenhouse. Elevation 4200 ft. Open all year.

Natural mineral water flows out of several springs at 185° and supplies six private-space tubs which are maintained between 95-105°. The mineral water also fills a large, 80-foot pond. All the pools operate on a flow-through basis so that no chemical treatment of the water is necessary. Bathing suits are not required in the private-space pools.

Future plans include overnight facilities, RV hookups and a vegetarian restaurant. Call for status of construction.

Camping is permitted on the premises. It is four miles to the nearest store and 24 miles to all other services in Burns.

Directions: From Burns, drive 24.5 miles east on OR 78 and watch for signs.

256   SNIVELY HOT SPRINGS

●   **Southwest of the town of Owyhee**

Easily-accessible, primitive hot spring on the river's edge in the Owyhee River canyon. Elevation 2,400 ft. Open all year.

Natural mineral water flows out of several springs and a concrete standpipe at temperatures of more than 150˚ and then flows toward the river where volunteers have built several rock-and-sand soaking pools. The temperature in the pools is controlled by varying the amount of cold river water permitted to enter. The pools are visible from the road, so bathing suits are advisable.

There are no services available on the premises except for a large parking area on which overnight parking is not prohibited. It is ten miles to a cafe, store and service station, and 18 miles to a motel and RV hookups. Owyhee Lake, 11 miles south of this hot spring, offers excellent fishing .

Directions: From the town of Owyhee, on OR 201, follow signs west toward Owyhee State Park. When the road enters Owyhee Canyon look for a large metal water pipe running up a steep slope on the west side of the road. 1.4 miles beyond that metal pipe, look on the other side of the road for a low concrete standpipe from which steaming water is flowing.

Source map: USGS *Owyhee Dam, Oregon.*

 Snively Hot Springs: This river-edge soaking pool escapes spring washouts because the river is controlled by an upstream dam.

257   WHITEHORSE RANCH HOT SPRING

●   **Southeast of Alvord Desert**

A very remote, primitive hot spring requiring about 28 miles of unpaved-road travel in the dry, southeastern corner of Oregon.

Natural mineral water flows out of a spring at 114˚ and into a small, volunteer-built soaking pool which ranges in temperature from 104-112˚. The overflow runs into a larger second pool which ranges in temperature from 70-90˚, depending on air temperature and wind conditions. The apparent local custom is clothing optional.

There are no services on the premises, but there is plenty of level space on which overnight parking is not prohibited. It is 45 miles to all services.

Directions: From Burns Junction on US 95, go 21 miles south on US 95, then turn west on a gravel road and go 21 miles to Whitehorse Ranch. Cross a channel and pass by two roads which turn off to the left. At approximately five miles from the ranch, turn left on the third road which is marked by an orange flag on a power pole. Continue on that road for approximately three miles, curving around a butte. The spring is on the northwest side of the second butte.

Source map: BLM *Southern Malheur* (URA-MFP).

 Whitehorse Ranch Hot Springs: This natural spring is about as far from the city as you can get without hiking into the wilderness.

10-10-92

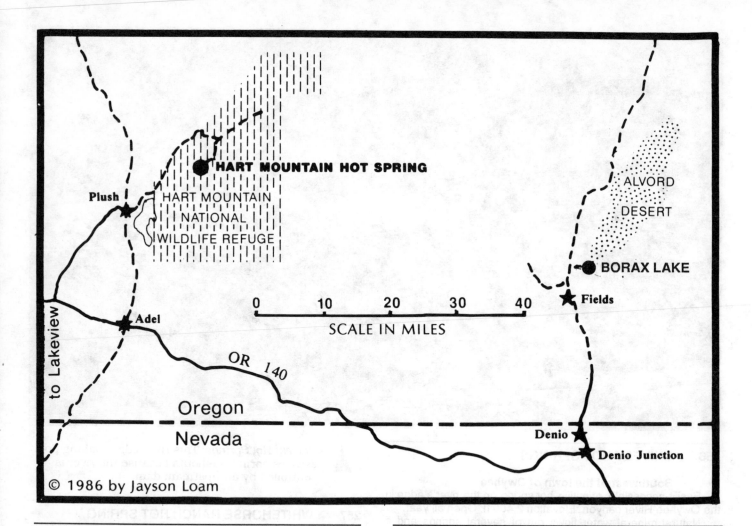

HART MOUNTAIN HOT SPRING

HART MOUNTAIN
NATIONAL
WILDLIFE REFUGE

Plush

ALVORD
DESERT

BORAX LAKE

Fields

Adel

to Lakeview

0   10   20   30   40
SCALE IN MILES

OR 140

Oregon

Nevada

Denio

Denio Junction

© 1986 by Jayson Loam

258 BORAX LAKE (see map)

● **North of the town of Fields**

A five-acre warm pond surrounded by grassland at the edge of the Alvord Desert. Elevation 4,000 ft. Open all year.

Natural mineral water (97°) flows out of the pond bottom at hundreds of gallons per minute, maintaining the pond temperature at approximately 90°. To reach swimming-depth water, it is necessary to slog through squishy mud shallows around the edge. The apparent local custom is clothing optional.

There are no services available, but there is plenty of level ground on which overnight parking is not prohibited. It is seven miles to a store, cafe, motel and garage.

Directions: From Denio, Nevada, drive north 20 miles on a good gravel road to the town of Fields, Oregon. Five miles north of Fields, on the east side of the road, is a grove of trees which makes and excellent camping area. A bumpy road (not good for low-clearance cars) leads east two miles from the trees to Borax Lake.

259 HART MOUNTAIN HOT SPRING (see map)

● **North of the town of Adel**

Semi-improved hot spring enclosed by a roofless, cement block wall and surrounded by miles of barren plateau within the Hart Mountain National Antelope Refuge. Elevation 6,000 ft. Open all year.

Natural mineral water flows out of a spring at 98°. The edge of the spring has been cemented to create a soaking pool which maintains that temperature. There is no posted clothing policy, which leaves it up to the mutual consent of those present.

There are no services available on the premises, but there is an abundance of level ground on which overnight parking is not prohibited. It is 20 miles to a cafe and store, and 40 miles to all other services.

Source map: *Hart Mountain National Antelope Refuge.*

SP-01-01

260 HUNTER'S HOT SPRING RESORT
■ P.O. Box 911   (503) 947-2127
    Lakeview, OR 97630   PR+MH+CRV

Historic spa in the process of a major expansion and tasteful remodeling into a destination resort. Located in the rolling southern Oregon hills, two miles north of Lakeview. Elevation 4,200 ft. Open all year.

Natural mineral water flows out of several springs at temperatures up to 203˚ and into cooling ponds, from which it is piped to the pool and to a heat exchanger for the hot-water system in the buildings. Natural mineral water also erupts out of a geothermal geyser once every minute and 20 seconds and flows into two large cooling ponds. An outdoor swimming pool is maintained at approximately 105˚ on a flow-through system with a minimum of chlorine treatment. Bathing suits are required.

A restaurant, store, service station, overnight camping and motel rooms are available on the premises. Pickup service to a private airport four miles away is also provided. Golf, hunting and fishing are available in the area. Visa and MasterCard are accepted.

Expansion plans include major museum buildings and a full-hookup RV park. Phone or write ahead for current brochure and status of construction.

Location: Two miles north of the town of Lakeview on US 395.

Hunter's Hot Spring Resort: This geyser is hardly as large as Yellowstone's Old Faithful, but it erupts every two minutes.

Hart Mountain Hot Spring: The mineral water in this spring is so pure that the bottom step of the ladder is clearly visible.

Jackson Hot Springs: Thanks to an abundance of geothermal water this swimming pool remains warm and open all winter.

Summer Lake Hot Springs: Chlorine treatment is not needed in this flow-through pool.

261   SUMMER LAKE HOT SPRINGS

Summer Lake, OR 97640

(503) 943-3931
PR+CRV

Small, indoor plunge in the wide open spaces south of Summer Lake. Elevation 4,200 ft. Open all year.

Natural mineral water flows out of a spring at 118° and cools as it is piped to the pool building. Water temperature in the indoor pool is maintained at 102° in the winter and 100° in the summer on a continuous flow-through basis that requires no chemical treatment of the water. Bathing suits are required.

Dressing rooms, overnight camping and RV hookups are available on the premises. It is six miles to all other services. No credit cards are accepted.

Location: Six miles northwest of the town of Summer Lake on OR 31. Watch for sign on north side of road.

262   JACKSON HOT SPRINGS

2253 Hwy 99 N.
Ashland, OR 97520

(503) 482-3776
PR+MH+CRV

Older resort with public plunge, indoor soaking tubs, picnic grounds and RV park. Elevation 1,800 ft. Open all year.

Natural mineral water flows out of a spring at 86° and directly into an outdoor swimming pool which is treated with chlorine and maintains a temperature of 84°. There are three indoor individual soaking tubs large enough for two persons each, in which additional heated natural mineral water can be controlled up to 110°. These tubs are drained and cleaned after each use so that no chemical treatment of the water is necessary. Bathing suits are required, except in private rooms.

Locker rooms, picnic grounds, cabins, overnight camping and RV hookups are available on the premises. There is a cafe, store and service station within two blocks. Visa and MasterCard are accepted.

Location: On US 99, two miles north of Ashland.

263 UMPQUA WARM SPRING

● **Northwest of Crater Lake**

Popular, small, semi-improved hot spring on a wooded bluff overlooking North Umpqua River. Located in the Umpqua National Forest at the end of a fairly steep, one-quarter-mile hike. Elevation 2,600 ft. Open all year.

Natural mineral water flows out of a spring at 108° and directly into a sheltered, six-foot by six-foot pool which volunteers have carved out of the spring-built travertine deposit. There are no posted clothing requirements, and the location is quite remote, so a clothing-optional custom would be expected. However, the location is so popular, especially on summer weekends, that it is advisable to take a bathing suit with you. You may have to wait your turn to share a rather crowded pool.

There are no services available on the premises. It is three miles to a Forest Service campground and 25 miles to all other services.

Directions: Drive 60 miles east of Roseburg on OR 138 to Toketee Junction. Turn north on paved road FS 34. Drive 2.3 miles, turn right on FS 3401 and go two miles to the parking area. Walk across the new bridge over the North Umpqua River, bear right on the North Umpqua Trail and climb 1/4 mile east to springs.

Source map: *Umpqua National Forest.*

Umpqua Warm Spring: This rustic shelter is perched in verdant trees above Loafer Creek. However, the pool is so small that it is frequently full of wall-to-wall bodies.

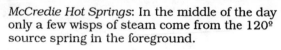 *McCredie Hot Springs*: In the middle of the day only a few wisps of steam come from the 120° source spring in the foreground.

During morning hours the entire soaking pool is enveloped in delicate clouds which soften the forms of *McCredie's* riveredge rocks.

When Forest Rangers get a complaint about the nudity at *McCredie Hot Springs*, they tell the complainers. "So don't go back."

264   MCCREDIE HOT SPRINGS

● **East of the town of Oakridge**

Easily-accessible, primitive hot springs with a strong skinny-dipping tradition, located on the north and south banks of Salt Creek in the Willamette National Forest. Elevation 2,100 ft. Open all year.

Natural mineral water flows out of several springs on the north bank at 120°, and on the south bank at 140°. The water is channeled into a series of shallow, volunteer-built, rock-and-mud pools where it cools as it flows toward the creek. Despite the proximity to a main highway, the apparent local custom is clothing optional.

There are no services available on the premises, but there is a large level area nearby in which overnight parking is not prohibited. It is less than one mile to a Forest Service campground and ten miles to all other services.

Directions: To reach the springs and pools on the north bank, drive from the town of Oakridge on OR 58, approximately ten miles east past Blue Pool Campground. At 0.1 of a mile past mile marker 45, turn right (south) into a large parking area between the road and the creek. Walk to the upstream (east) end of the parking area and follow a well-worn path 40 yards to springs.

To reach the springs and soaking pools on the south bank, drive 1/2 mile east on OR 58, turn right across the bridge and stay right on FS 5875. Park at the first curve. Look for an opening in the shrubbery, walk down the embankment to the trail and walk downstream 1/2 mile to the springs.

WARNING! Do not try to wade across Salt Creek to reach the south bank—the water is very deep and flows rapidly.

These south bank pools at *McCredie Hot Springs* are less crowded because they are harder to find and require a half-mile hike.

265   MEDITATION POOL (WALL CREEK) WARM SPRING

● **Northeast of the town of Oakridge**

Idyllic, primitive warm spring on the wooded banks of Wall Creek at the end of a short, easy trail in the Willamette National Forest. Elevation 2,200 ft. Open all year.

Natural mineral water flows up through the gravel bottom of a volunteer-built, rock-and-sand pool at 104°. The pool temperature ranges up to 96° depending on air temperature and wind conditions. While the water is not hot enough for therapy soaking, it is ideal for effortless lolling. The apparent local custom is clothing optional.

There are no services available on the premises. It is five miles from the trailhead to a Forest Service campground and nine miles to all other services.

Directions: On OR 58 in the town of Oakridge at the "city center" highway sign, turn north on Rose St. over the train tracks. At First St., turn east and keep going as that street becomes FS 24. Approximately ten miles from Oakridge on FS 24, turn north on FS 1934 for 1/2 mile and watch for trailhead sign on west side of the road. There is no name or number given for the trail at the trailhead area. Follow a well-worn path along Wall Creek for 600 yards to the creekside pool. Source map: *Willamette National Forest*.

Meditation Pool Warm Spring: The gentle tumbling sound of Wall Creek, a few feet away, is just enough for quiet centering.

 This official *Terwilliger* sign is not visible from the road, but confirms that hikers are on the trail to one of the most beautiful multi-pool hot spring locations.

Terwilliger Hot Spring: Log rounds, cut from fallen trees by a volunteer group, now give dry footing in an otherwise muddy gully.

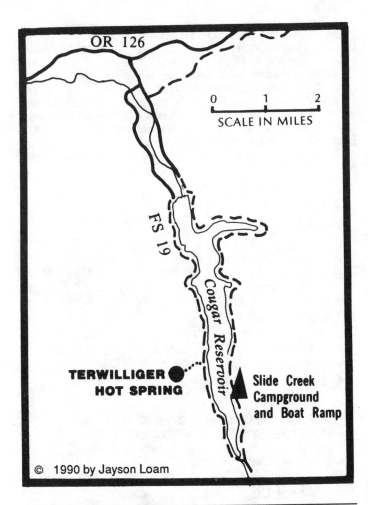

© 1990 by Jayson Loam

SCALE IN MILES

OR 126

FS 19

Cougar Reservoir

TERWILLIGER HOT SPRING

Slide Creek Campground and Boat Ramp

---

267   SPRINGFIELD SPAS

1100 Main St.   (503) 741-1777
Springfield, OR 97477   PR

Well-maintained, suburban, rent-a-tub establishment located on the main street.

Private-space hydrojet pools using chlorine-treated tap water are for rent to the public by the hour. Twelve fiberglass tubs in open-roof enclosed spaces are maintained at 102°. Each unit includes a covered dressing area.

Two tanning beds are available on the premises. No credit cards are accepted. Phone for rates, reservations and directions.

▲ *Springfield Spas:* The walls around most urban rental tubs, such as this one, provide privacy and convenience, but no scenery.

---

266   TERWILLIGER (COUGAR) HOT SPRING

(see map)

● **Southeast of the town of Blue River**

A lovely series of user-friendly, log-and-stone soaking pools in a picturesque, forest canyon at the end of an easy one-quarter-mile trail in the Willamette National Forest. Elevation 3,000 ft. Open all year.

Natural mineral water flows out of a spring at 116° and directly into the first of a series of volunteer-built pools, each of which is a few degrees cooler than the one above. An organized group of volunteers has also built access steps and railings and provides a full-time resident caretaker to protect and maintain the location. The apparent local custom is clothing optional.

There are no services available on the premises. There is a walk-in campground within one-half mile, and overnight parking is not prohibited in the roadside space near the trailhead. It is four miles to a Forest Service campground and eight miles to all other services.

Directions: From OR 126 approximately five miles east of Blue River, turn south on FS 19 along the west side of Cougar Reservoir. The unmarked hot-springs trailhead is on the west side of the road, 0.3 mile south of Boone Creek. A large parking area is on the east side of the road, 0.1 mile beyond the trailhead.

Reference map: *Willamette National Forest* (hot springs not shown).

Onsen Hot Tub Rentals: These open-roof hydro-pool spaces at least provide fresh air and sunshine along with personal privacy.

268A ONSEN HOT TUB RENTALS
1883 Garden Ave. (503) 345-9048
Eugene, OR 97403 PR

Well-maintained, enclosed-pool, rent-a-tub establishment located near the University of Oregon.

Private-space hydrojet pools using chlorine-treated tap water are for rent to the public by the hour. Fourteen fiberglass tubs in open-roof enclosed spaces are maintained at 102°. Each unit includes a covered dressing area.

No credit cards are accepted. Phone for rates, reservations and directions.

OUR RULES
- NO DRUGS OR ALCOHOL ON THE PREMISES.
- NO FOOD IN THE SPA ROOMS.
- NO GLASS CONTAINERS IN SPA ROOMS.
- NO SOAPS OR OILS IN SPAS.
- MINORS MUST BE ACCOMPANIED BY PARENTS OR LEGAL GUARDIAN.
- PLEASE HELP US MAINTAIN A QUIET & RELAXING ATMOSPHERE BY KEEPING VOICES LOW.

THE WATER
- TEMPERATURE MAINTAINED AT 102°F.
- AUTOMATIC CHLORINATORS MAINTAIN FREE CHLORINE AT 2-3 PPM.
- PH MAINTAINED AT 7.2 ~ 7.6.
- FILTERS ARE DIATOMACEOUS EARTH WITH A 10 MINUTE SYSTEM TURN OVER RATE.
- GROUPS ARE SCHEDULED 15 MINUTES APART TO INSURE PROPER FILTRATION.

BE CAREFUL
- THE SURFACE AROUND SPAS IS SLIP RESISTANT, BUT ENTER & EXIT SPAS WITH CAUTION.
- WE RECOMMEND A MOMENT'S PAUSE WHEN LEAVING SPA TO LET YOUR BODY ADJUST.
- WE ARE NOT RESPONSIBLE FOR LOST ITEMS LEFT ON THE PREMISES.
- WE WILL CHECK WITH YOU ON THE HALF HOUR TO INSURE EVERYTHING IS SATISFACTORY.

ONSEN trusts your stay with us will be relaxing and enjoyable. Thank You!

Each rent-a-tub establishment has its own set of rules, similar to this Onsen list.

268B EMERALD PARK AND RIVER ROAD POOL
1400 Lake Dr.   (503) 688-4052
☐ Eugene, OR 97404   PR

Two spotless, outdoor hydrojet pools included in a public recreation complex near downtown Eugene. Open all year.

Large tile pools using chlorine-treated tap water are available to the public for a fee, except when reserved for special group use. Water temperature is maintained at 104° in the winter and 102° in the summer. The complex includes an outdoor wading pool and a large indoor swimming pool, as well as a fitness center with weight equipment. One of the hydrojet pools has a roof, and both of them are within a grassy, fenced patio area adjoining the indoor pool. Bathing suits are required. Visa and MasterCard are accepted only for quarterly passes.

Phone to find out the hours when the hydrojet pools are available to the public.

269 WILLAMETANS
P.O. Box 1054   (503) 933-9955
☐ Eugene, OR 97401   PR+MH+CRV

Large, well-equipped nudist park in the forested foothills east of Eugene. Elevation 1,200 ft. Open all year.

One indoor hydrojet pool using chlorine-treated tap water is maintained at 102°. The outdoor swimming pool is maintained at 78° in the summer and is not heated in the winter. There is also a coin-operated sauna. Clothing is prohibited in the pools and sauna and is optional elsewhere.

Overnight camping and RV hookups are available on the premises. It is five miles to all other services. Visa is accepted for payment of ground fees.

Note: This is a membership organization not open to the public for drop-in visits, but interested visitors may be issued a guest pass by prior arrangement. Telephone or write for information and directions.

▲ *Emerald Park and River Road Pool:* This was one of the first community-owned plunges to add outdoor gas-heated hot pools.

▲ *Willametans:* While urban rent-a-tub sites near Eugene put their hot pools outside, these nudists built their pool indoors.

270 BELKNAP HOT SPRINGS
P.O. Box 1
McKenzie Bridge, OR 97413

(503) 822-3535
MH+CRV

Attractive, riverside resort in a rustic setting with in-room jettubs, campground and RV park, surrounded by the lush greenery of Willamette National Forest. Elevation 1,700 ft. Open all year.

Natural mineral water flows out of a spring at 196° and is piped into a combination reservoir and heat exchanger where heat is extracted for space heating and for the hot water supply in the lodge and the RV park. The cooled mineral water is piped to outdoor pools at the lodge and the RV park. Both pools are treated with chlorine and maintained at a temperature of 102° in the winter and 93° in the summer. Six lodge rooms have indoor hydrojet tubs controllable up to 110°. These tubs are drained and cleaned after each use so that no chemical treatment of the water is needed. The use of the pools is limited to registered guests. Bathing suits are required, except in private rooms.

Rooms, overnight camping and RV hookups are available on the premises. It is six miles to all other services. Visa and MasterCard are accepted.

Location: On OR 126, 6 miles east of the town of McKenzie Bridge. Follow signs.

Belknap Hot Springs: Hot mineral water is piped across the river through the pipes visible beyond the far edge of pool area.

In addition to the main swimming pool by the lodge, *Belknap Hot Springs* has this smaller pool for customers in the RV park area.

 Bigelow Hot Spring: This pool cannot be seen from the road 100 feet away, so those who wish to skinny-dip may do so safely.

271   BIGELOW HOT SPRING

● **Northeast of the town of McKenzie Bridge**

A small, rock-and-sand pool in a fern-lined grotto on the west bank of the McKenzie River. Elevation 2,000 ft. Open all year.

A small flow of natural mineral water (130°) bubbles up from the bottom of a volunteer-dug pool. Temperature is controlled by adding river water as needed. The apparent local custom is clothing optional.

There are no services available on the premises. It is 1 1/2 miles to a campground (Ollalie), three miles to a motel and RV hookups (Belknap Hot Springs), and six miles to all other services.

Directions: From the town of McKenzie Bridge on OR 126, drive nine miles northeast and turn left onto Deer Creek Road (FS 2654). Park just beyond the bridge over the McKenzie River and walk approximately 100 ft. downstream to the pool.

272   DIG YOUR OWN HOT SPRINGS
c/o Paulina Lake Resort, Box 7   (503) 536-2240
● La Pine, OR 97739

Unique, underground, geothermal flow which may be tapped by digging a hole in the lakeshore gravel. Located at Paulina Lake in Newberry Crater, south of the city of Bend. Elevation 6,300 ft. Open all year.

Natural mineral water does not flow out of the ground but rather flows up at the northeast edge of the lake, joining the lake water without emerging on the surface. When the lake level is just right, a hole dug in the lake-edge gravel will fill with water ranging up to 110°. Access is via a 2 1/2 mile trail or, in the summer, by boat. There are no posted clothing requirements, leaving it up to the mutual consent of those present.

Boat rental, cabins, cafe, store and gas pumps are available at Paulina Lake Resort, and overnight camping is available nearby. Fishing, hiking, skiing and snowmobiling are also available in the area. No credit cards are accepted.

Phone Paulina Lake Resort to find out if the lake level is right and to get information on boat rental rates.

Directions: On 97 approximately 20 miles south of Bend, follow signs east to Paulina Lake.

 Dig Your Own Hot Springs: The magic place to dig is just below the treeless rock slide on the far side of Lake Paulina.

67

 Kah-Nee-Ta Vacation Resort Village: Part of the fun of visiting this Indian reservation resort is living in surprisingly comfortable canvas teepees instead of in motel rooms.

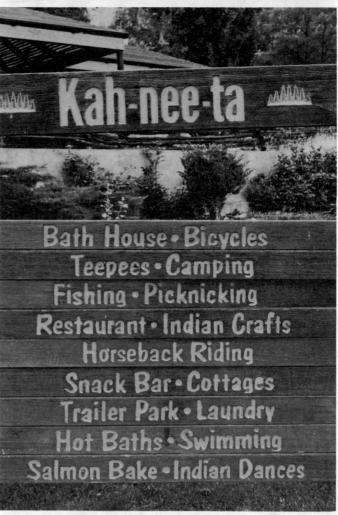

 This outdoor-oriented destination resort, with a variety of activities, is a major source of income for the Indian tribes.

 Kah-Nee-Ta is on the dry side of the Cascade Mountains, so the hills have very few trees. However, the extra days of sunshine are very welcome to residents and visitors in Oregon.

273   KAH-NEE-TA VACATION RESORT VILLAGE
P.O. Box K   **(503) 553-1112**
■ **Warm Springs, OR 97761**   **PR+MH+CRV**

A modern resort owned and operated by the Confederated Tribes of the Warm Springs Indian Reservation. In these foothills on the east side of the Cascade Mountains, the sun shines 340 days a year. Elevation 1,500 ft. Open all year.

Natural mineral water flows out of a spring at 140° and is piped to the bathhouse and swimming pool. The large outdoor swimming pool is chlorinated and maintained at a temperature of 95°. The men's and women's bathhouses each contain five tiled Roman tubs in which the soaking temperature is individually controlled up to 110°. Tubs are drained and filled after each use. Pools and bathhouses are available to the public as well as to registered guests. Bathing suits are required in public areas.

Massage, dressing rooms, restaurant, cabins, teepees, overnight camping, RV hookups and miniature golf are available on the premises. Resort hotel and golf course are located nearby. It is 11 miles to a store and service station. Visa, MasterCard, American Express, Diner's Club and Carte Blanche are accepted.

Directions: From US 26 in Warm Springs, follow signs 11 miles northeast to resort.

▲ *Breitenbush Hot Springs Retreat and Conference Center:* This location is superb for quiet riverside meditation.

▲ The holistic community which operates *Breitenbush Hot Springs* sponsors groups such as this Summer Solstice Healing Gathering.

**274   BREITENBUSH HOT SPRINGS
         RETREAT AND CONFERENCE CENTER**
■ **P.O. Box 578**   **(503) 854-3314**
Detroit, OR 97342   **PR+MH**

A rustic, older resort being renovated by a residential holistic community on the banks of the Breitenbush River, surrounded by the Willamette National Forest. Elevation 2,000 ft. Open all year.

Natural mineral water flows out of springs and artesian wells at temperatures up to 180°. There are four outdoor soaking pools maintained at 104°, with flow-through mineral water requiring no chemical treatment. There are three outdoor foot baths in the meadow, which operate on a flow-through basis with temperatures averaging between 100-110°, depending on weather conditions. The steambath building is supplied with 180° water direct from an adjoining well and spring. Plans to renovate the swimming pool are pending. Phone ahead for status of construction. The pools are available to the public as well as to registered guests, but prior reservations are advised. Bathing suits are required in the hot tub and sauna areas from 9 A.M. to noon, optional thereafter.

Massage (by reservation), vegetarian meals and cabins are available on the premises. It is 11 miles to a store, service station and phone, 1 1/2 miles to overnight camping and 70 miles to RV hookups. Organizations and individuals are invited to request the newsletter describing rates and facilities suitable for seminars and conferences. Visa and MasterCard are accepted.

Location: 11 miles northeast of Detroit. Phone for rates, reservations and directions.

 Although Bagby Hot Springs has a clothing-optional policy in the communal bathhouse, a sign is posted on the access trail asking skinnydippers to be considerate of others.

FELLOW FRIENDS OF BAGBY -
PLEASE CONSIDER THE FEELINGS
OF PEOPLE WHO ARE OFFENDED BY NUDITY.
· · · THANK YOU · · ·

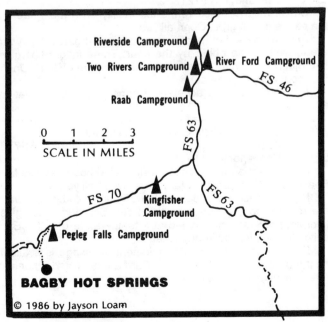

275 BAGBY HOT SPRINGS

● **Southeast of the town of Estacada**

A world class, deep-in-the-woods, soaking opportunity, springing from the ashes of a burned-out Forest Service bathhouse. Half-roofed buildings, hollow-log tubs, and geothermal water delivered by wooden flumes contribute to the rustic atmosphere, as does the beautiful 1 1/2-mile access path through a rain forest. Elevation 2,100 ft. Open all year.

Natural mineral water emerges from two springs at 135° and flows through wooden flumes to an outdoor, round cedar tub on its own deck near the upper spring, and to two half-roofed bathhouse buildings near the lower spring. One building has five private stalls containing hollow-log tubs cut from local giant cedar trees. The adjoining building is a communal area containing three more hollow-log tubs plus a round redwood tub. A flume diversion gate at each tub brings in more hot water whenever desired, or buckets of cold creek water may be added. All tubs are drained and cleaned daily so that no chemical treatment of the water is necessary. There are no posted clothing requirements, and the apparent local custom in the communal bathhouse is clothing optional.

Friends of Bagby, Inc., is the volunteer organization which, in cooperation with the Forest Service, planned and accomplished all of the construction. The Friends also staff a caretaker's cabin at the location 365 days per year. You can support the work of this pioneering organization by sending tax-deductible contributions to Friends of Bagby, Inc., P.O. Box 15116, Portland, OR 97215

There is a picnic area in the Bagby Natural Area, but no overnight camping is permitted. A walk-in campground is located at Shower Creek, 1/3 mile beyond Bagby. There is no overnight parking at the Bagby trailhead on FS 70, but a Forest Service Campground (Pegleg Falls) is located 1/2 mile northeast of the trailhead. All other services are available 32 miles away in Estacada.

Four Seasons Hot Tubbing: This newer facility features shiny acrylic tubs and a toilet in each private-space dressing room.

276 FOUR SEASONS HOT TUBBING

19059 S.E. Division   (503) 663-3411
❑   Gresham, OR 97030   PR

Attractive, suburban rent-a-tub facility featuring enclosed outdoor tubs. Open all year.

Private-space hot pools using chlorine-treated tap water are for rent to the public by the hour. Six enclosed, outdoor fiberglass hydrojet pools are maintained at a temperature of 104˚. Each unit includes indoor dressing room, shower and toilet.

Visa and MasterCard are accepted. Phone for rates, reservations and directions.

277A OPEN AIR HOT TUBBING

11126 N.E. Halsey   (503) 257-8191
❑   Portland, OR 97220   PR

Unique, suburban rent-a-tub featuring open-roofed wood patios. Open all year.

Private-space hot pools using chlorine-treated tap water are for rent to the public by the hour. Six enclosed, outdoor fiberglass hydrojet pools are maintained at temperatures ranging from 102-104˚. Each unit has an outdoor water spray over the pool and an indoor dressing room with shower and toilet. Three of the units can be combined to accommodate a party of 24. There is a sauna in one unit.

An open-air tanning salon is available on the premises. Visa and MasterCard are accepted. Phone for rates, reservations and directions.

277B INNER CITY HOT SPRINGS

2927 N.E. Everett   (503) 238-4010
❑   Portland, OR 97232   PR

Open-air, family-style pools and sauna in a garden setting near downtown Portland.

Two communal hydrojet pools, cold pool, sauna and sundeck are for rent to the public by the hour. Both hot pools use gas-heated tap water treated with chlorine and are maintained at 104˚. Bathing suits are optional in the pool and sauna areas.

Massage, chiropractic care, homeopothy, rebirthing and accupressure are available on the premises. No credit cards are accepted. Phone for rates, reservations and directions.

277C THE FAMILY HOT TUB

4747 S.E. Hawthorne   (503) 239-TUBS
❑   Portland, OR 97215   PR

Small, neighborhood rent-a-tub facility on a main street in the east-side suburbs. Open all year.

Private-space hot pools using chlorine-treated tap water are for rent to the public by the hour. Three indoor fiberglass hydrojet pools are maintained at a temperature of 104˚. One of the rooms also has a sauna.

No credit cards are accepted. Phone for rates, reservations and directions.

278 ELITE TUBBING AND TANNING

4240 S.W. 10th   (503) 641-7727
❑   Beaverton, OR 97005   PR

Private rent-a-tub suites in a remodeled house across from Beaverton's Montgomery Ward store. Open all year.

Private-space hot pools using chlorine-treated tap water are for rent to the public by the hour. Six indoor fiberglass hydrojet pools are maintained at a temperature of 103˚. Each suite includes a shower and toilet.

Facilities include tanning equipment. Massage is available on the premises. Visa and MasterCard are accepted. Phone for rates, reservations and directions.

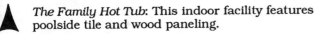
The Family Hot Tub: This indoor facility features poolside tile and wood paneling.

SAVE WATER

BATHe WITH A FRIEND

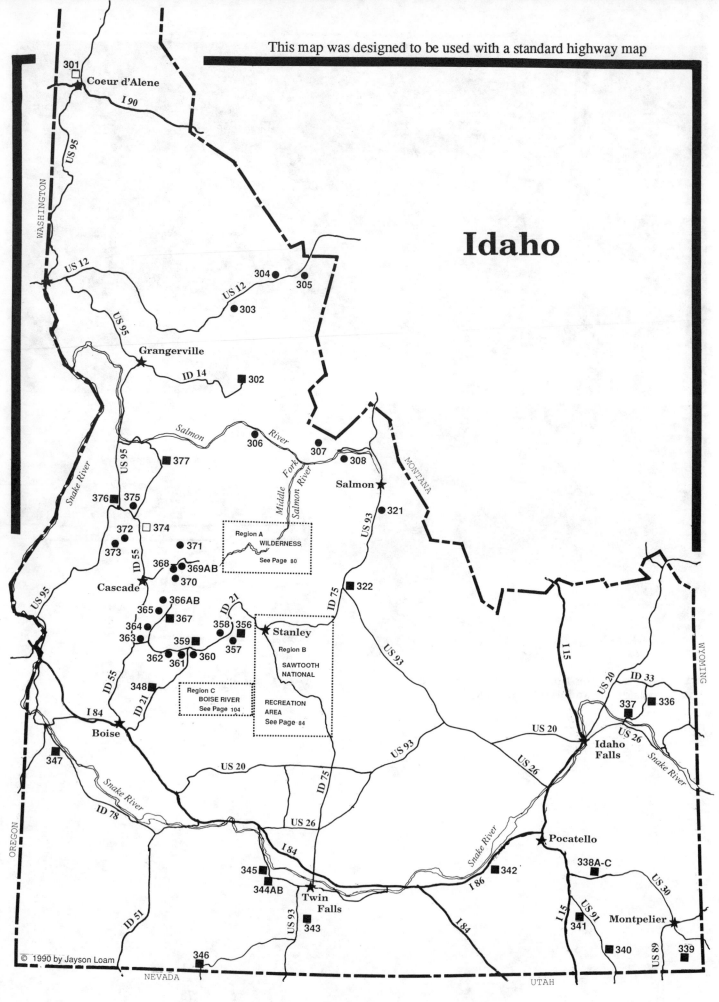

Idaho

301

Coeur d'Alene

I 90

US 95

WASHINGTON

US 12

US 95

US 12

304

305

303

Grangerville

ID 14

302

Salmon   River

306

307

308

377

Middle   Fork

Salmon   River

Salmon

321

US 93

376 375

372   374

373

371

ID 55

368   369AB

370

Cascade

366AB

365 367

364

363

362 361 360

359

358 356

Stanley

357

ID 21

ID 75

322

US 93

Region A
WILDERNESS
See Page 80

Region B

SAWTOOTH
NATIONAL

RECREATION
AREA
See Page 84

348

ID 55

ID 21

Region C
BOISE RIVER
See Page 104

I 84

Boise

347

US 95

Snake River

ID 78

US 20

US 20

US 93

US 26

ID 75

US 26

US 20

ID 33

337   336

US 26

Idaho
Falls

Snake River

I 15

MONTANA

WYOMING

Snake River

I 86

342

Pocatello

338A-C

US 30

US 91

341

Montpelier

340

US 89

339

345

344AB

Twin
Falls

US 93

343

I 84

I 15

ID 51

346

NEVADA

UTAH

OREGON

Snake River

74

● Non-commercial mineral water pool

■ Commercial (fee) mineral water pool

☐ Gas-heated tap or well water pool

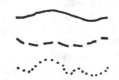

〰 Paved highway

- - - Unpaved road

⋯⋯ Hiking route

PR = Tubs or pools for rent by hour, day or treatment

MH = Rooms, cabins or dormitory spaces for rent by day, week or month

CRV = Camping or vehicle parking spaces, some with hookups, for rent by day, week, month or year

---

301	BENNETT BAY INN	
	E 5144 I-90	(208) 664-6168
☐	Coeur D'Alene, ID 83814	PR+MH

Modern motel with hot-pool theme suites, store and boat dock on Lake Coeur D'Alene, three miles from the town of Coeur D'Alene and 30 miles from Spokane, Washington.

Pools in motel suites are for rent to the public by the hour and by the day. Lake water is heated by electricity, treated with chlorine, and maintained at 102°. There are six indoor, fiberglass pools, five of them in spectacular theme rooms. Adult movies are available with room rentals. The outdoor swimming pool is filled with unheated lake water and treated with chlorine.

Facilities include free rowboat use with room rental. Visa, MasterCard, American Express and Diners Club are accepted. Phone for rates, reservations and directions.

302	RED RIVER HOT SPRINGS	
		(208) 983-0452
■	Elk City, ID 83525	PR+MH+CRV

Friendly, remote, rustic resort featuring both public and private-space pools surrounded by the tall timber in the Nezperce National Forest. Elevation 4,500 ft. Open all year.

Natural mineral water flows out of ten springs at temperatures up to 130°. The chlorine-treated swimming pool temperature varies from 88° in the summer to 72° in the winter. The outdoor flow-through soaking pool is maintained at 104° and requires no chemical treatment. There are also three, claw-footed bathtubs located in private spaces. These are drained and cleaned after each use. In a fourth private space, there is an authentic galvanized horse trough which is surprisingly comfortable for a two-person soak. Pools are available to the public as well as to registered guests. Bathing suits are required in public areas.

Locker rooms, a cafe, store, rustic cabins and overnight camping are available on the premises. Hiking, fishing, cross-country skiing, snowmobiling, and horse trails are nearby. It is 30 miles to a service station and 150 miles to RV hookups. No credit cards are accepted.

Directions: From the town of Grangeville, take ID 14 to Elk City, then go 25 miles east to the resort. The last 11 miles are on an easy gravel road.

 Red River Hot Springs: The restaurant area in the background overlooks the swimming pool and the soaking pool in the foreground.

 This metal horse trough at *Red River Hot Springs* has been installed in a private space, becoming a cozy soaking pool for two.

303   STANLEY HOT SPRING

● **Northeast of the town of Lowell**

Several shallow pools in the Huckleberry Creek canyon at the end of a rugged five-mile trail in the Selway-Bitterroot Wilderness. Elevation 3,600 ft. Open all year.

Natural mineral water flows out of a canyon-bank spring at 110° and into a series of volunteer-built, rock-and-sand pools which range in temperature from 90-100°, depending on air temperature and wind conditions. The apparent local custom is clothing optional.

There are no services available on the premises. There is a Forest Service campground at the trailhead. All other services are 49 miles from the trailhead.

Directions: On US 12, drive 26 miles northeast of Lowell to the Wilderness Gateway Compound (ranger station and visitor center). From there, on FS Trail 211, hike 5 miles east, then 1/2 mile south on FS 221 to spring.

Source map: *Clearwater National Forest.*

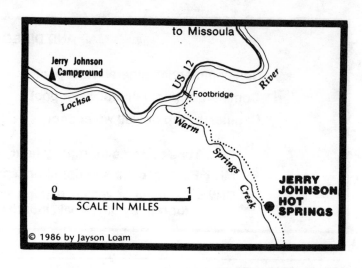

© 1986 by Jayson Loam

304   WEIR CREEK HOT SPRINGS

● **Northeast of the town of Lowell**

Secluded, primitive hot springs and creekside soaking pools reached via a sometimes difficult half-mile path in Clearwater National Forest. Elevation 2,900 ft. Open all year.

Natural mineral water flows out of several springs at 117° and is channeled through a wooden gutter to a volunteer-built pool lined with split logs and located above the creek. Temperature can be controlled by moving the gutter to add or divert the flow of hot water. The apparent local custom is clothing optional.

There are no services available on the premises. It is eight miles to a campground, 16 miles to a restaurant and motel, and 35 miles to all other services.

Directions: From Lowell, drive 45 miles northeast on US 12 to mile marker 142. Park in pull-out area just east of that mile marker at a bridge spanning Weir Creek. Follow an unmarked, unmaintained path up the west side of the creek for slightly less than 1/2 mile to the springs. Wherever it appears that the path divides, stay with the fork that keeps the creek in sight.

Source map: *Clearwater National Forest.*

▶ *Jerry Johnson Hot Springs*: These upper pools overlooking a forest meadow maintain a 106° temperature without a creek water mix.

76

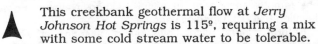
This creekbank geothermal flow at *Jerry Johnson Hot Springs* is 115°, requiring a mix with some cold stream water to be tolerable.

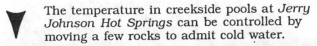
The temperature in creekside pools at *Jerry Johnson Hot Springs* can be controlled by moving a few rocks to admit cold water.

305   JERRY JOHNSON HOT SPRINGS   (see map)

● **Southwest of the town of Missoula, Montana**

Delightful series of user-friendly, primitive hot springs at the end of an easy, one-mile hike through a beautiful forest along the east bank of Warm Springs Creek. Elevation 3,200 ft. Open all year.

Odorless natural mineral water flows out of many fissures in the creek bank at 114° and also out of several other springs at temperatures up to 110°. Volunteers have constructed rock-and-mud soaking pools along the edge of the river and near the springs. The temperature within each pool is controlled by admitting cold creek water as needed or by diverting the hotter flow to let a pool cool down. The apparent local custom is clothing optional.

There are no services on the premises. Overnight camping is permitted, but excessive vandalism may force the Forest Service to adopt a policy of day use only for this site. However, there are three uncrowded Forest Service campgrounds within five miles of the Jerry Johnson Hot Springs trailhead. It is ten miles to a cafe, service station and all other services.

Directions: Drive on US 12 to Warm Springs Park bridge trailhead, which is located 1/2 mile west of mile marker 152. Park in large area on north side of US 12, walk over bridge and follow FS 49 one mile southeast to springs.

Source map: *Clearwater National Forest.*

 Horse Creek Hot Spring: A roofless enclosure provides soaking privacy but you can't see the lovely scenery while you are inside.

306   BARTH HOT SPRINGS

● **West of the town of North Fork**

A truly unexpected, claw-footed bathtub in a remote section of the main Salmon River known as the *River of No Return*. Elevation 2,700 ft. Open all year.

Natural mineral water flows out of many small seeps at temperatures up to 140˚ and cools as it is gathered into a PVC pipe carrying it to the outdoor bathtub. There are no posted clothing requirements, which leaves that matter up to the mutual consent of those present.

There are no services available on the premises, nor are there any roads to this area. Access is by raft or jet boat. It is 65 miles by river to and from all services.

The Forest Service issues licenses to a limited number of outfitters who operate raft and boat trips on an individual seat and charter basis. For more information, write to Idaho Outfitter's and Guides Association, Inc., Peck, Idaho, 83545.

Source maps: Forest Service, *The Salmon, River of No Return*.

307   HORSE CREEK HOT SPRING   (see map)

● **Northwest of the town of North Fork**

Rock-lined, primitive hot spring enclosed by four walls in a very remote section of beautiful Salmon National Forest. Elevation 6,200 ft. Open all year.

Natural mineral water flows out of a spring at 97˚ and directly into the pool, which is surrounded by a roofless bathhouse. The apparent local custom is clothing optional.

There is a picnic area with table and rest rooms available at the springs. It is one mile to a campground and 35 miles to all other services.

Directions: From the town of North Fork, go west on FS 030, north on FS 038, west and north on FS 044, then west and south on FS 065 to the spring.

Source map: *Salmon National Forest*.

▲ At *Horse Creek Hot Spring* the soaking pool is the spring itself, which has been excavated large enough to accomodate four good friends.

78

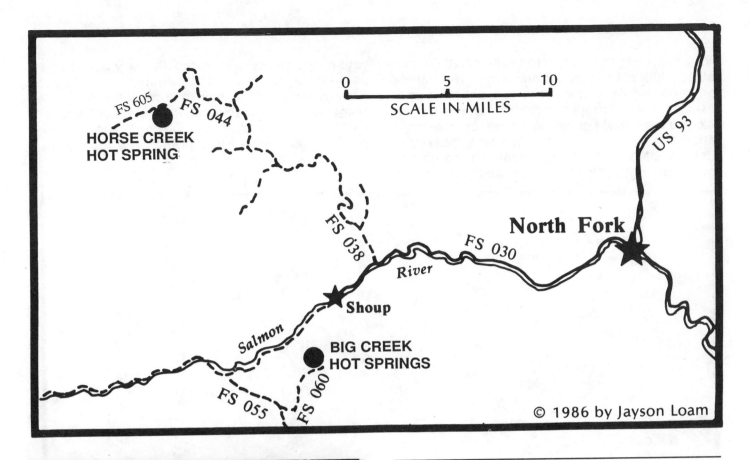

SCALE IN MILES

FS 605 FS 044
HORSE CREEK
HOT SPRING

FS 038

FS 030

North Fork

US 93

River

Salmon

Shoup

BIG CREEK
HOT SPRINGS

FS 055   FS 060

© 1986 by Jayson Loam

Big Creek Hot Springs: A good gravel road
leads to within 50 yards of this location.

308   BIG CREEK HOT SPRINGS   (see map)

● **West of the town of North Fork**

Dozens of high-temperature geothermal outflows along Warm Springs Creek in a remote, rocky canyon in Salmon National Forest. Elevation 4,800 ft. Open all year.

Natural mineral water flows out of many small fissures in the rocks at more than 170° toward a series of volunteer-built rock pools along the bed of Warm Springs Creek. Pool temperature is controlled by admitting cold water piped from a nearby cold spring. There are no services available on the premises. It is 33 miles to all services.

Source maps: *Salmon National Forest*; USGS *Shoup, Idaho-Montana.*

This is the region in which to totally escape urban noise pollution, because the only way to reach these springs is to hike or float in on a raft, or both. It is possible to plan a rugged backpack route which will take you to several springs over a two or three day period. It is equally possible to find packaged river-raft trips, featuring hot springs, which fly you to an upriver airstrip, carry all your food and gear, cook all your meals and even wash the dishes, while you sit back and enjoy unsurpassed beauty.

In any case, the first step is to consult with a ranger station in Challis National Forest or Salmon National Forest. For information on charter or single-seat raft trips, write to Idaho Outfitter's and Guides Association, Inc. Peck, ID 83545

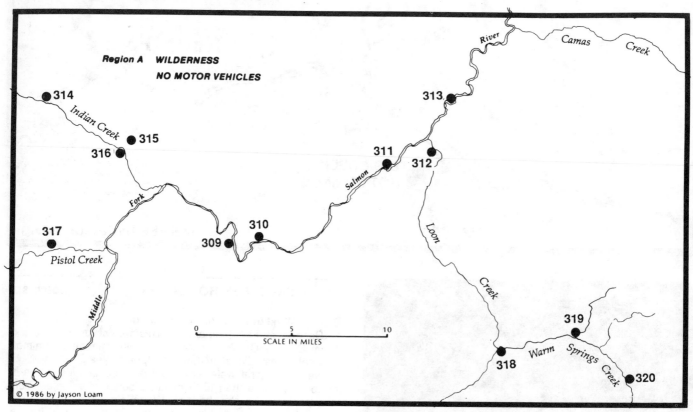

WILDERNESS HOT SPRINGS ACCESSIBLE BY RAFT

309   SUNFLOWER FLATS HOT SPRINGS

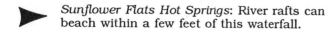

Natural mineral water from a group of hot springs (109°) flows through some shallow, cliff-top pools before dropping to the river's edge in the form of a hot waterfall.

► *Sunflower Flats Hot Springs*: River rafts can beach within a few feet of this waterfall.

80

 Hood Ranch Hot Springs: Even in a wilderness area it is sometimes necessary to use conventional galvanized iron pipe.

 Whitey Cox Hot Springs: Except for its remoteness, this soaking pool comes very close to meeting the ideal image.

310   HOOD RANCH HOT SPRINGS

●

The geothermal water from springs with temperatures up to 149˚ cools as it flows through pipes to a crude shower-bath and soaking pool within 100 yards of the river.

311   WHITEY COX HOT SPRINGS

●

A beautiful riverside meadow contains several classic, natural soaking pools supplied from nearby hot springs (131˚) through channels where the water cools on the way.

312   LOWER LOON CREEK HOT SPRINGS

●

A large, log soaking pool on the edge of Loon Creek is supplied by several springs with temperatures up to 120°. This pool does require a 1/4-mile hike from the raft-landing beach where the creek joins the river.

▲ *Lower Loon Creek Hot Springs*: Some hardy individuals go back and forth between this hot pool and the adjoining cold creek.

313   HOSPITAL BAR HOT SPRINGS

●

Dozens of fissures in the riverbank rocks emit 115° geothermal water which is collected for soaking in a few shallow pools next to a favorite landing spot for rafts.

▲ *Hospital Bar Hot Springs*: At this final geothermal stop in the wilderness, the sky is so blue, the air so clear, and the water so warm, that everyone is reluctant to leave.

WILDERNESS HOT SPRINGS ACCESSIBLE BY TRAIL ONLY

314   KWIS KWIS HOT SPRINGS

●

Hot mineral water flows out at 156° and cools while flowing toward Indian Creek. You get to build your own pool at the creek's edge.

315   MIDDLE FORK INDIAN CREEK HOT SPRINGS

●

Outflow temperature—162°.

316   INDIAN CREEK HOT SPRINGS

●

Outflow temperature—190°.

317   PISTOL CREEK HOT SPRINGS

●

Outflow temperature—115°.

318   OWEN CABIN HOT SPRINGS

●

Five springs (133°) flow into rock-and-sand pools at the edge of the creek. The best one is against the cliff under a hot waterfall.

319   FOSTER RANCH HOT SPRINGS

●

Outflow temperature—135°.

320   SHOWER BATH HOT SPRINGS

●

Creekside pools fed by 200-foot high hot waterfalls (122°) and warm streams winding through a grassy meadow.

 Challis Hot Springs: This is one of the few large swimming pools with a sufficiently large flow-through to avoid chlorination.

▼ *Goldbug Hot Springs*: At the end of a rugged uphill hike, this warm cascade is both a welcome sight and needed physical therapy.

321   GOLDBUG HOT SPRINGS

● **Southwest of the town of Salmon**

Unusual underground mix of geothermal and creek water, emerging as warm cascades through shallow, rocky, canyon pools reached by a steep, two-mile trail in Salmon National Forest. Elevation 5,200 ft. Open all year.

Natural mineral water flows out of several springs and also combines with creek water flowing under the rocky creekbed. Volunteers have added rock-and-sand dams to deepen the water-worn cascade pools where the combined water flow reemerges. Temperatures in these cascade pools are determined by the rate of runoff in the canyon. Volunteers have also built a rock-and-sand pool fed by a small spring, resulting in temperatures in the range of 90-100°. The apparent local custom is clothing optional.

There are no services available on the premises. Parking is available at the trailhead, and it is 19 miles to all other services.

Directions: On US 93 approximately 23 miles south of Salmon, look for mile marker 282. Go east on a short gravel road to the trailhead parking area. Cross Warm Springs Creek at the trailhead and follow the trail up the canyon to the springs.

322   CHALLIS HOT SPRINGS

■ H/C 63 Box 1779   (208) 879-4442
Challis, ID 83226   PR+CRV

Older, community plunge and campground on the banks of the Salmon River. Elevation 5,000 ft. Pools open all year; campground open April 1 to November.

Natural mineral water flows from several springs at temperatures up to 127° and is piped to flow-through indoor and outdoor pools which require no chemical treatment. The temperature of the outdoor pool is maintained at approximately 90°, and the temperature of the indoor pool ranges from 108-110°. Bathing suits are required.

Changing rooms, picnic areas, camping and RV hookups are available on the premises. All other services are available within seven miles. No credit cards are accepted.

Directions: From intersection of US 93 and ID 75 near Challis, go southeast on US 93 and watch for signs to hot springs.

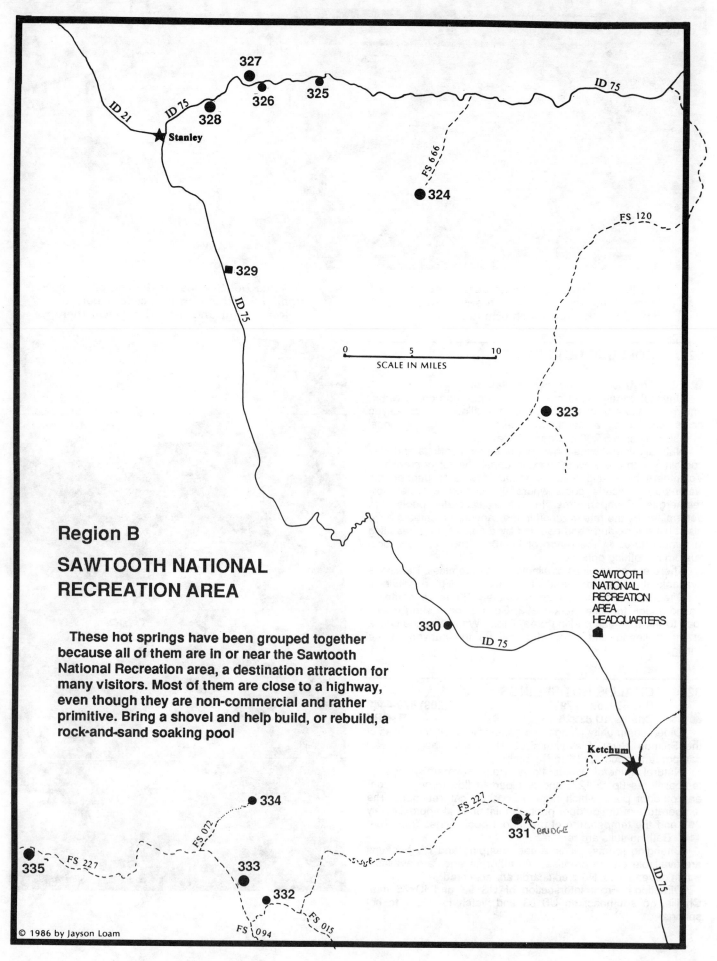

Region B

SAWTOOTH NATIONAL
RECREATION AREA

These hot springs have been grouped together because all of them are in or near the Sawtooth National Recreation area, a destination attraction for many visitors. Most of them are close to a highway, even though they are non-commercial and rather primitive. Bring a shovel and help build, or rebuild, a rock-and-sand soaking pool

▲ *Slate Creek Hot Spring*: After the original volunteers built these enclosures another volunteer cut a window to enjoy the view.

▼ *Sunbeam Hot Springs*: It would be possible to sit in these riveredge pools and cast a line into one of our best fishing streams.

323 WEST PASS HOT SPRING

● **Southeast of the town of Stanley**

A semi-improved hot springs in the Sawtooth National Recreation Area (temporarily unreachable by vehicle due to lack of legal right-of-way on access road). Elevation 7,000 ft. Open all year.

Natural mineral water flows out of a spring at approximately 125° and is piped to an outdoor bathtub at West Pass. Temperature is controlled by diverting the flow of hot water whenever desired.

Note: Personal inspection for more details was not possible due to road closure. The Forest Service staff is negotiating with the private-property owner involved to clear the right-of-way. Contact Sawtooth National Recreation Area Headquarters (eight miles north of Ketchum on ID 75) for latest information.

Source map: *Sawtooth National Recreation Area.*

324 SLATE CREEK HOT SPRING

● **East of the town of Stanley**

Two spring-fed tubs at the end of a 300-yard hike in Sawtooth National Forest. Elevation 7,000 ft. Open all year.

Natural mineral water flows out of a spring at 122°, and is piped to two soaking boxes inside two homemade baththouses. Water temperature is controlled by diverting the flow of hot water into the tub when the desired soaking temperature has been reached. The apparent local custom is clothing optional.

There are no services available on the premises. It is 30 miles to all services.

Directions: From US 93, 1 1/2 miles west of Holman Creek Campground, go south on FS 666 along Slate Creek for approximately seven miles to the end of the gravel road. Follow footpath for the remaining 300 yards.

Source map: *Sawtooth National Recreation Area.*

325 SUNBEAM HOT SPRINGS

● **East of the town of Stanley**

Several rock-and-sand pools on the edge of the Salmon River in Challis National Forest. Elevation 6,000 ft. Open all year.

Natural mineral water flows out of several springs on the north side of the road at temperatures up to 160°. The water flows under the road to several volunteer-built rock pools along the north bank of the river, where hot and cold water mix in a variety of temperatures. As all pools are easily visible from the road, bathing suits are advisable.

There are no services available on the premises. It is one mile to a store and cabins at Sunbeam Resort (summer only) and 11 miles to all other services in Stanley.

Location: On ID 75, one mile west of Sunbeam Resort, northeast of the town of Stanley.

Source map: *Sawtooth National Recreation Area.*

Kem (Basin Creek Bridge) Hot Springs: If the first in a series of pools is built over the source spring, it may be too hot for comfort.

326   KEM (BASIN CREEK BRIDGE) HOT SPRINGS

● **East of the town of Stanley**

Small, primitive spring and soaking pools on the edge of the Salmon River in Sawtooth National Recreation Area. Elevation 6,000 ft. Open all year.

Natural mineral water flows out of a spring at 110° and cools as it flows through several volunteer-built, rock-and-sand soaking pools along the edge of the river. Pool temperatures may be controlled by diverting the hot water or by bringing a bucket for adding cold river water. Because the spring is at the east end of a popular, unofficial campground, bathing suits are advisable in the daytime unless you check the situation out with your neighbors.

Except for the camping area, there are no services on the premises. It is seven miles to all services.

Directions: On ID 75, 0.7 of a mile east of mile marker 197, turn off the highway toward the river and down a short gravel road into the camping area.

Source map: *Sawtooth National Recreation Area* (hot springs not shown).

Basin Creek Campground Hot Spring: This is one of those rare opportunities to camp within an easy walk of a hot spring pool.

327   BASIN CREEK CAMPGROUND HOT SPRING
JULY 6, 1991

● **East of the town of Stanley**

Several small pools located on a creek adjacent to a campground in the Sawtooth National Recreation Area. Elevation 6,100 ft. Open all year.

Natural mineral water at 137° flows out of the ground and cools as it runs downhill to several rock-and-sand pools at the edge of the creek. The water can be further cooled by adding creek water. It is advisable to wear a bathing suit as the pools are near the campground.

There is an adjoining campground, and it is seven miles to all other services in Stanley.

Directions: Drive seven miles east of Stanley to Basin Creek Campground. Walk from campsite #4 through the bushes to the creek. The pools are hidden on the opposite side.

Source map: *Sawtooth National Forest* (hot springs not shown).

HOT WATER TOP 1" OF POOL, COLD H2O
BENEATH, NOT THAT GREAT
SULPHUR SMELLING HOT SPRING W/ SOURCE
AT BASE OF SLOPE, VERY HOT!!!
JULY 6, 1991
NOT WORTH A RETURN VISIT UNLESS
VASTLY IMPROVED!

 Elkhorn (Boat Box) Hot Spring: Fine tuning the temperature of this soaking pool involves adding buckets of cold river water followed by small squirts of scalding mineral water. It is also handy to have a willing helper.

328   ELKHORN (BOAT BOX) HOT SPRING

● **East of the town of Stanley**

Small, wood soaking box perched on a rock between the road and the Salmon River in the Sawtooth National Recreation Area. Elevation 6,100 ft. Open all year.

Natural mineral water flows out of a spring at 136° and is piped under the road to the soaking box. The temperature in the box is varied by diverting the flow of hot water and pouring in buckets of cold river water. Bathing suits are advisable as the location is visible from the road.

There are no services on the premises. It is two miles to all services.

Directions: On ID 75, 0.7 of a mile east of mile marker 192, watch for a small turnout (two car limit) on the river side of the road. The box is visible from the turnout.

Source map: *Sawtooth National Recreation Area* (hot springs not shown).

▲ *Idaho Rocky Mountain Ranch:* Guests are housed in an elegant lodge but the mineral-water pool adjoins the fields of a working ranch.

329   IDAHO ROCKY MOUNTAIN RANCH

H/C 64 Box 9934   (208) 774-3544
Stanley, ID 83278   MH

Attractive guest ranch with rustic authenticity and peaceful ambience nestled in the heart of the breathtaking Sawtooth National Recreation Area. Elevation 6,500 ft. Open June through September; November through April.

Natural mineral water flows out of a spring at 106° and is piped to a flow-through, outdoor swimming pool that is maintained at 103-105° and requires no chemical treatment. Pool is available to lodging guests only. Bathing suits are required.

Dressing rooms, restaurant, rooms and cabins are available on the premises. A bed and breakfast cabin is available close to the pool. Hiking, fishing, boating and horse trails are available nearby. All other services are available within two miles. Visa and MasterCard are accepted.

Phone for rates, reservations and directions.

330   RUSSIAN JOHN HOT SPRING

● **Northwest of the town of Ketchum**
Remains of an old sheepherder soaking pool on a slope 200 yards above the highway in Sawtooth National Recreation Area. Elevation 6,900 ft. Open all year.

Natural mineral water flows out of a spring at 89° and directly into a small, clay-bottom pool which maintains a temperature of no more than 86°. Despite the cool temperature, this pool is so popular you may have to wait your turn. The apparent local custom is clothing optional.

There are no services available on the premises. It is 18 miles to all services.

Directions: On ID 75, 30 yards south of mile marker 146, turn west and then south to parking area.

Source map: *Sawtooth National Recreation Area.*

331   WARFIELD HOT SPRING - JULY 6, 1991

● **West of the town of Ketchum**
Roadside, volunteer-built soaking pool on the north bank of Warm Springs Creek. Elevation 6,400 ft. Open all year.

Natural mineral water seeps out of the ground at 102° just above the creek level and accumulates in a shallow, rock-and-sand pool large enough for several persons. Bathing suits are advisable.

No services are available on the premises. It is 11 miles to all services.

Directions: From ID 75 (Main St.) in Ketchum, drive 10.6 miles west along Warm Springs Road. Spring is visible from the road.

Source map: *Sawtooth National Forest.*

ANOTHER STREAMSIDE POOL THAT IS HOT ON THE SURFACE AND COLD BELOW. EXTREMELY HOT AT THE ~~WHERE~~ SOURCE! POOL IS ONLY 1½" DEEP AT DEEPEST POINT, VERY SHALLOW. NOT WORTH A RETURN VISIT UNLESS VASTLY IMPROVED!

Worswick Hot Springs: On a chilly day the entire upper slope is dotted with steam plumes from many small geothermal fissures.

332   WORSWICK HOT SPRINGS

● **West of the town of Ketchum**

Dozens of primitive springs send a large flow of geothermal water tumbling down several acres of rolling hillside in the Sawtooth National Forest. Elevation 6,400 ft. Open all year.

Natural mineral water flows out of many springs at temperatures of more than 150° supplying a series of volunteer-built, rock-and-log pools in the drainage channels. The water cools as it flows downhill so the lower the pool the lower the temperature. The apparent local custom is clothing optional.

There are no services available on the premises. It is two miles to overnight camping and 14 miles to all other services.

Directions: From the intersection of FS 227 and FS 094, go 2.2 miles east of FS 227. Alternate route: From the town of Fairfield on US 20, go north on FS 094 to intersection with FS 227, the follow above directions.

Source map: *Sawtooth National Forest*.

Russian John Hot Spring: This easy-access idyllic primitive spring has only one big drawback: you can't get warm in 86º water.

Preis Hot Spring: Dedicated volunteers will go to a lot of bother to make a usable soaking pool from even a very small spring.

333   PREIS HOT SPRING

● **West of the town of Ketchum**

Small, two-person soaking box near the side of the road in Sawtooth National Forest. Elevation 6,000 ft. Open all year.

Natural mineral water flows out of the spring at 94° and directly into a small pool that has been given board sides and is large enough to accommodate two very friendly soakers. Bathing suits are advisable.

There are no services on the premises. It is two miles to overnight camping and 14 miles to all other services.

Directions: From the intersection of FS 227 and FS 094, go 2.1 miles north on FS 227 and watch for spring ten yards from the east side of the road. Alternate route: From the town of Fairfield on US 20, go north on FS 094 to intersection with FS 227, then follow above directions.

Source map: *Sawtooth National Forest*.

334   SKILLERN HOT SPRINGS

● **East of the town of Featherville**

Primitive hot spring on Big Smokey Creek, three miles by trail from Canyon Campground. Elevation 5,800 ft. Open all year.

Natural mineral water flows south from a spring at more than 110°, supplying a volunteer-built rock pool at the edge of the creek. Pool temperature is controllable by varying the amount of cold creek water admitted. The local custom is clothing optional.

There are no services on the premises. It is three miles to the campground and trailhead and 24 miles to all other services.

Directions: From Featherville, go 21 miles east on FS 227. About two miles beyond the South Fork Boise River, turn north to Canyon Campground. Trailhead is at the north end of the campground. The trail fords the stream several times and might not be passable during high water.

Source maps: *Sawtooth National Forest*; USGS *Sydney Butte* and *Paradise Peak, Idaho*.

Baumgartner Hot Spring: Over the years thousands of campers have enjoyed the benefits of this thoughtful gift.

335   BAUMGARTNER HOT SPRINGS

● **East of the town of Featherville**

Well-maintained soaking pool in popular Baumgartner Campground in Sawtooth National Forest. Elevation 5,000 ft. Open all year.

Natural mineral water flows out of a spring at 105°, supplying the soaking pool on a flow-through (no chlorine) basis and maintaining the temperature at 104°. Because of the pool's location in a campground, bathing suits are advisable.

Campground facilities are on the premises. It is 11 miles to a motel, restaurant, service station and grocery store, and 48 miles to RV hookups.

Location: On FS 227, 11 miles east of Featherville.

Source map: *Sawtooth National Forest*.

Baumgartner Hot Springs: These local residents are cleaning the shallow soaking pool under National Forest contract.

This is an ideal campground for city folk who prefer solid smooth concrete pools over sandy-bottom primitive hot springs pools.

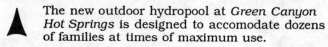

▲ *Green Canyon Hot Springs*: The original indoor swimming pool, with its snack bar and arcade games, is a year-round social center.

▲ The new outdoor hydropool at *Green Canyon Hot Springs* is designed to accomodate dozens of families at times of maximum use.

336 GREEN CANYON HOT SPRINGS
■ Box 96   (208) 458-4454
   Newdale, ID 83436   PR+CRV

Rural, indoor plunge and RV park in a really green canyon. Elevation 6,000 ft. Open every day except Sunday from mid-April to the end of September; open weekends the rest of the year.

Natural mineral water flows out of a spring at 118° and is piped to pools and a geothermal greenhouse. The indoor swimming pool is maintained at 90°, and the outdoor hydrojet pool is maintained at 105°. Both pools are treated with chlorine, and bathing suits are required.

Locker rooms, snack bar, picnic area and RV hookups are available on the premises. It is 21 miles to all other services. No credit cards are accepted.

Directions: From the town of Driggs, go north and west 17 miles on ID 33. At Canyon Creek bridge, turn south and follow signs four miles to resort.

337 HEISE HOT SPRINGS
■ Box 417   (208) 538-7312
   Ririe, ID 83443   PR+CRV

Modernized, family-oriented resort with spacious, tree-shaded picnic and RV grounds on the north bank of the Snake River. Elevation 5,000 ft. Open all year except the month of November.

Natural mineral water flows out of a spring at 126° and is piped to an enclosed hydrojet pool which is maintained at 105°and requires no chemical treatment required. Tap water, treated with chlorine and heated by geothermal heat exchangers, is used in the other pools. An outdoor soaking pool is maintained at 92-93°, the large swimming pool at 82°, and the waterslide pick-up pool at 85°. Bathing suits are required in all areas.

Locker rooms, cafe, overnight camping, RV hookups, picnic area and golf course are available on the premises. It is five miles to a store, service station and motel. No credit cards are accepted.

Directions: From the town of Idaho Falls, go east 22 miles on US 26 and then follow signs four miles north across river to resort.

▲ *Heise Hot Springs*: A giant water slide is one of the main attractions at this large and popular resort near Idaho's eastern border.

▼ This is the only *Heise Hot Springs* pool which contains mineral water, but the other pools use geothermal energy via heat exchangers.

▲ Recreation, rather than medicinal therapy, is the promotion theme at *Heise Hot Springs*.

LAVA HOT SPRINGS

LONG BEFORE WHITE MEN DISCOVERED THESE SPRINGS, SEPT. 9, 1812, INDIANS GATHERED HERE TO USE THE FREE HOT WATER.

Except where they found hot springs, pre-historic Indians had a hard time getting hot water. They wove watertight baskets into which they put heated rocks. Here they had plenty of hot water for baths and for processing hides without going to all the work of heating baskets. This was one of their major campgrounds, especially in winter. After 1868, when they began to stay mostly on the Fort Hall Indian reservation, this spot lost its importance as a winter camp.

338A   LAVA HOT SPRINGS FOUNDATION
P.O. Box 668   (208) 776-5221
Lava Hot Springs, ID 83246   PR

Two attractive and well-maintained recreation areas operated by a self-supporting state agency in the town of Lava Hot Springs. Elevation 5,000 ft.

GEOTHERMAL POOLS: (East end of town; open 363 days per year.) Natural mineral water flows out of the ground at 110° and directly up through the gravel bottoms of two large, partly shaded soaking pools. No chemical treatment is necessary. Pool temperatures range down to 107° at the drain end of the lower soaking pool. The same water is pumped to two partly shaded hydrojet pools that maintain an average temperature of 106°. Bathing suits are required in all pools. Massage is available on the premises.

SWIMMING POOLS: (West end of town; open Memorial Day to Labor Day.) Chlorinated city water is used in the TAC-size pool and in the Olypmic-size pool. Hot mineral water piped from the geothermal pools is run through a heat exchanger to maintain the pool temperatures at 88°. The pool complex is surrounded by a large, level lawn. Bathing suits are required.

Locker rooms are available at both locations, and it is less than three blocks to all other services. No credit cards are accepted.

▲ *Lava Hot Springs Foundation:* A nominal use-charge produces enough income to maintain these modern geothermal soaking pools.

▲ Many seniors are attraced by the availability of massage on the premises, and by the numerous nearby RV parks and motels.

338B RIVERSIDE INN
212 Portneuf Ave.   **(208) 776-9906**
■ **Lava Hot Springs, ID 83246**   **PR+MH**

A picturesque, historic hotel once known as the *Elegant Grand*, visible on the main street between the two Lava Hot Springs Foundation locations. Elevation 5,400 ft. Open only Friday and Saturday and long weekends.

Natural mineral water is pumped out of a well at 118°, then piped to five indoor private soaking pools which are drained and filled after each use, making chemical treatment unnecessary. Two rock-lined pools, each large enough for six people, are in one room; and three cement pools, each large enough for two people, are in another private room. Water temperature in each pool is controllable by mixing in cold tap water as desired. The pools are available to the public as well as to registered guests. No one under 19 is admitted.

Hotel rooms are available on the premises. It is less than three blocks to all other services. Visa and MasterCard are accepted.

338C HOME HOTEL AND MOTEL
305 E. Main   **(208) 776-5507**
■ **Lava Hot Springs, ID 83246**   **MH**

Remodeled, older hotel featuring hot mineral baths in all units, on the main street between the two Lava Hot Springs Foundation locations. Elevation 5,400 ft. Open all year.

Natural mineral water flows out of a spring at 121° and is piped to two-person tubs in all rooms. Temperature in each tub is controllable by the customer. The eight rooms in the hotel are non-smoking; the 13 rooms in the motel section permit smoking.

It is less than three blocks to a cafe, store, service station, overnight camping and RV hookups. Visa and MasterCard are accepted.

▲ *Riverside Inn:* This historic location offers historic multi-person concrete pools.

▲ *Lava Hot Springs Foundation:* This swimming and diving complex was built to host Olympic Games trials, and then to become available to the public at low fees. Operating expenses are minimized by using hot springs geothermal energy to heat the tap water in these pools.

 Bear Lake Hot Springs: This indoor pool and recreation complex is popular during a short summer season at this mile-high elevation.

▼ *Riverdale Resort*: This unique location has a flow of mineral water is so large that all pools can be drained and filled every day.

339   BEAR LAKE HOT SPRINGS
■ Box 75   (208) 945-2494
St. Charles, ID 83272   PR+CRV

Large pool building and campground on a remote section of the lakeshore. Elevation 6,000 ft. Open May to September.

Natural mineral water flows out of a spring at 120° and is piped to two indoor pools which operate on a flow-through basis requiring no chemical treatment. The swimming pool is maintained at 75-85° and the ten-person soaking pool at 110-115°. Bathing suits are required.

Locker rooms, cafe, overnight parking and a boat dock are on the premises. It is seven miles to a store, service station and motel. No credit cards are accepted.

Directions: From US 89 on the north side of the town of St. Charles, follow signs across the north end of Bear Lake to the resort.

340   RIVERDALE RESORT
■ 3696 N. 1600 E.   (208) 852-0266
Preston, ID 83263   PR+CRV

New commercial development in a rural valley subdivision. Elevation 4,000 ft. Open all year.

Natural mineral water is pumped from a geothermal well at 122°, then cooled with tap water as needed to maintain temperatures in various outdoor pools. All pools are drained daily, eliminating the need for chemical treatment of the water. The partly shaded hydrojet pool is maintained at 103-105°, and a large soaking pool is maintained at 96-100° in the summer and 102-104° in the winter. The Junior Olympic swimming pool is maintained at 86° in the summer and 92° in the winter. Two waterslide catch pools are maintained at approximately 80°. Bathing suits are required.

Locker rooms, massage by appointment, snack bar, overnight camping and RV hookups are available on the premises. It is less than six miles to a cafe, store, service station and motel. No credit cards are accepted.

Directions: From Preston on US 91, go 6 miles north on ID 34 and watch for resort signs.

▲ *Downata Hot Springs*: Swinging from ring to ring is one of the most popular challenges at this summertime community resort.

SUPER SLIDE RULES

• OBEY ATTENDANTS
• RIDE AT OWN RISK

• ANYONE CAUGHT STOPPING
  OR STANDING IN SLIDE

  WILL FORFEIT THEIR PASS
• MOVE PROMPTLY FROM POOL

• NO RUNNING, PUSHING ETC.
• NO CUT OFFS

• NO METAL ON SUITS
         WARNING

LIGHTWEIGHT SUITS
MAY BE DAMAGED

WEAR AT OWN RISK
MAY THE FORCE BE WITH YOU

▲ At friendly *Downata Hot Springs*, even the official rules end with encouragement.

341   DOWNATA HOT SPRINGS
■ 25901 Downata Rd.   (208) 897-5736
   Downey, ID 83234   PR+CRV

Expanded, older, rural plunge and picnic grounds in the rolling hills of southeastern Idaho. Elevation 4,000 ft. Open May 1 to Labor Day.

Natural mineral water flows out of a spring at 112° and is piped to outdoor pools treated with chlorine. The main swimming pool and the waterslide catch pool are maintained at 85-95°. Bathing suits are required.

Locker rooms, snack bar, picnic grounds, overnight camping and miniature golf are available on the premises. It is three miles to a store, service stations and motel. No credit cards are accepted.

Directions: On US 91, drive 3 miles south from the town of Downey and watch for signs.

▲ *Indian Springs Natatorium*: Convenient changing rooms are built into the fence.

▲ *Nat-Soo-Pah Hot Springs*: Two of the soaking pools as seen from the top of the slide.

342 INDIAN SPRINGS NATATORIUM

■ 3249 Indian Springs Rd.   (208) 226-2174
American Falls, ID 83211   PR+CRV

Older, rural picnic ground and plunge with RV accommodations. Elevation 5,200 ft. Open April 1 to Labor Day.

Natural mineral water flows out of a spring at 90° and is piped to an outdoor swimming pool which is treated with chlorine and maintains a temperature of 90°. Bathing suits are required.

Locker rooms, picnic area and full-hookup RV spaces are available on the premises. It is three miles to all other services. No credit cards are accepted.

Location: On Idaho Route 37, three miles south of the city of American Falls.

343 NAT-SOO-PAH HOT SPRINGS

■ Route 1   (208) 655-4337
Hollister, ID 83301   PR+CRV

Clean and quiet community plunge with soaking pools and acres of tree-shaded grass for picnics and overnight camping. Located on the Snake River plain, south of Twin Falls. Elevation 4,400 ft. Open May 1 to Labor Day.

Natural mineral water flows out of a spring at 99° and is piped to three outdoor pools. The swimming pool is maintained at 92-94°, using flow-through and some chlorine treatment. Part of the swimming pool flow-through is heated with a heat pump to supply the soaking pool which is maintained at a temperature of 104-106°. The hydrojet pool, supplied by direct flow-through from the spring, maintains a temperature of 99° and requires no chemical treatment. There is also a small waterslide at the side of the swimming pool. Bathing suits are required.

Locker rooms, snack bar, picnic area, overnight camping and RV hookups are available on the premises. It is four miles to a store and service station and 16 miles to a motel. No credit cards are accepted.

Directions: From US 93, 1/2 mile south of Hollister and 1/2 mile north of the Port of Entry, go east three miles on Nat-Soo-Pah Road directly into the location.

▲ The *Nat-Soo-Pah* circular slide and swimming
pool as seen from the smaller soaking pool.

99

 Banbury Hot Springs: The log tethered in the middle of the pool is an idestructible toy which gets lots of action from teenagers.

 Timer-controlled hydrojets are built into the sunken roman baths at *Banbury Hot Springs*.

344A   BANBURY HOT SPRINGS
Route 3   (208) 543-4098
■   Buhl, ID 83316   PR+CRV

Community plunge on the Snake River with soaking pools and spacious, tree-shaded area for picnics and overnight camping. Elevation 3,000 ft. Open weekends from Easter weekend to May 1; open every day from May 1 to Labor Day.

Natural mineral water flows out of a spring at 141°. The large, outdoor, chlorine-treated pool is maintained at temperatures ranging from 89-95°. The three indoor soaking pools and the two indoor hydrojet pools are in private rooms. The temperatures of the pools are individually controlled. Each pool is drained and refilled after each use requiring no chemical treatment of the water. Bathing suits are required in the outside pool.

Locker rooms, snack bar, overnight camping, RV hookups, and a boat ramp and dock are located on the premises. It is four miles to a restaurant and 12 miles to a store, service station and motel. No credit cards are accepted.

Directions: From the town of Buhl, go ten miles north on US 30. Watch for sign and turn east 1 1/2 miles to resort.

100

Miracle Hot Springs: In the background can be seen the drain pipe, which also acts as a skimmer, in this private flow-through pool

Even this main pool at Miracle Hot Springs is supplied on a continuous flow-through basis, eliminating the need for chlorination.

344B MIRACLE HOT SPRINGS
Route 3, Box 171   (208) 543-6002
■ **Buhl ID 83316**   **PR+CRV**

Older health spa surrounded by rolling agricultural land. Elevation 3,000 ft. Open all year.

Natural mineral water is pumped out of a well at 139° and into an outdoor swimming pool and 19 roofless, enclosed soaking pools, all of which operate on a flow-through basis requiring no chemical treatment. The swimming pool is maintained at a temperature of 95°, and the temperature in the individual pools is controllable. Bathing suits are required in public areas. All buildings and dressing rooms are supplied with geothermal heat.

Massage by appointment, RV hookups and overnight camping are available on the premises. A restaurant is available within three miles, and all other services are available within ten miles. No credit cards are accepted.

Location: On US 30, ten miles north of the town of Buhl.

Sligar's Thousand Springs Resort: Even the small fry want a chance at the tethered log.

345 SLIGAR'S THOUSAND SPRINGS RESORT
Route 1 Box 90   (208) 837-4987
■ **Hagerman, ID 83332**   **PR+CRV**

Indoor plunge with private-space hydrojet tubs and green, shaded RV park with a view of multiple waterfalls on cliffs across the Snake River. Elevation 2,900 ft. Open all year.

Natural mineral water flows out of a spring at 200° and is piped to an indoor swimming pool, 17 indoor hydrojet pools large enough for eight people, and one indoor hydrojet pool large enough for 20 people. The temperature in the swimming pool is maintained between 90-96°, while the temperature in the hydrojet pools is individually controllable. All the pools are chlorinated. Bathing suits are required in public areas.

Locker rooms, boat dock, shaded picnic area, overnight camping and RV hookups are available on the premises. A restaurant is within one mile, and all other services are within 5 miles. No credit cards are accepted.

Directions: On US 30, eight miles south of the town of Hagerman.

346 MURPHY'S HOT SPRINGS

Rogerson, ID 83302

(208) 857-2233
PR+MH+CRV

Western-style pool, bathhouse, bar and RV park in a remote section of the Jarbridge River Canyon. Elevation 5,100 ft. Open all year.

Natural mineral water flows out of two springs at 129° and into an outdoor, chlorine-treated pool and into three indoor, flow-through soaking pools requiring no chemicals. The swimming pool is maintained at temperatures ranging from 80-90°. The large indoor pool for use by six people is maintained at 96°, and the two smaller, two-person tubs are maintained at 104° and 107°. Pools are open to the public in addition to registered guests. Bathing suits are required in the pool and public areas.

Dressing rooms, cafe, gas pump, cabins, overnight camping and RV hookups are available on the premises. It is 49 miles to a store and service station. No credit cards are accepted.

Directions: From Twin Falls, go approximately 37 miles south on US 93. Watch for highway sign and turn southwest 1/2 mile into Rogerson. At main intersection, watch for Murphy Hot Springs highway sign and follow signs 49 miles to location. Only the last few miles are gravel.

347 GIVENS HOT SPRINGS

Star Route Box 103
Melba, ID 83641

(208) 495-2433
PR+CRV

Rural plunge, picnic grounds and RV park on agricultural plateau above the Snake River. Elevation 3,000 ft. Open all year.

Natural mineral water flows out of an artesian spring at 120° and is piped to a chlorine-treated, indoor swimming pool and six indoor, private-space soaking pools which operate on a drain-and-fill basis requiring no chemicals. The swimming pool is maintained at a temperature of 99° in the winter and 85° in the summer. The temperature in the tubs is individually controllable, with temperatures ranging from 105-110°. Bathing suits are required.

Dressing rooms, a snack bar, picnic grounds, softball diamond and overnight camping are available on the premises. It is 11 miles to all other services. No credit cards are accepted.

Location: Eleven miles southeast of the town of Marsing on ID 78.

▲ *Murphy's Hot Springs*: The meandering creek alongside the pool is just right for this informal outpost of civilization.

▲ *Givens Hot Springs*: Swimming and diving lessons are a year-round activity in this heated building with a geothermal pool.

Warm Springs Resort: A popular all year resort with one of the largest flow-through (no chlorination) swimming pools in Idaho.

348   WARM SPRINGS RESORT
■   P.O. Box 28   **(208) 392-4437**
      Idaho City, ID 86361   **PR+MH+CRV**

Rural plunge and RV park surrounded by Boise National Forest. Elevation 4,000 ft. Open all year.

Natural mineral water flows out of a spring at 110º and through an outdoor swimming pool maintained at a temperature of 94º in summer and 97º in winter. Chemical treatment of the water is not required. The pool is open to the public as well as to registered guests. Bathing suits are required.

Locker rooms, snack bar, cabins, overnight camping and RV hookups are available on the premises. A cafe, store and service station are located within two miles. No credit cards are accepted.

Location: On ID 21, 1 1/2 miles south of Idaho City.

Region C   BOISE RIVER — MIDDLE FORK

The common thread connecting these hot springs is a gravel road FS 268, which winds along the riverbank for 50 miles, often only one lane wide. Loaded logging trucks coming downstream have the inside lane, while upstream traffic must make do with turnouts on the edge toward the river—not recommended for trailers and motor homes. It is possible to reach Atlanta by taking FS 384, FS 327 and FS 268 from ID 21, 15 miles south of Lowman. Then, when you head downstream from Atlanta to Arrowroot Reservoir on FS 268, you will at least have the inside lane and will not be meeting any loaded logging trucks.

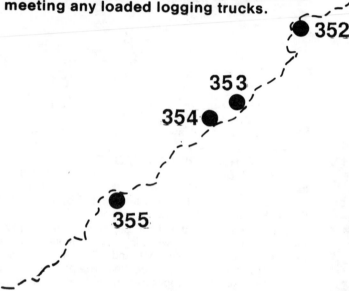

The hot springs below are listed in sequence, working downstream from Atlanta Hot Springs.

© 1986 by Jayson Loam

---

349   ATLANTA HOT SPRINGS   (see map)

● **North of the town of Atlanta**

Primitive spring and a small, rock-and-sand soaking pool on a wooded plateau in Boise National Forest. Elevation 5,400 ft. Open all year.

Natural mineral water flows out of a spring at 110° and cools as it travels to a nearby, volunteer-built pool. The pool temperature is approximately 100°, depending on air temperature and wind conditions. This site is easily visible from the nearby road, so bathing suits are advisable.

No services are on the premises.

It is one-half mile to a campground, one mile to cabins, cafe, service station and store, and 62 miles to RV hookups.

Source maps: *Boise National Forest*; USGS *Atlanta East* and *Atlanta West*.

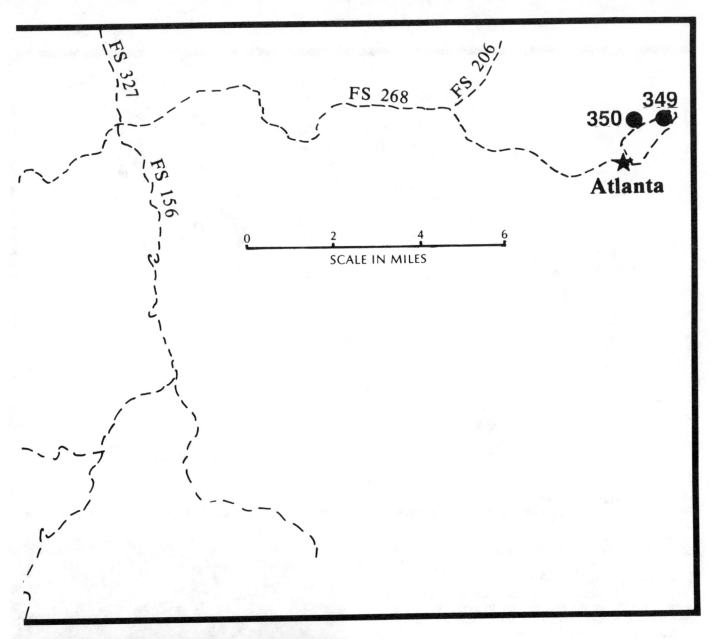

FS 327

FS 268

FS 206

FS 156

350 ● ● 349

★
Atlanta

0   2   4   6
SCALE IN MILES

◄ *Atlanta Hot Springs:* Runoff from the hot pool flows to the larger cold pond which is visible across the road in the background.

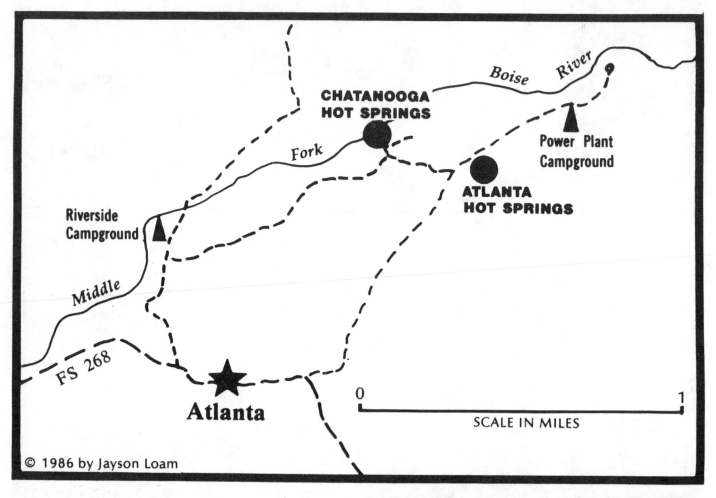

© 1986 by Jayson Loam

CHATANOOGA HOT SPRINGS

Boise River

Fork

Middle

FS 268

Riverside Campground

Power Plant Campground

ATLANTA HOT SPRINGS

Atlanta

0   1

SCALE IN MILES

350   CHATANOOGA HOT SPRINGS   (see map)

● **North of the town of Atlanta**

Large, comfortable, sand-bottom pool at the foot of a geothermal cliff surrounded by the tree-covered slopes of Boise National Forest. Elevation 5,400 ft. Open all year.

Natural mineral water flows out of fissures in a 100-foot high cliff at 120° and cools as it tumbles toward a volunteer-built, rock-and-sand soaking pool which retains a temperature of more than 100°. The apparent local custom is clothing optional.

There are no services on the premises. It is one-half mile to a campground, one mile to a cafe, cabins, service station and store, and 62 miles to RV hookups.

Note: The pool is visible from the north edge of the unmarked parking area at the top of the cliff. Several well-worn, steep paths lead down to the pool.

Source maps: *Boise National Forest;* USGS *Atlanta East* and *Atlanta West.*

 Chatanooga Hot Springs: This site, with its natural cooling-tower cascade, is one of the most dramatic settings along the Middle Fork.

106

 Dutch Frank Hot Springs: Unlimited opportunities for volunteers who would like to experiment with building soaking pools.

 Loftus Hot Springs: A charming waterfall and grotto pool, just right for meditating on nature and the sound of splashing water.

(see map on preceding pages)

351 DUTCH FRANK HOT SPRINGS

●

Scattered, geothermal flows along 200 yards of riverbank. Located on the south bank of the river, immediately east of the Roaring River bridge.

352 NEINMEYER HOT SPRINGS

●

Several primitive hot springs on the south bank of the river, across from Neinmeyer Campground.

353 LOFTUS HOT SPRINGS

●

Intimate, leafy, volunteer-built soaking pool with 100° water, ten yards from a small parking area on the north side of the road. It is located 0.2 of a mile east of the bridge

354   SMITH CABIN HOT SPRINGS

●

    Volunteer-built, river's-edge pools on both sides of the river, 0.7 of a mile west of the above described bridge.

355   SHEEP CREEK BRIDGE HOT SPRINGS

●

    Volunteer-built pool with rock screen containing algae-laden water at temperatures up to 100°, depending on weather conditions. It is located 20 yards from the south end of the bridge over which the road returns to the north side of the river.

▲ *Sheep Creek Bridge Hot Spring*: One of the plentiful, but seldom used, non-commercial hot springs along the Boise Middle Fork.

▲ *Smith Cabin Hot Springs*: As is the case with many volunteer-built soaking pools, this one needs more work to acheive a usable depth.

▲ *Sawtooth Lodge*: This rustic site is the farthest upstream on the South Fork of the Payette River at the Sawtooth Range gateway.

▼ *Sacajawea Hot Springs*: Hot mineral water seeps out of this entire river bank, creating spectacular steam clouds on chilly mornings.

---

356   SAWTOOTH LODGE

■ **Grandjean, ID 83637**

(208) 344-6685
PR+MH+CRV

Historic mountain resort in the Sawtooth Recreation Area. Elevation 5,100. Open June through October.

Natural mineral water flows out of several springs with temperatures up to 150° and into an outdoor, chlorinated swimming pool maintained at approximately 80°. The pool is available to the public as well as to registered guests. Bathing suits are required.

Dressing rooms, cafe, cabins, overnight camping and RV hookups are available on the premises. It is 28 miles to a store and service station. Visa and MasterCard are accepted.

Directions: From the town of Lowman, go 22 miles east on ID 21, then follow signs six miles on gravel road to lodge.

 Father fishes in the icy river while mother and children soak in a comfortable 100° pool of runoff water from *Sacajawea Hot Springs*.

▼ Some of the *Sacajawea Hot Springs* runoff pools are within a few yards of roaring rapids in the South Fork of the Payette.

357   SACAJAWEA HOT SPRINGS

● **West of the town of Grandjean**

Popular, large geothermal area on the north bank of the South Fork of the Payette River in Boise National Forest. Elevation 5,000 ft. Open all year.

Natural mineral water flows out of many springs at temperatures up to 108° and cools as it cascades into a series of volunteer-built rock pools along the river's edge. Because the pools are visible from the road, bathing suits are advisable.

There are no services available on the premises. It is one mile to a cafe, cabins, overnight camping and RV hookups, and 27 miles to a store and service station.

Directions: From Lowman, drive 21 miles east on ID 21 to Grandjean turnoff (FS 524) on right. Follow gravel road 4.6 miles to Wapiti Creek Bridge. Look for springs on right side of road, 0.6 of a mile past the bridge.

 Bonneville Hot Springs: This single-tub one-person bathhouse is for those who are too civilized to sit in a natural-bottom pool.

 Where the main *Bonneville* runoff reaches the creek, volunteers have used fallen timber to build an unusually large soaking pool.

358 BONNEVILLE HOT SPRINGS

● **West of the town of Grandjean**

Popular, semi-remote geothermal area on a tree-lined creek in Boise National Forest. Elevation 4,800 ft. Open all year.

Natural mineral water flows out of a multitude of springs with various temperatures up to 180°. Be careful not to step into any of the scalding runoff channels. There is one small, wooden bathhouse with an individual tub supplied from a nearby spring at a temperature of 103°. Soakers drain the tub after each use. There are also many volunteer-built, rock-and-sand soaking pools along the edge of the creek where the geothermal water can be mixed with cold water. Bathing suits are advisable.

No services are available on the premises. It is one-quarter mile to a campground, eight miles to a cafe, cabins and RV hookups, and 19 miles to a store and service station.

Directions: From Lowman, drive 19 miles northeast to Bonneville Campground (formerly Warm Springs Campground). From the north edge of the campground, follow the unmarked but well-worn path 1/4 mile to geothermal area.

 Some of the lesser *Bonneville* runoff streams are used to supply small rock-and-sand pools.

112

359 HAVEN LODGE
General Delivery
Lowman, ID 83637

(208)259-3345

The 1989 Lowman area fire burned out this motel and RV park, along with the swimming and soaking pools. Only the service station was spared. A major rebuilding program is being planned. Phone for status of construction and a current report on available services.

▲ One of the attractions at *Kirkham Hot Springs* is the availabiity of hot showers, as well as soaking pools, 24 hours of every day.

360   KIRKHAM HOT SPRINGS

● **East of the town of Lowman**

Popular geothermal area with many hot waterfalls and pools adjoining a National Forest campground on the South Fork of the Payette River. Elevation 3,900 ft. Open all year.

Natural mineral water flows out of many springs and fissures along the south bank of the river at temperatures up to 120° and cools as it cascades toward the river. Volunteers have built several rock-and-sand soaking pools in which temperatures can vary above or below 100° depending on air temperature and wind conditions. Bathing suits are advisable, especially in the daytime.

Overnight camping is available in the adjoining campground. It is four miles to a cafe, store, service station and cabins, and 34 miles to RV hookups.

Directions: From the town of Lowman, go four miles east on ID 21 and watch for Kirkham Hot Springs Campground sign.

Source map: *Boise National Forest.*

▲ *Kirkham Hot Springs*: Insects destroyed many of the trees in the campground, but this is still a very popular overnight site.

Pine Flats Hot Spring: This unique soaking pool combines a sweeping view of the river with the sound of a geothermal cascade.

Hot Springs Campground: One volunteer-built pool is visible at the end of the cement foundations which used to be a bathhouse.

361   PINE FLATS HOT SPRING

● **West of the town of Lowman**

Spectacular, geothermal cascade and cliffside soaking pool overlooking the South Fork of the Payette River in Boise National Forest. Elevation 4,100 ft. Open all year.

Natural mineral water with temperatures up to 125° flows from several springs on top of a one-hundred-foot high cliff, cooling as it spills and tumbles over the rocks. There is one volunteer-built, tarp-lined rock pool 30 feet above the river immediately below a hot shower-bath which averages 104°. Other rock pools at the foot of the cliff have lower temperatures. The apparent local custom is clothing optional.

The hot springs are located one-third mile from the Pine Flats Campground and parking area. It is four miles to a cafe, store, service station and motel, and 27 miles to RV hookups.

Directions: From the west edge of Pine Flats campground, follow an unmarked but well-worn path 1/3 mile west down to and along a large riverbed, rock-and-sand bar. Look for geothermal water cascading down the cliff onto the bar.

Source map: *Boise National Forest.*

362   HOT SPRINGS CAMPGROUND

● **East of the town of Crouch**

The cement foundations of a long-gone bathhouse and some small, volunteer-built soaking pools are intended to use some of the continuing hot-water flow. Located on a riverbank across the highway from a National Forest campground. Elevation 3,800 ft. Open all year.

Natural mineral water flows out of several springs at 105° and into volunteer-built, shallow, rock-and-sand pools near the south side of the highway. Bathing suits are advisable.

Overnight camping is available on the premises. All other services are available four miles away.

Directions: From the town of Crouch, go four miles east toward Lowman. Look for Hot Springs Campground one mile after entering Forest Service land.

Source map: *Boise National Forest.*

114

363 DEER CREEK HOT SPRINGS

● **West of the town of Crouch**

Small, volunteer-built soaking pool in a gully 20 yards from a paved highway, combining the flow from several springs, a test well and a creek. Elevation 3,000 ft. Open all year.

Natural mineral water flows out of multiple springs and an abandoned well casing at temperatures ranging up to 176˚. Volunteers have built a shallow, plastic-and-sand soaking pool on one side of the creek to mix the hot and cold water. There are no posted clothing requirements, but the proximity to the highway makes bathing suits advisable.

There are no services available on the premises, but all services are available four miles away.

Directions: From the town of Crouch, go 4 1/2 miles west toward the town of Banks, watching for a steep dirt road on the north side of the highway. Do not drive up the road—it deadends in just a few yards. Park in a turnout on the river side of the highway and walk back to the springs, which are just below the steep side road.

Source map: *Boise National Forest.*

364 ROCKY CANYON (ROBERTS) HOT SPRING
(see map)

● **North of the town of Crouch**

Primitive hot spring on the Middle Fork of the Payette River in Boise National Forest. Elevation 4,000 ft. Open all year.

Natural mineral water flows out of a spring at 120˚, then down a steep slope toward the river. To reach the spring, you must ford the river, which might not be safe during high water. Volunteers have built a series of primitive rock pools, each cooler than the one above. All pools are visible from the road, so bathing suits are advisable.

There are no services available on the premises. It is 1/2 mile to a picnic are, one mile to a campground, and ten miles to all other services in Crouch.

Source map: *Boise National Forest.*

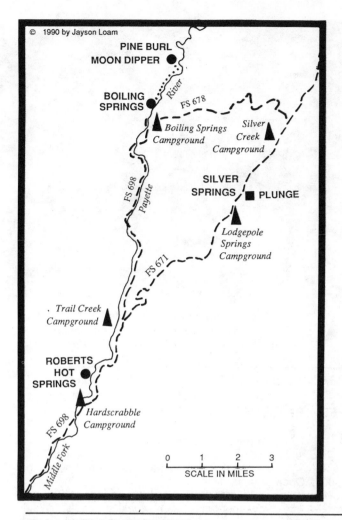

365 BOILING SPRINGS   (see map)

● **North of the town of Crouch**

Large, geothermal water flow on the Middle Fork of the Payette River in Boise National Forest. Elevation 4,000 ft. Open all year.

Natural mineral water flows out of a cliff at more than 130˚, into a pond adjacent to the Boiling Springs guard station. The water cools as it flows through a ditch to join the river. Summer volunteers usually build a rock-and-mud dam at the point where the water is cool enough for soaking. Because of the nearby campground, bathing suits are advisable.

No services are available on the premises. It is one-quarter mile to a campground and 19 miles to all other services.

Directions: From the north edge of Boiling Springs campground, follow the path 1/4 mile to the guard station and spring.

Source map: *Boise National Forest.*

 Rocky Canyon (Roberts) Hot Spring: On this steep slope some form of plastic sheeting is needed to hold the hot water in a rock pool.

 Moon Dipper Hot Spring: This delightful pool is on the south bank of Dash Creek, near where it joins the Payette Middle Fork.

366A MOON DIPPER HOT SPRING AND
            (see map on preceding page)
366B PINE BURL HOT SPRING

● **North of the town of Crouch**

Two remote and primitive hot springs on the bank of Dash Creek, very close together in Boise National Forest. Elevation 4,000 ft. Open all year.

Natural mineral water flows out of two springs at 120° and directly into volunteer-built, rock soaking pools. Water temperature in the pools is controlled by mixing cold creek water with the hot water. The apparent local custom is clothing optional.

No services are available on the premises. It is a two-mile hike to overnight camping and 21 miles to all other services.

Directions: From the Boiling Springs guard station, follow a well-used but unmarked path along the river for a two-mile hike to the springs.

Source maps: *Boise National Forest*; USGS *Boiling Springs, Idaho*.

Note: There are several more primitive hot springs with potential for volunteer-built soaking pools further upstream from Moon Dipper and Pine Burl. However, all of them require that the river be forded many times with a high risk of losing the faint, unmarked path. Consult with a Boise National Forest ranger station before attempting to find any of these springs.

 Pine Burl Hot Spring: This smaller pool, with beautiful scenery, can be found by following Dash Creek upstream for two hundred yards.

116

▲
▼

Silver Creek Plunge: A very large warm water pool makes this location especially suitable for vacationing families with teenage children. For those who are not equipped to camp out, there are rooms available in the lodge building visible in the background.

367   SILVER CREEK PLUNGE

■   **(208) 344-8688 (unit 1942)**
H/C 76 Box 2666   **(see map on preceding page)**
Garden Valley, ID 83622   PR+MH+CRV

Remote, mountain resort surrounded by Boise National Forest. Elevation 4,600 ft. Open all year; snowmobile access in winter.

Natural mineral water flows out of a spring at 101˚ and is piped to an outdoor swimming pool which is maintained at 84˚. The pool operates on a flow-through basis and requires no chemical treatment. The pool is available to the public as well as to registered guests. Bathing suits are required.

Dressing rooms, snack bar, rooms, cabins and overnight camping are available on the premises. It is 23 miles to a store, service station and RV hookups. No credit cards are accepted.

Directions: From the town of Crouch, go north 14 miles on FS 698, then bear northeast on FS 671 for nine miles to plunge.

Source map: *Boise National Forest*.

368   BREIT (TRAIL CREEK) HOT SPRING
(see map)

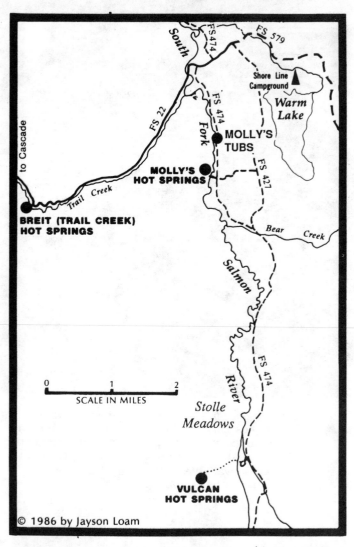

© 1986 by Jayson Loam

● **West of Warm Lake**

Small, scenic hot spring and soaking pool in a narrow canyon down a steep, 60-yard path from a paved highway in Boise National Forest. Elevation 5,900 ft. Open all year.

Natural mineral water flows out of a fissure in the rocks at more than 115°. Volunteers have built a primitive, rock-and-sand soaking pool on the edge of Trail Creek where the hot and cold water can be mixed by controlling the amount of cold creek water admitted. The apparent local custom is clothing optional.

No services are available on the premises. It is two miles to a campground and 25 miles to all other services.

Directions: From the intersection of FS 22 and FS 474 west of Warm Lake, go west 3.7 miles and look for an especially large parking area on the south side of the road. From the west edge of this parking area, the pool is visible at the bottom of Trail Creek canyon. There is no maintained trail, so be careful scrambling down the steep. path.

Source map: *Boise National Forest.*

 Breit (Trail Creek) Hot Spring: Volunteers have made it possible for soakers to have either a rock-and-sand primitive pool or this de luxe porcelain bathtub from the big city.

---

369 A   MOLLY'S TUBS
(see map)

● **West of Warm Lake**

An unusual collection of bathtubs on the South Fork of the Salmon River in Boise National Forest. Elevation 5,200 ft. Open all year.

Natural mineral water flows out of several springs at approximately 120° and is piped through hoses to eight bathtubs. Buckets are used for adding cold water. The apparent local custom is clothing optional.

There are no services available on the premises. It is 1 1/2 miles to a campground and 24 miles to all other services in Cascade.

Directions: From the intersection of FS 22 (paved) and FS 474 (gravel), go 1.3 miles south on FS 474 to pullout on right. Take path down to tubs.

Source map: *Boise National Forest.*

▲ *Vulcan Hot Springs*: Insects and storms have ravaged this pool and scenery, but the hot creek is still there, waiting for volunteers.

369B MOLLY'S HOT SPRING   (see map)

● **West of Warm Lake**

Makeshift pools perched on a steep, geothermal hillside in Boise National Forest. Elevation 5,300 ft. Open all year.

Natural mineral water flows out of several springs at more than 120° and is gathered by several pipes and hoses. The pool temperature is controlled by diverting or combining the hotter and cooler flows. The apparent local custom is clothing optional.

No services are available on the premises. It is three miles to overnight camping and 25 miles to all other services.

Directions: From the intersection of FS 22 (paved) and FS 474 (gravel), go 1.7 miles south on FS 474 to intersection with a road leading east toward Warm Lake. The road leading west from this intersection has been blocked to vehicle traffic, but it is passable on foot. Follow the road 300 yards to an old vehicle bridge, cross the bridge, and immediately turn right onto an unmarked path which leads 100 yards north to the geothermal area.

Source map: *Boise National Forest.*

370   VULCAN HOT SPRINGS   (see map)

● **South of Warm Lake**

Once-popular, geothermal creek pool showing signs of neglect in an insect-ravaged part of Boise National Forest. Elevation 5,600 ft. Open all year.

Natural mineral water flows out of many small bubbling springs at boiling temperature, creating a substantial hot creek which gradually cools as it runs through the woods toward the South Fork of the Salmon River. Volunteers have built a log dam across this creek at the point where the water has cooled to approximately 105°. This dam has been partly wiped out by high-water runoff, and the one-mile trail to it is no longer maintained. The apparent local custom is clothing optional.

One mile south of Stolle Meadows there is an unmarked, unofficial camping area where the head of the trail to the springs begins. It is six miles to a Forest Service campground and 32 miles to all other services.

Directions: At the west edge of the camping area is a log footbridge built by the Corps of Engineers. Cross this bridge and follow the path across two more log bridges. It is approximately one mile to the dam and pool.

Source maps: *Boise National Forest;* USGS *Warm Lake, Idaho.*

119

White Licks Hot Springs: Although not a Forest Service Campground, there is plenty of level ground for legal overnight parking.

Sugah (16 mile) Hot Spring: This idyllic spot is ten yards from a gravel road, but it is 16 miles from a paved road, so is seldom used.

371   SUGAH (MILE 16) HOT SPRING

● **North of Warm Lake**

A sweetie of a remote soaking pool located on the edge of the South Fork of the Salmon River in Payette National Forest. Elevation 4,000 ft. Open all year.

Natural mineral water flows out of a spring at 115° and cools as it goes through makeshift pipes to the volunteer-built, rock-and-masonry pool at the river's edge. Pool temperature is controlled by diverting the water when not needed, or by adding a bucket of cold river water. The apparent local custom is clothing optional.

There are no services available on the premises. There is a campground within two miles and it is 40 miles to all other services.

Directions: From the intersection of FS 22 (paved) and FS 474 (gravel), go north on FS 474 along the South Fork of the Salmon River for 16 miles to the spring. At 1.7 miles past Poverty Flats Campground there is small (two-car) turnout on the side of the road toward the river. Look for an unmarked, steep path down to the pool.

Source maps: *Payette National Forest; Boise National Forest.*

372   WHITE LICKS HOT SPRINGS   (see map)

● **West of the town of Donnelly**

A large, geothermal seep serving two small bathhouses in an unofficial camping area at a wooded site surrounded by Payette National Forest. Elevation 4,800 ft. Open all year.

Natural mineral water flows out of many small springs at temperatures up to 120°, supplying two small, wood shacks, each containing a cement tub. Each tub is served by two pipes, one bringing in 110° water, the other bringing in 80° water. The tub temperature is controlled by plugging up the pipe bringing in the water not desired. Soakers are expected to drain the tub after each use. Bathing suits are not required inside the bathhouses.

A picnic area and camping area are available on the premises. It is 16 miles to all other services.

Directions: From ID 55 in Donnelly, follow signs west toward Rainbow Point Campground. After crossing the bridge across Cascade Reservoir, follow FS 186 (gravel) as it starts north, curves west and then goes south. Watch for hot spring on the west side of FS 186, 3 1/2 miles south of the intersection of FS 245 and FS 186.

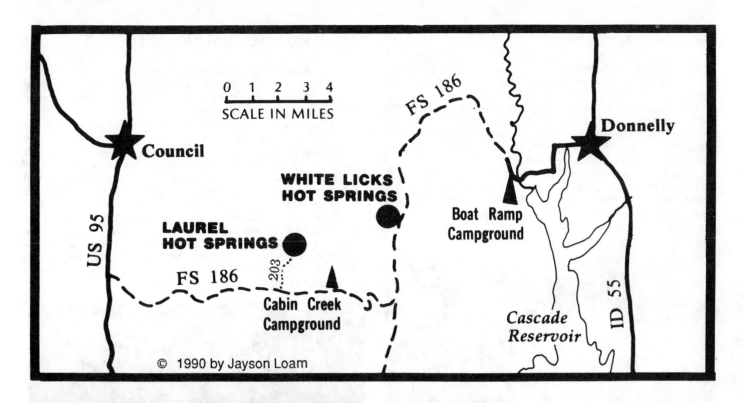

373   LAUREL HOT SPRINGS   (see map)

●   **East of the town of Council**

Several primitive, thermal springs in a wooded canyon at the end of a rugged, two-mile hike in Payette National Forest. Elevation 4,300 ft. Open all year.

Natural mineral water flows out of several springs at temperatures up to 120° and into progressively cooler, volunteer-built soaking pools along the bottom of Warm Springs Creek. The local custom is clothing optional.

There are no services available on the premises. It is two miles to a campground and 23 miles to all other services.

Directions: From Cabin Creek Campground on FS 186, go two miles west to Warm Springs Creek. Follow trail number 203 two miles north to Springs. Water is very hot where the trail crosses the creek.

Source map: *Payette National Forest*.

 Laurel Hot Springs: This is more than an ideal hot spring; it is an ideal hot creek, which cools as flows through the woods.

121

374 WATERHOLE #1

P.O. Box 676   (208) 634-7758
Lake Fork, ID 83635   PR+MH+CRV

Tavern, lodge and unique hot tubs with a view of the mountains. Located five miles south of McCall.

Private-space hot pools using bromine-treated tap water are for rent to the public by the hour. There are six redwood hydrojet tubs in covered patios with one side that opens toward a mountain view. Pool temperatures range from 102-106°. Each unit has an inside, heated dressing room.

A cafe, tavern, rooms and overnight camping are available on the premises. A store and service station are within five blocks, and RV hookups are within five miles. Visa and MasterCard are accepted. Phone for rates, reservations and directions.

375 KRIGBAUM HOT SPRINGS

●   **East of the town of Meadows**

Primitive hot springs and soaking pool on the east bank of Goose Creek, surrounded by Payette National Forest. Elevation 4,000 ft. Open all year.

Natural mineral water flows out of a spring at 102° and is piped to a volunteer-built, rock-and-sand pool where the temperatures range from 85-95°, depending on weather conditions. The apparent local custom is clothing optional.

There are no services available on the premises. It is two miles to a store, service station, overnight camping and RV hookups, and nine miles to a motel and restaurant.

Directions: On ID 55, go one mile east from Packer Johns Cabin State Park and turn north on the gravel road along the east bank of Goose Creek. Just before the road crosses a bridge over Goose Creek, park and hike 300 yards north along the east bank to the pool.

Source map: *Payette National Forest*.

▲ *Waterhole #1*: In one way these rent-a-tubs are better than the real thing; the doors may be closed in winter for cozy warm soaking.

▲ *Krigbaum Hot Springs*: This unfenced private-property location goes through cycles of being destroyed by vandals and restored by volunteers. Here it is on a good day.

376 ZIM'S HOT SPRINGS

P.O. Box 314　　　　　　　　**(208) 347-9447**
New Meadows, ID 83654　　　　　　　**PR+CRV**

Older, rural plunge and picnic grounds in an agricultural valley. Elevation 4,200 ft. Open all year.

Natural mineral water flows out of an artesian well at 151° and is cooled as it is sprayed into the chlorine-treated pools. The temperature in the outdoor swimming pool ranges from 90-100° and from 103-106° in the outdoor soaking pool. Bathing suits are required.

Locker rooms, snacks, picnic area, overnight camping and RV hookups are available on the premises. A store, service station and motel are located within four miles. No credit cards are accepted.

Directions: From the town of New Meadows, take US 95 four miles north, then follow signs to plunge.

377 BURGDORF HOT SPRINGS

McCall, ID 83638　　　　　　　　　　**MH**

Picturesque, mountain-rustic resort without electricity or telephone, surrounded by Payette National Forest. Elevation 6,000 ft. Open all year.

Natural mineral water flows out of a spring at 112° and directly into and through a sandy-bottom swimming pool which averages 100° and requires no chemical treatment. There is also one indoor, claw-footed enamel bathtub which is drained after each use. The pools are available only to registered guests. Bathing suits are required during the daytime.

Dressing rooms, a communal kitchen and cabins are available on the premises. Write first for reservations and information on current status and what to bring. Overnight camping is within 1/4 mile. It is 30 miles to all other services. Hiking, skiing, snowmobiling and boating are nearby. No credit cards are accepted.

Directions: From ID 55 at the west end of McCall, take Warren Wagon Road 30 miles north to Burgdorf Junction, then follow signs two miles west to resort. For wintertime pick-up by snowmobile, write to the resort manager.

 Burgdorf Hot Springs: This rustic resort dates back to the days when logs were used to build everything, including swimming pools.

 Zim's Hot Springs: Spray jets are used to cool incoming hot water to the right level for maintaining pool temperature.

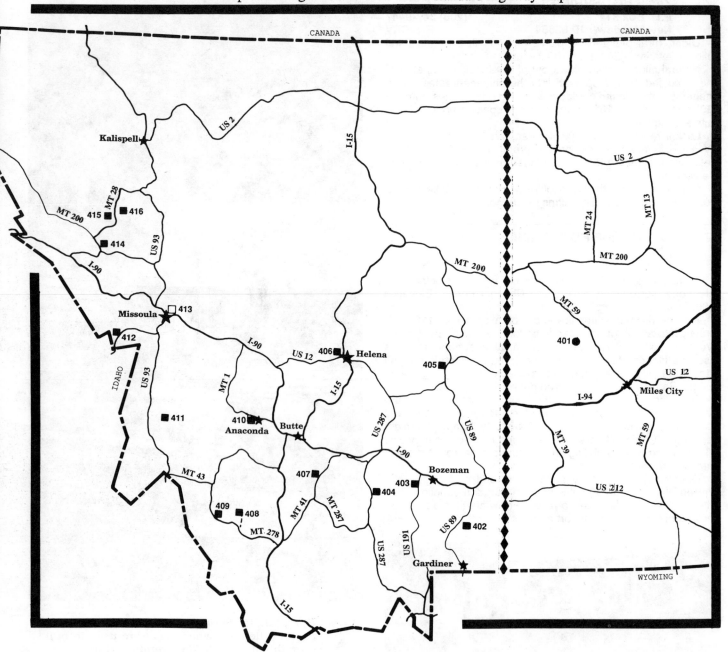

Montana

MAP AND DIRECTORY SYMBOLS

● Non-commercial mineral water pool

■ Commercial (fee) mineral water pool

□ Gas-heated tap or well water pool

〰 Paved highway

- - - Unpaved road

∙∙∙∙ Hiking route

PR = Tubs or pools for rent by hour, day or treatment

MH = Rooms, cabins or dormitory spaces for rent by day, week or month

CRV = Camping or vehicle parking spaces, some with hookups,
        for rent by day, week, month or year

401   ANGELA HOT WELL

● **West of the town of Angela**

An artesian mineral water well building its own cooling ponds on the plains of eastern Montana. Elevation 3,000 ft. Open all year.

An oil exploration well hit geothermal water and now gushes 1,200 gallons per minute at 179°. Travertine deposits have built spectacular terraces and a constantly shifting series of shallow cooling ponds. A comfortable soak is possible when you find that section of an outer pond which has cooled below 109°. The apparent local custom is clothing optional.

There are no services available on the premises but there is ample level ground on which overnight parking is not prohibited. It is six miles to gas and snacks in Angela, and 46 miles to all other services in Miles City.

Directions: On MT 22 drive one mile north of Angela and turn left (west) on dirt road. Drive 6.2 miles and turn left (south) on dirt road. Drive four miles to the well, staying with the most-traveled route whenever the road forks.

402   CHICO HOT SPRINGS

P.O. Box 127   (406) 333-4933
Pray, MT 59065   PR+MH

Large, older resort surrounded by Gallatin National Forest. Elevation 5,000 ft. Open all year.

Natural mineral water flows out of several springs at 110°. The outdoor swimming pool is maintained at 90°, the covered soaking pool at 105°, and two private-space redwood hot tubs that are at 105°. All pools operate on a flow-through basis so that no chemical treatment is needed. Pools are available to the public as well as to registered guests. Bathing suits are required except in private spaces.

Changing rooms, restaurant, hotel rooms, saddle horses and a private trout lake are available on the premises. It is four miles to a store and service station and 15 miles to overnight camping and RV hookups. Visa and MasterCard are accepted.

Directions: From the town of Emigrant on US 89 south of Livingston, take MT 362 southeast for three miles. Follow signs to resort.

Chico Hot Springs: This all-year destination resort near Yellowstone National Park offers public pools full of pure mineral water, a luxury which is not available in the Park.

 Bozeman Hot Springs: The multi-temperature pools in the foreground help make this one of the most popular KOA campgrounds in the west.

Bear Trap Hot Springs: Hot artesian well water pressure supplies this self-operating cooling-tower effect 24 hours per day.

403 BOZEMAN HOT SPRINGS

133 Lower Rainbow Rd.   (406) 587-3030
Bozeman, MT 59715   PR+RV

Tree-shaded KOA campground with mineral water pools. Elevation 4,500 ft. Open all year. Pools closed from sundown Fridays to sundown Saturdays.

Natural mineral water flows out of a spring at 141° and is piped to an indoorpool building. The swimming pool is maintained at 90°, and adjoining soaking pools are maintained at temperatures ranging from 100-110°. There is also a 60° cold pool. All pools operate on a flow-through basis, including cold tap water for controlling temperatures, so no chemical treatment is needed. Pools are available to the public as well as to registered guests. Bathing suits are required.

Locker rooms, grocery store, laundromat, picnic area, RV hookups and tent-trailer rentals are available on the premises. It is one mile to a restaurant and service station and eight miles to a motel. Visa and MasterCard are accepted.

Location: On US 191, eight miles southwest of the town of Bozeman.

404 BEAR TRAP HOT SPRINGS
P.O. Box 2944   **(406) 685-3303**
■ **Norris, MT 59745**   **PR+CRV**

Small RV park in foothills below Tobacco Root Mountains. Elevation 5,000 ft. Open all year.

Natural mineral water flows out of artesian springs at 128˚. The outdoor soaking pool is maintained at 101˚ in the summer and 106˚ in the winter. The water contains no sulfur, and no chemical treatment is added because the pool operates on a flow-through basis. The pool is available to the public as well as to registered guests. Bathing suits are required.

A store, picnic area, overnight camping and RV hookups are available on the premises. It is 1/4 mile to a cafe and service station and ten miles to a motel. No credit cards are accepted.

Directions: From US 287 in the town of Norris, go 1/4 mile east on MT 84.

405 SPA MOTEL
P.O. Box 370   **(406) 547-3366**
■ **White Sulphur Springs, MT 59645**   **PR+MH**

Remodeled, older resort at the foot of the Castle Mountains. Elevation 5,100. Open all year.

Natural mineral water flows out of a spring at 135˚ and is piped to two pools which operate on a flow-through basis, requiring no chemical treatment. The outdoor swimming pool is maintained at 94˚ in the summer and 104˚ in the winter. The indoor soaking pool is maintained at 106-108˚. Bathing suits are required.

Rooms and a picnic area are available on the premises. It is less that five blocks to all other services. Visa and MasterCard are accepted.

Location: On US 89 at the west end of White Sulphur Springs.

406 BROADWATER ATHLETIC CLUB
4920 Hwy 12 W.   **(406) 443-5777**
■ **Helena, MT 59601**   **PR**

Large well-equipped health center on the outskirts of Helena. Elevation 5,000 ft. Open all year.

Natural mineral water flows out of a spring at 153˚ and is piped to several pools where it is treated with bromine. The outdoor swimming pool is maintained at 93˚, and the outdoor lap pool is maintained at 87˚. The three indoor hydrojet pools, (men's, women's and coed) are maintained at 104˚. The men's and women's sections each contain a sauna and steambath. Facilities are available to the public as well as to members and guests. Bathing suits are required in public areas. There is also a park containing a swimming pool, children's spray pool, picnic area, BBQ pits, volleyball court and a giant waterslide. The park is open to the public.

Locker rooms, massage by appointment, juice bar, weight room, racquet ball and running tracks (indoor and outdoor) are available on the premises. It is three miles to a cafe, store, service station and motel, and seven miles to overnight camping and RV hookups. Visa, MasterCard and American Express are accepted.

Location: On US 12, two miles west of Helena.

Barkell's Hot Springs: In good old Montana tradition, this hot spring attracted the building of a swimming pool with a bar.

407 BARKELL'S HOT SPRINGS
SUPPER CLUB AND LOUNGE   **(406) 287-9919**
■ **Silver Star, MT 59751**   **PR**

Community plunge with adjoining bar and restaurant. Elevation 4,500 ft. Open all year.

Natural mineral water flows out of a spring at 180˚ into a cooling pond. It is then piped to an indoor swimming pool maintained at a temperature of 75-100˚ by the addition of cold tap water as needed. The pool is drained and refilled weekly so that no chemical treatment is needed. Bathing suits are required.

A store, service station, overnight camping and RV hookups are located within one mile. It is 10 miles to a motel. Visa and MasterCard are accepted.

Location: On MT 41 between Twin Bridges and Whitehall, 1/4 mile south of the town of Silver Star.

408 ELKHORN HOT SPRINGS
P.O. Box 514   (406) 834-3434
Polaris, MT 59746   PR+MH+C

Beautifully restored mountain resort, lodge and rustic cabins, situated among the tall trees of Elkhorn National Forest. Elevation 7,400 ft. Open all year.

Natural mineral water flows out of nine springs with temperatures ranging from 107-160°. The outdoor swimming pool is maintained at 88-95° and the outdoor soaking pool at 95-104°. There are two coed Roman saunas maintained at 110°. All pools are drained and refilled weekly so that no chemical treatment is needed. Pools are available to the public as well as to registered guests. Bathing suits are required.

Locker rooms, cafe, gasoline, tent spaces, picnic area, overnight camping and cabins are available on the premises. Hunting, fishing, backpacking, rock and mineral hunting, skiing and snowmobile trails are available nearby. Pick-up service is provided from the city of Butte by prior arrangement. No credit cards are accepted.

Directions: From I-15, three miles south of Dillon, take MT 278 west 27 miles to large sign, turn north, and follow gravel road 13 miles to resort.

409 JACKSON HOT SPRINGS
P.O. Box 808   (406) 834-3151
Jackson, MT 59736   PR+MH+CRV

Renovated lodge and cabins on the main street of a small town. Elevation 6,400 ft. Open all year.

Natural mineral water flows out of a spring at 137° and is piped to cabins and an indoor pool. The indoor swimming pool is maintained at 98-100° and operates on a flow-through basis, so no chemical treatment is necessary. Water temperatures in cabin bathtubs may be controlled by adding cold tap water as needed. The swimming pool is available to the public as well as to registered guests. Bathing suits are required.

Dressing rooms, restaurant, cabins, overnight camping and RV hookups are available on the premises. It is one block to a store and service station. No credit cards are accepted.

Location: On MT 278 in the town of Jackson.

Elkhorn Hot Springs: These chlorine-free pools are a welcome sight after a rugged day of summer hiking or winter snowmobiling.

Fairmont Hot Springs: This major destination resort is a modern spin-off from the popular historic spa in British Columbia.

410 FAIRMONT HOT SPRINGS
1500 Fairmont Rd.   **(406) 797-3241**
Anaconda, MT 59711   **PR+MH**

Large hotel-type resort and real-estate development in a wide valley. Elevation 5,300. Open all year.

Natural mineral water flows out of a spring at 160˚ and is piped to a group of pools where it is treated with chlorine. The indoor and outdoor swimming pools are maintained at 80-85˚ and the indoor and outdoor soaking pools at 105˚. There are also men's and women's steam rooms. Facilities are available to the public as well as to registered guests. Bathing suits are required.

Locker rooms, restaurant, rooms, mini-zoo, tennis, golf course, waterslide and horseback riding are available on the premises. Overnight camping and RV hookups are available one block away. It is five miles to a store and service station. Visa, MasterCard and American Express are accepted.

Directions: From I-90, 12 miles west of Butte, take the Gregson-Fairmont exit and follow signs to the resort.

411 SLEEPING CHILD HOT SPRINGS
P.O. Box 768   **(406) 363-6250**
Hamilton, MT 59840   **PR+MH**

A small resort designed to provide "rustic elegance," surrounded by Bitterroot National Forest. Elevation 5,400 ft. Open all year.

Natural mineral water flows out of a spring at 125˚ and is piped to two outdoor soaking pools and one large outdoor swimming pool. The swimming pool is maintained at a temperature 95-99˚, and the soaking pools are maintained from 105-110˚. All pools are flow-through, so no chemical treatment is needed. There is also one coed sauna. Facilities are available to the public as well as to registered guests. Bathing suits are required.

Locker rooms, bar, restaurant and hotel rooms are available on the premises. Overnight camping, hiking, fishing, hunting and cross-country skiing are available nearby. A store, service station and RV hookups are located within 15 miles. Visa and MasterCard are accepted.

Directions: From the town of Hamilton, take US 93 south to MT 38, then go east to MT 501. Follow signs to resort. The last five miles are on gravel road.

Sleeping Child Hot Springs: The bar, restaurant, and many of the rooms, have a view of the pools at this remote location.

129

 Lolo Hot Springs: Giant boulders near the swimming pool serve as sundecks-with-a-view. Other facilities may be in a state of flux as a new owner rebuilds after years of closure.

412   LOLO HOT SPRINGS RESORT
38500 Highway 12   **(406) 273-2290**
Lolo, MT 59847   **PR+MH+CRV**

An historic resort being restored and expanded in a spectacular mountain setting 30 miles west of Missoula. Elevation 4,700 ft. Open all year.

Natural mineral water flows out of two springs at temperatures of 110° and 117° and is piped to two outdoor pools. The large pool maintains a temperature of 92° with a continuous flow-through system that requires a minimum of chlorination. The soaking pool maintains a temperature of 103-105° on a continuous flow-through basis that requires no chemical treatment of the water. Bathing suits are required.

Facilities include dressing rooms, camping spaces, RV hookups, deli and convenience store, bar, picnic area and trout stream. Future plans include several new cabins. Phone ahead for status of construction. No credit cards are accepted. All other services are available in Missoula. Phone for rates and reservations.

Location: On US 12, 30 miles west of Missoula.

413   NEW LIFE FITNESS CLUB
127 N. Higgins   **(406) 721-5117**
Missoula, MT 59801   **PR**

Combination rent-a-tub establishment and fitness center in downtown Missoula.

Private-space pools using bromine-treated tap water are for rent to the public by the hour. There are four indoor hydrojet pools in which the temperature is maintained at 103-105°. There are also two coed steam baths and two coed saunas. Bathing suits are not required in the saunas, steambaths or private spaces.

Locker rooms, weight rooms and massage are available on the premises. No credit cards are accepted. Phone for rates, reservations and directions.

414   QUINN'S PARADISE RESORT: A NATURAL HOT SPRINGS
P.O. Box 219   **(406) 826-3150**
Paradise, MT 59856   **PR+MH+CRV**

Complete family resort on the banks of the Clark Fork River. Elevation 2,700 ft. Open all year.

Natural mineral water flows out of a spring at 120°. The outdoor swimming pool is treated with chlorine and maintained at a temperature of 88°. The outdoor hydrojet pool is maintained at 100° and operates on a flow-through basis so that no chemical treatment of the water is needed. There are two indoor, private-space fiberglass tubs in which the water temperature can be controlled by the customer. These pools are drained and refilled after each use, so that no chemical treatment is necessary. Pools are available to the public as well as to registered guests. Bathing suits are required except in private spaces.

Dressing rooms, cafe, bar, store, service station, rooms and cabins, overnight camping, RV hookups and fishing are available on the premises. Visa and MasterCard are accepted.

Location: On MT 135, three miles south of the junction with MT 200, which is east of St. Regis.

415 SYMES HOTEL AND MEDICINAL SPRING

(406) 741-2361

■ **Hot Springs, MT 59845** PR+MH

Historic hotel with a long tradition of mineral water and other health treatments. Elevation 2,900 ft. Open all year.

Natural mineral water flows out of an artesian well at 80-90° and is heated as needed for use in soaking tubs. There are nine individual soaking tubs in the men's bathhouse and six in the women's bathhouse. There are also hotel rooms with mineral water piped to the room. Temperature is controllable within each tub, and no chemical treatment is added. Bathhouses are available to the public as well as to registered guests.

Locker rooms, hotel rooms and chiropractic services are available on the premises. It is two blocks to a cafe, store and service station and six blocks to overnight camping and RV hookups. No credit cards are accepted.

Directions: From MT 382 northeast of St. Regis, follow signs to the town of Hot Springs and then to the hotel.

416 CAMP AQUA

P.O. Box K

(406) 741-3480

■ **Hot Springs, MT 59845** PR+MH+CRV

Well-maintained, family rent-a-tub establishment with overnight facilities surrounded by rolling foothills. Elevation 4,000 ft. Open all year.

Natural mineral water flows out of an artesian well at 124° and is piped to the bathhouse building. There are six large indoor soaking pools in private rooms, each with steam bath, sauna, shower and toilet. Pool water temperature is controllable by each customer up to 110°, and the pools are drained and refilled after each use, so no chemical treatment is needed. Bathing suits are not required in private rooms. Geothermal heat is used in all buildings.

Cabins, picnic area, overnight camping and RV hookups are available on the premises. It is six miles to all other services. No credit cards are accepted.

Directions: From MT 28, 2 1/2 miles north of Hot Springs junction, follow signs two miles east on gravel road to resort.

 Quinn's Paradise Resort: Recreational use of mineral water, rather than medicinal use, is a key theme at this major family resort.

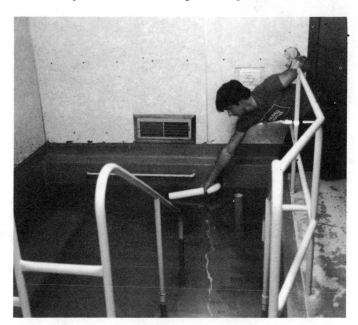

▲ *Camp Aqua:* This location deserves high marks for offering large family-size roman pools in private spaces equipped with toilets.

131

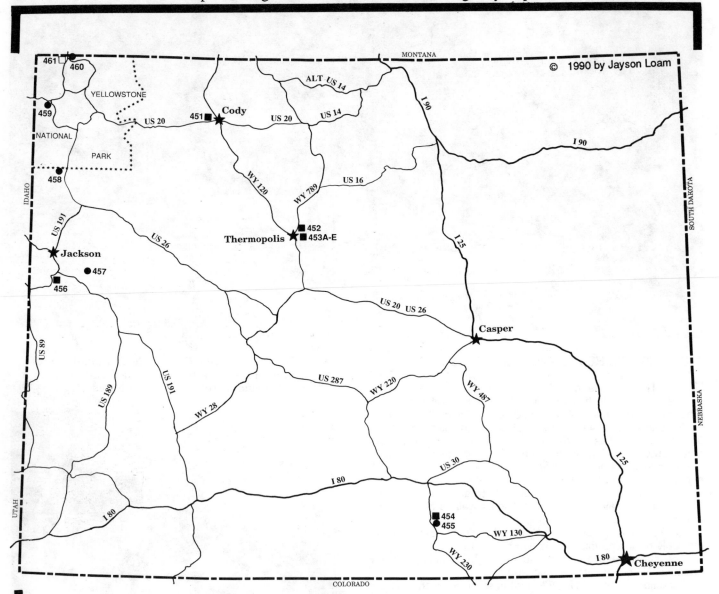

© 1990 by Jayson Loam

Wyoming

MAP AND DIRECTORY SYMBOLS

● Non-commercial mineral water pool

■ Commercial (fee) mineral water pool

☐ Gas-heated tap or well water pool

〰️ Paved highway

- - - Unpaved road

⋯ Hiking route

PR = Tubs or pools for rent by hour, day or treatment

MH = Rooms, cabins or dormitory spaces for rent by day, week or month

CRV = Camping or vehicle parking spaces, some with hookups, for rent by day, week, month or year

451 CODY ATHLETIC CLUB
515 W. Yellowstone   (303) 527-7131
Cody, WY 82414   PR+MH

Fully equipped health club and motel 31 miles east of Yellowstone National Park. Elevation 5,000 ft. Open all year.

Natural mineral water is piped out of a well at 87° and piped to an outdoor swimming pool which maintains a temperature of 86° and has no chemical treatment. The enclosed hydrojet pool uses gas-heated tap water treated with chlorine and is maintained at 105°. Bathing suits are required.

A coed steam bath, men's and women's exercise rooms with a sauna in each, and racquetball courts are available on the premises. Motel rooms are also available. It is 1/2 mile to all other services. Visa and MasterCard are accepted. Phone for rates, reservations and directions.

452 FOUNTAIN OF YOUTH
P.O. Box 711   (307) 864-9977
Thermopolis, WY 82443   PR+CRV

Well-kept RV park featuring a unique, large soaking pool. Elevation 4,300 ft. Open all year.

Natural mineral water flows out of the historic Sacajawea Spring at the rate of over one million gallons per day. Some of this 130° water is channeled through a cooling pond into a 200-foot-long soaking pool where the temperature varies from 104° at the inflow end to 99° at the outflow. The pool is available only to registered day campers and overnight campers. Bathing suits are required.

Restrooms, showers, overnight camping and RV hookups are available on the premises. It is two miles to all other services. No credit cards are accepted.

Location: On US 20, two miles north of the town of Thermopolis.

▲ *Fountain Of Youth*: From the Sacajawea Well, scalding water runs into a cooling pond (foreground), then into the large main pool.

▲ *Cody Athletic Club*: An elaborate health club and motel complex has been built up around this almost-hot warm spring. However, there is no mineral water in the small hot pool.

This square mile of land, with the Big Spring in the center, was presented to the State of Wyoming by the Federal Government after it had been purchased from the Shoshone and Arapahoe Indians in 1896. Elevation 4,300 ft. Open all year.

All of the establishments on the grounds are supplied with natural mineral water from the Big Spring, which flows out of the ground at 135º. Walkways have been provided through the large tufa terraces which have been built up by mineral deposits from the spring over the centuries. Facilities provided include a large tree-shaded picnic area in the center of the grounds.

All services not provided by an establishment within the State Park are available within 1/2 mile in the city of Thermopolis.

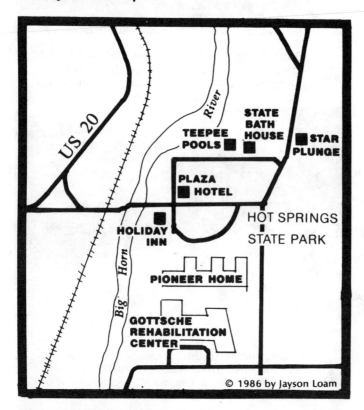

© 1986 by Jayson Loam

 State Bath House: These sparkling clean no-charge public pools and bathhouses are especially popular with seniors. The Big Spring tufa mounds are only yards away.

453A TEPEE POOLS (see map)
P.O. Box 750   (307) 864-9250
■ Thermopolis, WY 82443   PR

The outdoor swimming pool is maintained at 87-93°, and the indoor swimming pool is maintained at 93-97°. The indoor soaking pool is maintained at 104°, and the indoor steambath is maintained at 112-115°. All pools operate on a flow-through basis, so no chemical treatment is needed. Bathing suits are required.

Locker rooms and snack bar are available on the premises. No credit cards are accepted.

453B STATE BATH HOUSE (see map)
State Park   (307) 864-9902
● Thermopolis, WY 82443

The outdoor and indoor soaking pools are maintained at 104°. The temperature in 16 (eight men's and eight women's) individual soaking tubs is adjustable by the person using the tub. All pools use non-chlorinated, flow-through mineral water. No charge is made for pool or tub use.

Changing rooms are available and bathing suits are required in the communal pools. There is a nominal charge for renting suits or towels. No credit cards are accepted.

▲ *Star Plunge*: 105º water continuously overflows from the small foreground soaking pool into the large swimming pool.

453C STAR PLUNGE (see map)
P.O. Box 627   (307) 864-3771
Thermopolis, WY 82443   PR

The outdoor swimming pool is maintained at 92-96° and the indoor swimming pool is maintained at 96-98°. The hot pool also has a hydrojet section which is maintained at 105°. Included are an indoor and an outdoor waterslide which are open throughout the year. The coed steambath is maintained at 115°. All pools are flow-through requiring no chemical treatment. Bathing suits are required.

Locker rooms and snack bar are available on the premises. No credit cards are accepted.

453D PLAZA HOTEL AND APARTMENTS (see map)
P.O. Box 671   (307) 864-2251
Thermopolis, WY 82443   PR+MH

An older resort building with men's and women's bathhouses. Each bathhouse has four individual mineral-water tubs and two steambaths. Bathing suits are not required in bathhouses.

Hotel rooms, massage and sweat wraps are available on the premises. Visa and MasterCard are accepted.

453E HOLIDAY INN (see map)
P.O. Box 1323   (307) 864-313
Thermopolis, WY 82443   PR+MH

Conventional, major hotel with a unique adaptation of men's and women's bathhouses. Each bathhouse has private spaces for four individual soaking tubs, two saunas and two steambaths. The private spaces are rented to couples, even though they are in the men's and women's bathhouses.

The indoor soaking tubs are temperature controllable up to 110°, use natural mineral water, and are drained after each use so that no chemical treatment is needed. The outdoor hydrojet pool also uses natural mineral water without chemical treatment and is maintained at a temperature of 106°. The outdoor swimming pool uses gas-heated, chlorine-treated tap water and is maintained at a temperature of 78°. All pools and the athletic club facilities are available to the public as well as to registered guests. Bathing suits are required in all outdoor public areas.

Restaurant and hotel rooms are available on the premises. Visa, MasterCard, American Express and Carte Blanche are accepted.

▲ *Holiday Inn*: Only a major hotel chain would decide to install a chlorinated, gas-heated tap water swimming pool in a location which had unlimited odorless hot mineral water.

135

Hobo Pool: When the town built a swimming pool (fee required) it respected tradition by also building an adjoining no-charge pool.

The Saratoga Inn: It is apparent that the management does not want anyone attempting to do any moonlight swimming in this pool.

454   THE SARATOGA INN

P.O. Box 867
Saratoga, WY 82331

(303) 326-5261
MH

Modest golf and tennis resort surrounded by rolling ranch country. Elevation 6,800 ft. Open all year.

Natural mineral water is pumped out of a spring at 114° and piped to an outdoor swimming pool which is treated with chlorine and maintained at 100°. An outdoor, rock soaking pool is built over another spring and is maintained at 100-105°, with chlorine added as needed. Pool use is reserved for registered guests. Bathing suits are required.

Hotel rooms, restaurant, golf and tennis are available on the premises. It is four blocks to a store and service station and one mile to overnight camping and RV hookups. Visa, MasterCard and American Express are accepted.

Directions: From WY 130 in the town of Saratoga, go east on Bridge St. and follow signs four blocks to the resort.

455   HOBO POOL

● In the town of Saratoga

An improved but unfenced soaking pool and a fenced municipal swimming pool located on the banks of the North Platte River. Elevation 6,800 ft. Open all year.

Natural mineral water flows out of the source spring at 115°. A large cement soaking pool (no charge) maintains a temperature of 100-110°. Volunteers have channeled the soaking pool run-off into shallow rock pools along the edge of the river. A daily charge is made for the use of the swimming pool, which is maintained at 90°. Bathing suits are required.

There are no services on the premises. It is three blocks to all services. No credit cards are accepted.

Directions: On WY 130 in the town of Saratoga, watch for HOBO POOL sign, then follow signs four blocks east to the pool.

136

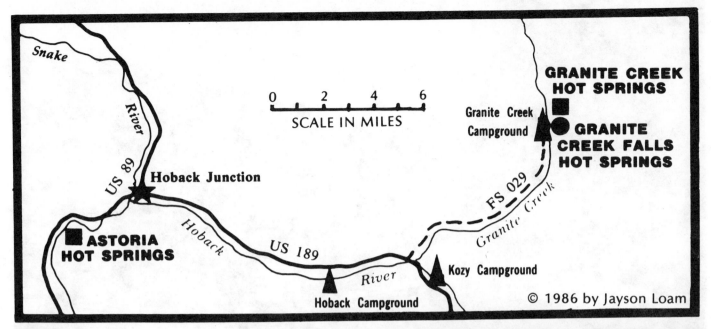

GRANITE CREEK HOT SPRINGS

Granite Creek Campground

GRANITE CREEK FALLS HOT SPRINGS

FS 029

Granite Creek

0 2 4 6
SCALE IN MILES

Snake

River

US 89

Hoback Junction

Hoback

US 189

River

Kozy Campground

ASTORIA HOT SPRINGS

Hoback Campground

© 1986 by Jayson Loam

456   ASTORIA MINERAL HOT SPRINGS (see map)
■   Star Route, Box 18   (307) 733-2659
    Jackson, WY 83001   PR+CRV

Large, well-kept RV resort on the south bank of the Snake River. Elevation 6,100 ft. Open mid-May to mid-September.

Natural mineral water flows out of a spring at 104° and is piped to an outdoor swimming pool which is treated with chlorine and maintained at a temperature of 84°-92°. The pool is available to the public as well as to registered guests. Bathing suits are required.

Locker rooms, picnic area, tent spaces, RV hookups, grocery store, horse rentals and river raft trips are available on the premises. It is two miles to a cafe, service station and motel. No credit cards are accepted.

Location: On US 26, 17 miles south of the town of Jackson.

▲ *Astoria Mineral Hot Springs*: The pool at this popular summer resort has a great view of the Snake River gateway to the Teton Mountains.

 Granite Creek Hot Springs: For those who like mountain streams and camping in the woods, but prefer to soak in a supervised cement hot pool, this is the place. It is also a supurb warm oasis in the middle of winter snow.

457   GRANITE CREEK HOT SPRINGS
(see map on preceding page)
East of Hoback Junction PR

Part of a major bonanza for lovers of natural beauty and natural mineral water. Elevation 7,000 ft. Open all year, including the winter season for those who have snow cats.

Natural mineral water flows out of a spring at 112° and tumbles directly into a large cement pool built by the CCC in the 1930's. Cold stream water is added as needed to maintain the pool temperature of 95° in the summer and 105° in the winter. The pool is drained and refilled each day, so no chemical treatment is needed. Bathing suits are required.

Changing rooms and rest rooms are available on the premises, which is operated under a lease with the Forest Service. The site is closed and gates are locked from 8 P.M. to 10 A.M. A large, wooded, creekside campground is one-half mile away. It is ten miles to a cafe and motel and 22 miles to all other services.

Fifteen minutes by trail from this site is Granite Creek Falls Hot Spring. Natural mineral water flows out of a creek bank immediately below the falls at 130° and meanders through creekbed rocks where volunteers have built soaking pools in which the hot and cold waters mix. These rock-and-sand pools must be rebuilt after each annual high-water washout. Although the spring is partly visible from the road, the apparent local custom is clothing optional.

Allow no less than one full day and night to enjoy these two hot springs, the campground, and the beautiful scenery of Granite Creek Valley.

458   HUCKLEBERRY HOT SPRINGS

● **North of the town of Jackson**

Large group of primitive hot springs along the north bank of Polecat Creek, near the south entrance to Yellowstone National Park. The site includes the remains of a resort dismantled by order to Teton National Park which administers this area. Elevation 6,800 ft. Open all year.

Natural mineral water flows out of many springs at temperatures up to 130° cooling as it follows various channels to the creek. Volunteers have built small rock-and-mud soaking pools at several places where the water is in the 100-105° range. Bathing suits are advisable, especially in the daytime.

There are no services available on the premises. There is a commercial campground within one mile, and all other services are within five miles.

Note: This location is in transition from a commercial campground with swimming pool to some form of daytime use which does not include the now-bulldozed swimming pool. There is no way to predict how future Park Service action may affect the volunteer-built pools described below.

Directions: From US 89 two miles south of the Yellowstone Park boundary, go west on the Flagg Ranch Campground road for one mile across a bridge, and then bear right on the road into Huckleberry. If the Huckleberry road is blocked off at the intersection with the Flagg-Ashton road, park and walk in 1/2 mile on the old paved road to Huckleberry.

Look for some volunteer-built pools among the hot springs on the slopes west of the destroyed swimming pool and adjoining large geothermal pond. Another soaking pool is on the north bank of Polecat Creek, 1/4 mile west of the north end of the bridge which is crossed by the Huckleberry road.

Huckleberry Hot Springs: While the Park Service is trying to decide what to do with the area, volunteers have built soaking pools below the tree near the pond (above) and on the bank of Polecat Creek (below).

 Madison Campground Warm Spring: The controversial volunteer-built dam which raises the water level in this soaking pool is visible at the far end of the channel.

 Boiling River: This is one of the places where cold river water flows in from the left to mix with hot mineral water cascading down the riverbank; a skin-tingling experience.

459   MADISON CAMPGROUND WARM SPRING

● **In Yellowstone National Park**

Shallow, mud-bottom ditch near a campground inside the west boundary of Yellowstone National Park. Elevation 6,800 ft. Open all year.

Natural mineral water combined with underground river water bubbles up through a mud flat on the north bank of the Firehole River, just south of the campground. Volunteers have built a small sod dam across a narrow channel in order to accumulate enough 100º water to be 18 inches deep. (The chief ranger wants it known that those volunteers were breaking officially posted park regulations when they built that dam and that anyone caught in the act will be cited and prosecuted.) Bathing suits are required.

No services, other than the campground, are available at the springs. Refer to the NPS Yellowstone Park map for the location of all services.

Directions: Park on Loop G in Madison Campground and walk 100 yards south toward the Firehole River.

460   BOILING RIVER

● **In Yellowstone National Park**

Turbulent confluence of hot mineral water and cold river water along the west bank of the Gardiner River, just below Park Headquarters at Mammoth Hot Spring. Elevation 5,500 ft. Open all year during daylight hours only.

Natural mineral water flows out of a very large spring at 140˚ and travels 30 yards through an open channel where it tumbles down the south bank of the Gardiner River. Volunteers have rearranged some rocks in the river to control the flow of cold water in an eddy pocket where the hot and cold water churn into a swirling mixture which varies from 50˚-110˚. (The chief ranger wants it known that those volunteers were breaking officially posted Park regulations when they rearranged the rocks in the river, and that anyone caught in the act will be cited and prosecuted). Bathing suits are required.

No services are available at this location. Refer to the NPS Yellowstone Park map for the location of all services.

Directions: On the North Entrance Road between Mammoth Hot Spring and the town of Gardiner, look for the 45th Parallel sign on the east side of the road. Turn into the parking lot behind that sign and hike 1/2 mile upstream to where Boiling River cascades over the riverbank.

IN YELLOWSTONE'S
THERMAL AREAS
IT IS UNLAWFUL TO

TRAVEL OFF BOARDWALKS OR TRAILS
TAKE PETS ON BOARDWALKS OR TRAILS
THROW OBJECTS INTO POOLS OR GEYSERS
MARK THERMAL FEATURES
BATHE IN THERMAL POOLS OR STREAMS.

461   MAMMOTH HOT SPRINGS HOTEL AND CABINS

Mammoth Hot Springs   (307) 344-7311
☐   Yellowstone National Park, WY 82190   MH

Four fiberglass, hydrojet pools filled with chlorinated, electrically heated tap water behind high board fences adjoining four small cabins. Elevation 6,200 ft. Open all year.

These pools are not available for public use by the hour or the day. During the winter they are available for communal use by registered guests in the hotel. Bathing suits are required. During the summer they are for the private use of the registered guests in each of the four cabins. Phone for rates and reservations.

 Mammoth Hot Springs Hotel: This chlorinated tub of tap water looks like an ordinary outdoor rent-a-tub in the middle of any city.

STONEWALL AT YELLOWSTONE

Ten years ago, when I started the field research for my hot spring guides, I looked forward to soaking in the abundance of geothermal water in Olympic National Park in Washington, in Hot Springs National Park in Arkansas, and especially in Yellowstone National Park in Wyoming.

Olympic National Park actually has primitive out-in-the-woods hot springs available to the public, and also has commercial cement-and-tile hot pools at Sol Duc Resort. In Arkansas, all the springs have been capped but the hot mineral water is piped to numerous public bathhouses and hotels in the Park and in the adjoining town.

By vivid contrast, the stated policy of Yellowstone National Park management is to discourage all human use of geothermal water. Here is what I found during my first visit in 1979 and subsequent return trips.

An official Yellowstone National Park Regulation prohibits bathing in, or other use of, all geothermal springs, *and their run-off streams,* until after the geothermal water has mixed with surface water in a creek or river. Therefore, soaking in any spring is illegal and volunteers are not permitted to build rock-and-sand soaking pools where run-off streams have cooled to tolerable temperatures.

There are just three places in the Park where a legal mix of hot geothermal water and cold river water is practical for human use:

1. Madison Campground Warm Spring (see preceding page).
2. Boiling River (see preceding page).
3. Midway Geyser Basin Bridge over the Firehole River. Although this location was (and is) a legal geothermal/surface water mix, the Park Service arbitrarily banned human use in 1979 on the grounds that the bathers were "too much of a distraction." Ten years later that ban is still in force.

The other two locations do not appear on the Yellowstone National Park map, or in the official literature provided to all visitors. Also, these two locations are not mentioned on signs along nearby roads, they are not served by maintained trails, and there are no guidance signs pointing the way from any parking area. The Park Service has deliberately chosen not to help visitors find the only two places where they can legally soak.

In 1979 I interviewed the Chief Ranger, and also interviewed his successor in 1985. My key question both times was, "Does the Park Service have any plans to find or provide opportunities for visitors to safely and legally soak in hot water in Yellowstone National Park?" During both interviews the answer was a categorical "No." Furthermore, the Chief Ranger emphasized that the volunteers who rearrange the rocks in the river at the two locations in order to soak more comfortably were breaking Park Service regulations against disturbing the "natural" condition of the Park.

I do not understand a Park Service "naturalness" policy which permits commercial construction projects such as a block-long concrete marina for power boats on Yellowstone Lake, and then condemns visitors for rearranging a few rocks in the river.

When I inquired at Old Faithful Inn about the availability of hot tubs or hot pools for hotel guests, I was informed that the only place in Yellowstone Park with such facilities was the Hotel at Mammoth Hot Springs. (see above). The thought of soaking in a plastic pool of tap water, heated by electricity, behind a high board fence, did not even come close to my expectation of enjoying the natural beauty of Yellowstone Park.

I do understand that the Mammoth Hot Springs Hotel operators had to build some kind, any kind, of hot pools in order to compete with the other major commercial resorts in the Rocky Mountains. However, I do not understand a Park Service policy which permits such artificial and inefficient construction while allowing thousands of gallons per minute of natural hot mineral water from Boiling River to waste into the Gardiner River only a thousand yards away from the hotel.

It is my unpleasant duty to report that Yellowstone Park management chooses to ignore the desire of leg-weary visitors to relax in a safe and legal hot soak, and that any suggestion that the Park Service should reconsider this policy of neglect is met with a blunt official stonewall.

Jayson Loam

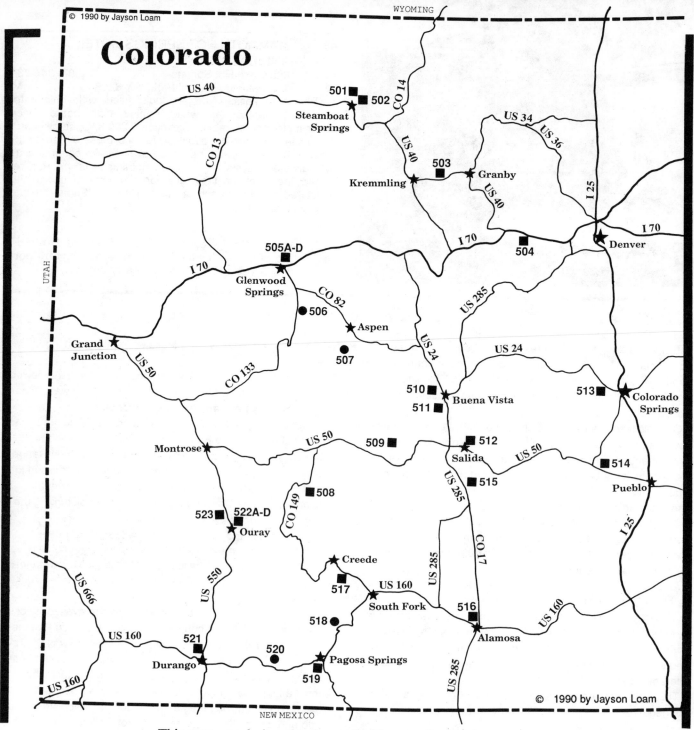

Colorado

WYOMING

US 40

501
502

Steamboat
Springs

CO 14

US 34
US 36

US 40

503 ● Granby

Kremmling

I 70

I 25

I 70

Denver

505A-D

I 70

Glenwood
Springs

CO 82

504

US 285

● 506

Aspen

UTAH

Grand
Junction

US 50

CO 133

● 507

US 24

US 24

510
511 Buena Vista

513 Colorado
Springs

Montrose

US 50

509

512
Salida

US 50

514

515

US 285

Pueblo

523 522A-D
Ouray

CO 149

508

US 550

US 285

CO 17

I 25

Creede

517

US 160
South Fork

516
Alamosa

US 160

518 ●

521

US 666

US 160

520 ●

519

Pagosa Springs

Durango

US 285

US 160

US 160

NEW MEXICO

This map was designed to be used with a standard highway map

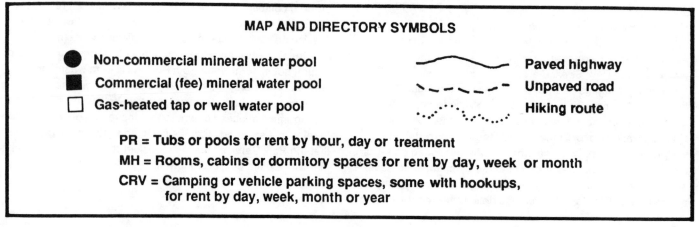

MAP AND DIRECTORY SYMBOLS

● Non-commercial mineral water pool

■ Commercial (fee) mineral water pool

□ Gas-heated tap or well water pool

〜〜〜 Paved highway

- - - Unpaved road

····· Hiking route

PR = Tubs or pools for rent by hour, day or treatment

MH = Rooms, cabins or dormitory spaces for rent by day, week or month

CRV = Camping or vehicle parking spaces, some with hookups,
for rent by day, week, month or year

501   STRAWBERRY PARK HOT SPRINGS

P.O. Box 773332   (303) 879-0342
■   Steamboat Springs, CO 80477   PR+MH+CRV

A unique hot spring which manages to retain a maximum of primitive naturalness while improving the services for a wide variety of modern hot-spring enthusiasts. Elevation 7,500. Open all year.

Natural mineral water flows out of many hillside fissures at 165° and is channeled into a series of creek-bank, rock-and-masonry pools where it is combined with creek water to provide a range of soaking temperatures. There is also a private-space hydrojet tub which is maintained at a temperature of 104-106°. Continuous flow-through in all pools eliminates the need for chemical treatment. There is a wood-burning sauna available near the pools. Bathing suits are required in the creekbed pool area during the day on Sunday, Tuesday, Thursday, Friday and Saturday, and are optional at other times and places.

Locker rooms, massage by appointment, cabins, overnight camping and catered private parties are available on the premises. By prior reservation there are also saddle-horse trips and cross-country skiing. It is seven miles to all other services. Visa and MasterCard are accepted.

Directions: From US 40 in the town of Steamboat Springs, go north on 7th St. and follow signs seven miles to location. Phone for rates, reservations and transportation in the winter.

Strawberry Park Hot Springs: A few years ago this was a primitive spring plagued with controversies about sanitation, nudity, behavior and trash. New ownership has preserved the primitive feel, including some controlled skinnydipping, while adding accomodations, hands-on administration and improved natural rock soaking pools.

143

502 STEAMBOAT SPRINGS HEALTH AND RECREATION

P.O. Box 1211   (303) 879-1828
Steamboat Springs, CO 80477   PR

Large community plunge, hot pool, water slide and sauna near the city center. Elevation 6,700 ft. Open all year.

Natural mineral water flows out of a spring at 104º and is piped to four pools which are treated with chlorine. The enclosed hydrojet pool is maintained at a temperature of 101º, the water slide pick-up pool at 99º, and the outdoor swimming pool at 80º. A large outdoor hydrojet pool is maintained at 102º. Bathing suits are required, even in the coed sauna.

Locker rooms, snack bar, exercise classes and tennis courts are available on the premises. It is three blocks to a cafe, store, service station and motel, and two miles to overnight camping and RV hookups. Visa and MasterCard are accepted.

Location: On the north side of US 40, at the east edge of the city of Steamboat Springs.

 Steamboat Springs Health and Recreation: One of the few publicly-owned plunges which has seen fit to add a popular super slide.

503 HOT SULPHUR SPRINGS

P.O. Box 175   **(303) 725-3306**
Hot Sulphur Springs, CO 80451   **PR+MH+CRV**

Older resort on US 40, which winds through the Rocky Mountains. Elevation 7,600 ft. Open all year.

Natural mineral water flows out of a spring at 115° and is piped to a variety of pools. The outdoor swimming pool is treated with chlorine and maintained at 85°. Two outdoor soaking pools are maintained at 100° on a flow-through basis that eliminates the need for chemical treatment. There are two indoor pools in private spaces that rent by the hour, and there are two indoor pools in separate men's and women's bathhouses. Temperatures in these pools are controllable up to 110°. Bathing suits are required except in indoor pools.

Dressing rooms, motel rooms, camping spaces and picnic area are available on the premises. It is three blocks to a cafe, store and service station, and 17 miles to RV hookups. No credit cards are accepted.

Directions: From US 40 in the town of Hot Sulphur Springs, follow signs north across the bridge to the resort.

Indian Springs Resort: A tropical garden has grown up under this famous translucent roof which covers the large main pool.

Hot Sulphur Springs: The variety of indoor and outdoor pools at this location attracts a wide range of mineral water customers.

504 INDIAN SPRINGS RESORT

P.O. Box 1300   **(303) 623-2050**
Idaho Springs, CO 80452   **PR+MH+CRV**

Popular historic resort just off I-70 in the Arapahoe National Forest. Elevation 7,300. Open all year.

Natural mineral water flows out of three underground springs at 124°. Within the men's cave are three walk-in soaking pools ranging in temperature from 104-112°. Within the women's cave are four similar pools. There are 12 private-space soaking pools large enough for couples or families, with temperatures ranging from 104-112°. All of the above pools operate on a flow-through basis so that no chemical treatment is necessary. A minimum of chlorine treatment is used in the large, landscaped indoor pool, which is maintained at 96° in the winter and 90° in the summer. Bathing suits are required in the swimming pool and prohibited in the caves.

Locker rooms, massage, chiropractor, dining room, hotel rooms, overnight camping and RV hookups are available on the premises. It is five blocks to a store and service station. Visa and MasterCard are accepted.

Directions: From I-70, take the Idaho Springs exit to the business district, then follow signs south of Soda Springs Road to resort.

▲ *Glenwood Hot Springs Lodge and Pool*: This two-block-long pool complex can accomodate hundreds of day-use and lodge customers and also have room for a full scale swim meet.

▼ *Glenwood Springs Vapor Caves*: This location specializes in providing feel-better therapy.

505A GLENWOOD HOT SPRINGS LODGE
AND POOL (see map)
P.O. Box 308 (303) 945-6571
■ Glenwood Springs, CO 81601 PR+MH

A very large commercial resort near the center of town on the north bank of the Colorado River. Elevation 5,700 ft. Open all year.

Natural mineral water flows out of a spring at 130° and is mixed with cold spring water to supply four pools, all of which are treated with chlorine. The two-block-long swimming pool is maintained at a temperature of 90°, the outdoor soaking pool, with jet therapy chairs at 104°, the water slide catch-pool at 85°, and the indoor hydrojet pool (in the athletic club) at 104°. There is also a sauna and steambath in the athletic club. Bathing suits are required everywhere.

Locker rooms, cafe, hotel rooms and miniature golf course are available on the premises. It is one block to a store and service station and two miles to overnight camping and RV hookups. Visa, MasterCard, Diners Club, Discover and American Express are accepted.

505B GLENWOOD SPRINGS VAPOR CAVES
(see map)
709 E. 6th (303) 945-5825
■ Glenwood Springs, CO 81601

Unique health center, one block from the large Hot Springs Lodge complex. Elevation 5,700. Open all year.

Natural mineral water and vapor emerge at 115° from several springs within three caves. There are no soaking pools, but a cold-water hose is available. All caves are coed and bathing suits are required.

Locker rooms and massage are available on the premises. It is three blocks to a cafe, store, service station and motel, and five miles to overnight camping and RV hookups. Visa, American Express and MasterCard are accepted.

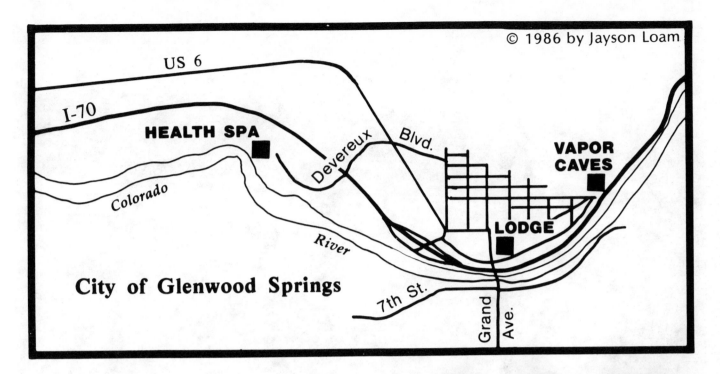

US 6

I-70

HEALTH SPA

Colorado

River

Devereux Blvd.

VAPOR CAVES

LODGE

City of Glenwood Springs

7th St.

Grand Ave.

505C   HEALTH SPA

P.O. Box 536
Glenwood Springs, CO 81601

(see map)
(303) 945-5021
PR

Chiropractic office and bathhouse part of old resort. Elevation 5,700 ft. Open all year.

Natural mineral water flows out of two springs at 110° and 124° and is piped to six individual tubs in private rooms. Customers can control tub temperature up to 112°. Bathing suits are not required in tub rooms.

Chiropractic adjustment and massage are available on the premises. It is 1/2 mile to a cafe, store, service station and motel, and five miles to overnight camping and RV hookups. No credit cards are accepted.

505D   SOUTH CANYON HOT SPRINGS

● **West of the city of Glenwood Springs**

A primitive, city-owned geothermal spring with a long history of controversy involving nudity, lack of sanitary facilities, and the dynamiting of volunteer-built soaking pools. Elevation 5,600 ft. Open all year.

Natural mineral water flows out of a spring at 118°. From time to time, volunteers build masonry soaking pools, then the city tests the water in the pools, finds it to be a health hazard (per state standards), and destroys the pools. The area is not fenced or posted, and there is no recent pattern of harassment. However, the police may choose to respond at any time to a complaint about drugs or nudity.

There are no services on the premises.

Directions: From I-70 west of Glenwood Springs, take the South Canyon exit and go approximately 1/2 mile up from the mouth of the canyon. You might or might not find a usable pool of geothermal water on the west side of the canyon.

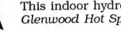 This indoor hydrojet pool is part of the *Glenwood Hot Springs Lodge* athletic club.

147

506   PENNY HOT SPRINGS

● **North of the town of Redstone**

Primitive, riverbank hot spring seasonally flooded by high water. Elevation 8,000 ft. Open all year.

Natural mineral water flows out of a spring at 133° and drops directly into the Crystal River. In between annual high-water washouts, volunteers build rock-and-sand pools in which hot mineral water and cold river water can be mixed to a comfortable soaking temperature. The location is close to the highway, so bathing suits are advisable.

There are no services on the premises. All services are within 25 miles.

Directions: On the east side of CO 133, 0.2 miles south of mile marker 57, there is a small parking area on the east side of the highway. A telephone cable strung across the river is visible from that area, and the springs are almost directly under the cable.

507   CONUNDRUM HOT SPRINGS

● **South of the town of Aspen**

Two primitive pools surrounded by spectacular Rocky Mountain scenery in a designated Wilderness Area of the White River National Forest. Elevation 11,200 ft. Open all year.

Natural mineral water flows out of a spring at 100° into two volunteer-built, rock-and-sand pools. The trail is so popular that the spring may be crowded. A long rugged climb will not necessarily give you quiet solitude. The local custom is clothing optional.

There are no services on the premises. It is eight miles of trail and five miles of rough road to a campsite. It is 20 miles to all other services.

This is a rewarding but hazardous location. Be sure to obtain directions, instructions and information about current trail conditions at a White River National Forest ranger station before attempting the trip.

 Youmans Store & Cabins (Cebolla Hot Springs): Each of the authentic log cabins contains a plank-lined soaking pit, excavated directly down into a source spring. The small building in the middle is an authentic privy, which must be shared by all patrons.

508   YOUMANS STORE & CABINS (CEBOLLA HOT SPRINGS)

County Road 27   (303) 641-0952
Powderhorn, CO 81243   MH

Something special. An old-fashioned soak in a plank-lined spring covered by an authentic log cabin on a rugged mountain slope in central Colorado. Elevation 8,100 ft. Open May to October.

Natural mineral water flows out of two springs at 106° directly up through the bottom planks of two wood-lined pits which have been built within each spring. The odorless geothermal water flows through continuously, maintaining a pool temperature of 105° and eliminating the need for any chemical water treatment. There are no hydrojets, but you will feel an occasional gas bubble rising to the surface as you soak in natural silence. The soaking pools and cabin floor are kept very clean, and one of the cabins has a wood stove. Bathing suits are not required within the cabins.

IMPORTANT NOTICE: These hot springs are reserved primarily for the use of registered guests in the nearby rental cabins. Phone ahead for reservations before attempting to drive to this remote location.

A store, service station, rental cabins and fishing are available on the premises. It is ten miles to a cafe and overnight camping and 20 miles to RV hookups. No credit cards are accepted.

Directions: From US 50 ten miles west of Gunnison, drive south on CO 149 approximately 15 miles and watch for Powderhorn turn off on left.

148

 Waunita Hot Springs Guest Ranch: In addition to supplying the swimming pool, hot spring water is used for geothermal heating in the lodge and for raising tropical fish.

---

509   WAUNITA HOT SPRINGS RANCH
    8007 County Road 887   (303) 641-1266
■   Gunnison, CO 81230   MH

    Rustic guest ranch surrounded by Gunnison National Forest. Elevation 9,000 ft. Open all year.

    Natural mineral water flows out of a spring at 175° and is piped to a swimming pool and to geothermal heating units in the buildings. The swimming pool is treated with chlorine and maintained at a temperature of 95°. Pool use is reserved for registered guests, with a minimum stay of six days by prior reservation only. Bathing suits are required.

    Guest-ranch services, including rooms, meals, saddle horses and fishing, are available on the premises. It is 15 miles to a store, service station and overnight camping, and 28 miles to RV hookups. No credit cards are accepted.

    Directions: From the town of Gunnison, go 19 miles east on US 50, then follow signs eight miles north to the ranch.

▲ *Mount Princeton Hot Springs*: The newer pools are on a grassy parklike knoll above the main lodge and individual hot-tub rooms.

▼ *Cottonwood Hot Springs Inn*: Urban-type fiberglass tubs have been given a rustic deck on the bank of a rushing mountain stream.

510   COTTONWOOD HOT SPRINGS INN
18999 Hwy 306   (719) 395-6434
Buena Vista, CO 81211   PR+MH

A small, rustic resort nestled in a high mountain valley, surrounded by the San Isabel National Forest. Elevation 8,500 ft. Open all year.

Odorless natural mineral water flows out of a well at 187°, cools to 120° in the 600-foot main conduit and is piped to three outdoor private-space hydrojet pools on a deck overlooking Cottonwood Creek. Individual pool temperatures range from 104-112° on a flow-through basis that requires no chemical treatment. Bathing suits are optional within the fenced private spaces. All pools are available to the public as well as to registered guests.

The mineral water is so pure that it is used as tap water throughout the resort. Facilities include dressing rooms, creekside cabins, lodge rooms, Jump Steady Bar & Restaurant, meeting rooms and an exercise room. Massage is available by appointment. Visa and MasterCard are accepted. It is 5 1/2 miles to all other services.

The rustic setting and facilities are well-suited to small seminar groups, reunions, retreats, etc. Phone or write for rates and reservations.

Directions: From US 24 in Buena Vista, go west 5 1/2 miles on CO 306, the road to Cottonwood Pass. Watch for resort signs on the right side of the road.

511   MOUNT PRINCETON HOT SPRINGS
County Road 162   (303) 395-2361
Nathrop, CO 81236   PR+MH

Large, modern resort surrounded by San Isabel National Forest. Elevation 8,500 ft. Open all year.

Natural mineral water flows out of a spring at 132°. Odorless and tasteless, this water is used in all pipes, including those which water the lawn. The outdoor swimming pool is maintained at 85° and the outdoor soaking pool at 95°. Both are treated with chlorine. There are two individual tubs in private rooms which are drained and refilled after each use, with temperatures controllable up to 110°. All pools and tubs are available to the public as well as to registered guests. Bathing suits are required everywhere except in private tub rooms.

Locker rooms, restaurant, hotel rooms, picnic area, saddle horses, fishing and hiking are available on the premises. It is five miles to all other services. Visa and MasterCard are accepted.

Directions: From US 285 in the town of Nathrop, go west five miles on CO 162 to resort.

512 SALIDA HOT SPRINGS

410 Rainbow Blvd. **(303) 539-6738**
Salida, CO 81201 **PR**

Modernized, indoor municipal plunge, hot baths, park and playground. Elevation 7,000 ft. Open all year.

Natural mineral water flows out of Poncha Springs at 150° and is piped five miles to Salida. The large indoor swimming pool is maintained at a temperature of 92-96° and is treated with chlorine. There are three private, family-size indoor soaking pools which are drained and refilled after each use and in which the water temperature is controllable by the customer. Bathing suits are required everywhere except in private soaking pools.

Locker rooms are available on the premises. It is less than five blocks to all other services. No credit cards are accepted.

Directions: From the junction of US 50 and US 285, go six miles east on US 50. Look for signs on the north side of the street.

513 MANITOU HEALTH SPA

934 Manitou Ave. **(719) 685-5431**
Manitou Springs, CO 80829

Historic old spa building being remodeled and restored by new owner on the main street in downtown Manitou Springs. Elevation 6,200 ft. Open all year.

Natural mineral water flows out of a spring at 68° and is heated to 104° for use in one of the private-room hydrojet pools. There are three other private-room hydrojet pools holding up to ten persons. These baths are filled with gas-heated tap water treated with bromine and are maintained at a temperature of 104°. Bathing suits are required at all times

Therapeutic Stress Massage is available on the premises at the Stress Massage Institute. It is less than three blocks to all other services. MasterCard and Visa are accepted. Phone for rates, reservations and directions.

Salida Hot Springs: The city of Salida bought a hot spring and piped the geothermal water five miles to supply this municipal pool.

Manitou Health Spa: In this historic spa traditional one-person tubs have been replaced by large fiberglass hydrojet tubs.

151

514   DESERT REEF BEACH CLUB
■   P.O. Box 503   (719) 661-1269
            Penrose, CO 81240   PR

A small, rustic recreation area which has grown up around a geothermal well in the desert foothills south of Colorado Springs. Elevation 5,200 ft. Open all year on Wednesday, Thursday, Friday, Saturday and Sunday, 10 A.M. to 10 P.M.

Natural mineral water flows out of an artesian well at 130° and is piped to two outdoor swimming pools and a separate hot tub on a flow-through basis so that no chemical treatment of the water is necessary. Flow rate is adjusted to maintain pool temperature within a comfortable range for bathing and soaking through all seasons. Bathing suits are optional.

A lawn area for picknicking is available on the premises. Visa and MasterCard are accepted. It is two miles to all other services. Phone during business hours for information on rates and directions.

▲ *Desert Reef Beach Club*: The waves at this mile-high beach may be small, but the water is warmer than is found at an ocean beach.

515   VALLEY VIEW HOT SPRINGS
■   P.O. Box 175   (719) 256-4315
            Villa Grove, CO 81155   PR+MH+CRV

Unique combination of primitive hot springs and primitive camping facilities, with clothing optional, on the west slope of the Sangre De Cristo mountains. Elevation 8,700 ft. Open all year.

Natural mineral water flows out of several springs at temperatures ranging from 85-100°. All pools are supplied on a flow-through basis so that no chemical treatment is needed. The outdoor cement swimming pool is maintained at 89°. The outdoor soaking pool is built right over a spring, so the water flowing up through the gravel bottom maintains a temperature of 96° in the pool. The small gravel-bottom upper pool is also built right over a spring, and the pool temperature varies from 80-105° depending on the volume of snow melt. There is also a small soaking pool at 83° inside the wood-fired sauna building. Clothing is optional everywhere on the extensive grounds.

Rustic cabins and tent spaces are available on the premises. It is 12 miles to all other services. Visa and MasterCard are accepted.

Note: This is primarily a membership facility, with the premises reserved for members and their guests on weekends. A limited number of guest passes are available during the week. Write or phone first for full information.

Directions: From the junction of US 285 and CO 17 near Mineral Hot Springs, take the gravel road due east seven miles to the location.

▲ *Valley View Hot Springs*: This beautiful upper pool can be reached only via a steep path, but it does have a grand view of the valley.

 The geothermal water in this *Valley View Hot Springs* pool is so clear that individual rocks can be seen on the gravel bottom.

For those members who wanted a modern swimming pool, with diving board and sun decks, this cement pool has been added.

516 SPLASHLAND HOT SPRINGS
Box 972 (303) 589-6307
Alamosa, CO 81101 PR

Large, rural community plunge in the center of a wide, high valley. Elevation 7,500 ft. Open Memorial Day through Labor Day.

Natural mineral water flows out of a spring at 106° and is piped to a large outdoor swimming pool which maintains a temperature of approximately 87°. The water is treated with chlorine. Bathing suits are required.

Locker rooms and snack bar are available on the premises. It is two miles to a cafe, store and service station, and five miles to all other services. No credit cards are accepted.

Location: On CO 17, one mile north of town of Alamosa.

 Splashland Hot Springs: At 7,500 ft. even summer days can be crisp, so a warm water pool is welcome, especially if that water comes out of the ground already heated.

517 4UR GUEST RANCH
P.O. Box 340 (719) 658-2202
Creede, CO 81130 MH

Modern, deluxe guest ranch surrounded by Rio Grande National Forest. Elevation 8,400 ft. Open June 1 to September 25.

Natural mineral water flows out of a spring at 140° and is piped into two pools where it is treated with bromine. The outdoor swimming pool is maintained at a temperature of 78° and the indoor hydrojet pool at 105°. Bathing suits are required. Pools are for the use of registered guests only, and the minimum stay is one week, by prior reservation only.

Rooms, meals, tennis, saddle horses, fishing and hiking are available on the premises. It is four miles to all other services. No credit cards are accepted.

Directions: From the town of South Fork on US 160, go 14 miles north on CO 149 to the village of Wagon Wheel Gap. Just 0.4 mile beyond Wagon Wheel Gap, watch for sign and turn left across bridge onto gravel road to the resort.

518　RAINBOW (WOLF CREEK PASS) HOT SPRINGS

● **Northwest of the town of Pagosa Springs**

A primitive riverside hot spring at the end of a rugged hike in the Weminuche Wilderness, northwest of CO 160. Elevation 9,000 ft. Open all year.

Natural mineral water flows out of a spring at 104° and flows directly into volunteer-built, rock-and-mud pools at the edge of the San Juan River. A high rate of geothermal flow maintains a temperature of more than 100° in these pools. The apparent local custom is clothing optional.

There are no services available on the premises. It is six miles to overnight camping and 25 miles to all other services.

The five-mile trail to this location includes new bridges over Beaver Creek and the West Fork of the San Juan River. For your own safety, inquire at a San Juan National Forest ranger station before starting this trip, and use the sign-in/sign-out board at the trailhead.

Source map: *San Juan National Forest.*

519　PAGOSA SPRINGS POOL
P.O. Box 37　　　　　　　　　　**(303) 264-5912**
■ **Pagosa Springs, CO 81147**　　　　　　**PR**

Older swimming pool and bathhouse formerly reserved for motel guests, now available to the public. Located near downtown Pagosa Springs. Elevation 7,100 ft. Open all year.

Natural mineral water is pumped from a well at 130° and piped to the swimming pool and bathhouse. The outdoor swimming pool is maintained at 90°. The two indoor soaking pools, in separate men's and women's sections, are maintained at 108°. All pools have continuous flow-through so that no chemical treatment is necessary. Each of the two bathhouse sections also has its own steambath. Bathing suits are required in the outdoor pools.

Locker rooms are available on the premises. It is less than three blocks to all other services. Visa, American Express and MasterCard are accepted.

Directions: In Pagosa Springs on US 160, 1/2 block west of the high school, turn south across the bridge and watch for pool on your left.

4UR Guest Ranch: The indoor hydrojet pool and dressing rooms are in the log building on the right, adjoining the outdoor swimming pool and barbecue pit building on the left.

Pagosa Springs Pool: This spot is within easy walking distance of the center of town.

155

Ouray Hot Springs: This city-owned facility makes the most of a large geothermal water flow and a spectacular natural setting.

Wiesbaden Motel and Health Resort: This group is dedicating a new deck and fiberglass pool.

520   PIEDRA RIVER HOT SPRING

● **West of Pagosa Springs**

A peaceful primitive spring in a beautiful mountain setting at the end of a rugged two-mile hike in the San Juan National Forest Elevation 7,400 ft. Open all year.

Natural mineral water, at approximately 110°, flows up from the bottom of several volunteer-built, rock-and-sand pools on the east bank of the Piedra River. When necessary, evaporation cooling is supplemented by adding cold river water. The apparent local custom is clothing optional.

No services are available on the premises. It is six miles to a Forest Service campground (Lower Piedra) on FS 622, one mile north of US 160. It is 26 miles to all other services in Pagosa Springs.

Directions: From US 160, between Pagosa Springs and Bayfield, drive north on FS 622 for six miles to a fork in the road. The parking area on the left is the signed trailhead for Sheep Creek Trail. Hike up this steep trail for approximately one mile to the bridge over the river. Do not cross, but rather turn right and follow a trail up the east bank of the river for approximately one mile to Coffee Creek. Turn left toward the river to reach the springs.

Source map: *San Juan National Forest* (springs not shown).

521   TRIMBLE HOT SPRINGS
■   6475 County Road 203   (303)259-0314
     Durango, CO 81301   PR

Recently restored older resort in the scenic Animas River Valley, below the La Plata mountains. Elevation 6,500 ft. Open all year.

Natural mineral water flows out of a spring at 111° and is piped to two outdoor pools where it is treated with ozone. The Olympic-size swimming pool is maintained at 85-90°, and the smaller therapy pool, equipped with hydrojets, is maintained at 104-106°. There are two indoor private hydrojet pools in which water temperature may be controlled. Bathing suits are required except in the private rooms.

Massage, physical therapy, locker rooms, snack bar, picnic area and gardens are available on the premises. It is two miles to a bed and breakfast inn and six miles to all other services. Visa and MasterCard are accepted.

Directions: From the city of Durango, go six miles north on US 550, then west 100 yards on Trimble Lane to springs.

156

522A OURAY HOT SPRINGS

■ **Ouray, CO 81427**

(303) 325-4638
PR

Large, city-owned swimming pool and visitor information complex. Elevation 7,800 ft. Open all year.

Natural mineral water flows out of a spring at 150° and is cooled with city tap water as needed to supply two large outdoor pools. The shallow soaking pool is maintained at 95-100° in the summer and 102-104° in the winter. The deep swimming and diving pool averages 85-95° in the summer and 75-80° in the winter. Both pools have continuous flow-through so that no chemical treatment is needed. Bathing suits are required.

Locker rooms, snack house, fitness center and swim shop with suit rentals are available on the premises. All other services are within six blocks. No credit cards are accepted.

Location: The entire complex is easily visible on the west side of US 550.

522B WIESBADEN MOTEL AND HEALTH RESORT

■ **P.O. Box 349**
Ouray, CO 81427

(303) 325-4347
PR+MH

Modern resort built to complement the spectacular canyon area of Uncompahgre National Forest. Elevation 7,700 ft. Open all year.

Natural mineral water flows from three springs at temperatures ranging from 108-130°. It is then mixed with cold spring water as needed to maintain desired pool temperatures on a flow-through basis, requiring no chemical treatment. The outdoor swimming pool ranges from 85° in the morning to 104° by evening. The soaking pool in the natural vapor cave is maintained at 108°. The soaking pool in the sauna is kept at 117°. Bathing suits are required.

A 105° flow-through soaking pool is supplied by a hot waterfall in a private area called "The Lorelei." In this beautifully landscaped space, which may be rented by the hour, clothing is optional.

Geothermal heat is used in all buildings. Rooms, massage, reflexology, facials and exercise equipment are available on the premises. It is two blocks to a cafe, store and service station, and eight blocks to overnight camping and RV hookups. Visa and MasterCard are accepted.

Location: In the town of Ouray, two blocks east of US 550. Follow signs.

522C BOX CANYON LODGE AND HOT SPRINGS

■ **45 3rd Ave.**
Ouray, CO 81427

(303) 325-4981
MH

Modern, off-highway lodge adjacent to Box Canyon Falls in a picturesque mountain town. Elevation 7,700 ft. Open all year.

Natural mineral water flows out of a spring at 140° and is piped to four redwood tubs where it is treated with bromine. There are four outdoor hydrojet tubs maintained at a temperature of 105° and reserved for the use of registered guests only. Bathing suits are required. Visa, MasterCard, Diners Club and Discover are accepted.

Location: Two blocks west of US 550 on 3rd Ave.

▲ *Box Canyon Motel and Hot Springs:* Hot tubbing in the winter can be quite enjoyable when your nice warm motel room is just steps away.

522D BEST WESTERN TWIN PEAKS MOTEL

■ **125 3rd Ave.**
Ouray, CO 81427

(303) 325-4427
MH

Modern, major hotel in a picturesque mountain town. Elevation 7,700 ft. Open April through October.

Natural mineral water flows out of a spring at 156° and is piped to two pools treated with bromine. The outdoor swimming pool is maintained at 92°, the indoor soaking pool at 107°. Pools are reserved for the use of registered guests. Bathing suits are required. Visa, MasterCard, American Express, Carte Blanche, Diners Club and Amoco are accepted.

Location: One block west of US 550 on 3rd Ave.

▼ *Orvis Hot Springs*: For those who like to alternate dry and wet heat, this soaking pool is located next to the sauna building.

▲ This enlarged hot spring pond at *Orvis Hot Springs* is the nearest thing to Indian-style soaking available at a commercial location.

523 ORVIS HOT SPRINGS
■ 1585 County Rd. #3   **(303) 626-5324**
Ridgway, CO 81432   **PR+MH**

Small and charming rustic lodge with multiple geothermal pools, located in a wide mountain valley. Elevation 7,000 ft. Open all year.

Mineral water flows from several springs at temperatures ranging from 112-127° and is piped to a variety of tubs and pools, all of which operate on a flow-through basis requiring no chemical treatment. All of them are available to the public for day use as well as to registered guests.

There are four private rooms with tiled soaking pools that have a water temperature of 105-109° that are drained and cleaned every day. Immediately adjoining the sauna building there is one outside soaking pool, built of stone, which has a water temperature of 105-108°. There is one large cement indoor soaking pool (three feet deep, 25 feet in diameter) which has a temperature of 101° in the summer and 104° in the winter. There is also one large, excavated soaking pond (six-feet deep, 30 feet in diameter) which has hot mineral water continuously flowing in from the bottom and the sides. This enlarged natural hot-spring maintains a year-round temperature of 103-105°. Clothing is optional in all pools except the 25-foot indoor soaking pool.

Facilities include six lodge rooms which share two baths. Room rates include unlimited use of sauna and pool facilities. Visa and MasterCard are accepted. It is less than two miles to the town of Ridgway and all other services. Phone for rates, hours, reservations and directions.

7-8-91   EXCELLENT !!!

 Orvis Hot Springs visitors can enjoy a clothing-optional pond, snow-capped mountains and lodge rooms only a few steps away.

Customers who prefer to avoid skinnydippers may use this indoor *Orvis Hot Springs* pool, where bathing suits are required.

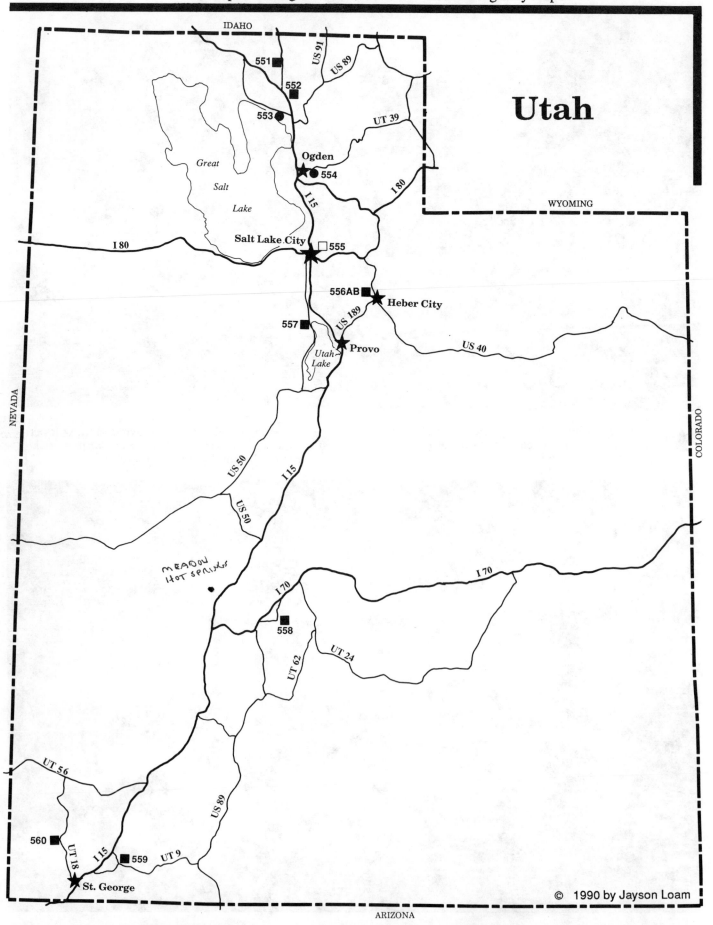

This map was designed to be used with a standard highway map

© 1990 by Jayson Loam

160

▲ *Belmont Springs*: The design of most new hot springs resorts includes group hydrojet pools first made popular as urban rent-a-tubs.

▲ Much more than just a plunge, *Belmont Springs* includes a golf course, an RV park and a recreation-oriented real estate development.

551   BELMONT SPRINGS
Box 36   **(801) 458-3200**
■ **Fielding, UT 84311**   **PR+CRV**

Modern, commercial plunge with RV park and golf course in a treeless northern Utah valley. Elevation 4,300 ft. Open April through September.

Natural mineral water flows out of artesian wells at 125° and is piped to four outdoor pools, all of which are treated with chlorine. The large swimming pool is maintained at 93°, a soaking pool at 106°, and two hydrojet pools at approximately 106°. Bathing suits are required.

Locker rooms, two picnic bowers, golf course, overnight parking and RV hookups are available on the premises. A cafe, store, service station and motel are available within ten miles. No credit cards are accepted.

Directions: From the town of Plymouth on I-15, go one mile south and watch for resort sign.

161

 Crystal Hot Springs: Tree-covered slopes on both sides of the pool area give this location the feeling of being user-friendly.

---

552 CRYSTAL HOT SPRINGS

■ 8215 North Hwy 69   (801) 279-8104
Honeyville, UT 84314   PR+CRV

Superbly remodeled, historical resort featuring the world's largest side-by-side hot and cold springs. The property includes spacious, tree-shaded lawns for picnics and camping. Elevation 4,700 ft. Open all year.

Natural mineral water flows out of a spring at 135° and is piped to three outdoor hydrojet pools which are maintained at 102°, 104° and 106° on a flow-through basis requiring no chemical treatment. A large outdoor soaking pool of natural mineral water is maintained at 100° with a minimum of chlorine treatment. Another large soaking pool uses chlorine-treated spring water maintained at a temperature of 95°. Similar water is used in the catch-pool at the bottom of two large waterslides. There is also an Olympic-size swimming pool using cold spring water, which is drained and filled weekly and reqirues a minimum of chlorine treatment. Bathing suits are required.

Locker rooms, snack bar, overnight camping and RV hookups are available on the premises. It is four blocks to a store and service station and 15 miles to a motel. No credit cards are accepted.

Directions: From I-15, take Honeyville exit. Go one mile east on UT 240 to UT 69, then 2 1/2 miles north to resort on west side of highway.

There are dozens of shaded tenting spaces at *Crystal Hot Springs* along the grassy ridge just north of the main pool area.

553 STINKY SPRINGS

● **West of the town of Brigham City**
A small, partly vandalized cement-block bathhouse alongside a highway in the flat country north of the Great Salt Lake. Elevation 4,000 ft. Open all year.

Natural mineral water flows out of a spring at 118°, through a culvert under the highway, and into three cement soaking pits in the abandoned building. Temperature within each pool is controlled by diverting the hot-water flow as desired. In recent years volunteers have kept the surrounding party trash to a minimum, but the water does have a sulfur-dioxide smell. The apparent local custom is clothing optional within the building.

There are no services available on the premises.

Directions: From I-15, take the Golden Spike exit, then go nine miles west through Corinne on UT 83. The building is on the south side of the road shortly before you reach Little Mountain, a rocky hill on the north side of the road.

554 OGDEN HOT SPRINGS

● **East of the city of Ogden**
Small, primitive hot spring in a river gorge subject to annual flooding. Elevation 4,800 ft. Open all year.

Natural mineral water flows out of a spring at 130° and through a pipe to a volunteer-built, rock-and-mud pool at the water's edge. The temperature is controlled by diverting the flow when desired. The apparent local custom is clothing optional.

There are no services available on the premises.

Directions: From I-15 in Ogden, go east 14 miles on UT 39 to the mouth of Ogden Canyon. The pool is 100 feet upstream from the water pipe suspended far above. Parking is upriver just past where the river crosses under the road for the first time.

▲ *Stinky Springs:* No one knows why this block house was built, or how it survives, but it continues to provide free soaks every day.

555 THE SPA CENTER (SOAK YOUR BODY)
3955 S. State St.   (801) 264-TUBS
☐   Salt Lake City, UT 84107   PR

Basic rent-a-tub establishment, plus spa sales and service, on a main street in Southern Salt Lake City.

Private-space hot pools using bromine-treated tap water are for rent to the public by the hour. Six indoor, fiberglass hydrojet pools are maintained at temperatures ranging from 102-104°. Visa and MasterCard are accepted. Phone for rates, reservations and directions.

Mountain Spaa Resort: The indoor pool, built in a large crater, is covered by the building on the far side of the swimming pool.

The Homestead: The proximity of Midway to several major ski slopes makes this indoor pool a popular wintertime attraction.

556A   THE HOMESTEAD

700 N. Homestead Road	(801) 654-1102
Midway, UT 84049	PR+MH+C

Remodeled, historic resort specializing in family reunions and group meetings, with extensive landscaping and a minimal use of natural mineral water. Elevation 5,600 ft. Open all year.

Natural mineral water flows from a tufa-cone spring at 92° and is piped to one small outdoor soaking pool which averages 90° and is not treated with chemicals. All other pools use chlorine-treated tap water. The large outdoor swimming pool is maintained at 82° and the indoor hydrojet pools at 98°. There is also a dry sauna available. Pool use is available to the public as well as to registered guests. Bathing suits are required.

Locker rooms, dining room, hotel rooms and overnight camping are available on the premises. It is two miles to a store, service station, RV hookups and a golf course. Visa, American Express and MasterCard are accepted for rooms and for dining, but not for public swimming.

Directions: From Heber City on US 189, go west on UT 113 to the town of Midway and follow signs to resort.

556B   MOUNTAIN SPAA RESORT

800 North 200 East	(801) 654-0721
Midway, UT 84049	PR+MH+CRV

Historic resort, formerly known as Luke's Hot Pots. Elevation 5,700 ft. Open April to October (mineral baths open all year).

Natural mineral water flows from cone-shaped tufa craters at 110° and is piped to three pools. The outdoor swimming pool is maintained at 90-95° and is treated with chlorine. The indoor swimming pool is built inside a large crater, maintains a temperature of 95-100°, and has a continuous flow-through requiring no chemical treatment of the water. The indoor soaking pool, large enough for eight persons, is drained after each use so that no chemical treatment is needed.

Locker rooms, cafe, bed and breakfast, rooms, overnight camping and RV hookups are available on the premises. Visa and MasterCard are accepted.

Directions: From Heber City on US 189, go west on UT 113 to the town of Midway. Turn north on River Road, go .7 mile to 600 North in Midway and follow signs to resort.

557 SARATOGA RESORT
Saratoga Rd. at Utah Lake   (801) 768-8206
Lehi, UT 84043   PR+CRV

Lakeside recreation resort with picnic grounds, rides and boat-launching facilities. Elevation 4,200 ft. Open May to September.

Natural mineral water is pumped out of a well at 120° and is piped to four outdoor pools, all of which are treated with chlorine. One large hydrojet pool is maintained at 100°. The swimming pool, diving pool and waterslide catch pool are maintained at 75-80°. Bathing suits are required.

Locker rooms, snack bar, overnight camping and RV hookups are available on the premises. There are also several amusement park rides. No credit cards are accepted.

Directions: From the town of Lehi on I-15, go west on UT 73 and follow signs to resort.

Saratoga Resort: This giant waterslide is the most popular of many recreation attractions at this famous lakeside hot springs resort.

558 MONROE HOT SPRINGS
575 East First North   (801) 527-4014
Monroe, UT 84754   PR+CRV

RV park with restaurant, swimming pool and hillside soaking pool overlooking an agricultural valley. Elevation 5,500 ft. Open all year; swimming pool open from Memorial Day to Labor Day.

Natural mineral water flows out of a spring at 135° and is piped into a heat exchanger, then into a soaking pool where the temperature ranges from 100-105°. The outdoor swimming pool and hydrojet pool use chlorinated tap water heated in the geothermal heat exchanger to approximately 90°. Bathing suits are required.

Locker rooms, dinner-house meals, store, picnic area, overnight camping and RV hookups are available on the premises. It is a short walk to the large and colorful Red Hill Spring and to the adjoining tropical fish pond. A service station and motel are within four blocks. Visa and MasterCard are accepted.

Directions: From the town of Richfield on I-70, go nine miles south on UT 118 to the town of Monroe. Follow signs to resort.

Monroe Hot Springs: This hot spring also supplies geothermal water for use in a space-heating project at the local high school.

▲ *Pah Tempe Hot Springs Resort*: Mineral water cascades into the shallow Virgin River, which becomes a giant run-and-splash playground.

---

559   PAH TEMPE HOT SPRINGS RESORT
■   **825 North 800 East**   **(801) 635-2879**
       Hurricane, UT 84737   **PR+MH+CRV**

A unique resort being remodeled by new owners and featuring a spectacular flow of geothermal water out of the sides and bottom of the Virgin River canyon, 20 miles southwest of Zion National Park. Elevation 3,000 ft. Open all year.

Natural mineral water flows out of rock grottos and up out of the riverbed at temperatures of 105° to 110°. There is one shaded, outdoor swimming pool which averages 100°. The seven riverbank soaking pools range from 102-106°, and the two private indoor hydrojet pools average 105°. The flow-through rate in all pools is sufficient to eliminate the need for chemical treatment of the water. Bathing suits are required.

Locker rooms, massage and bed and breakfast are available on the premises. There is also a special retreat facility for weddings and family reunions. It is two miles to a cafe, store and service station. Visa and MasterCard are accepted.

Directions: From the town of Hurricane, go one mile north on UT 9 and follow signs to resort.

▲ On the ledges, and in the caves, above the river, a series of comfortable soaking pools have been constructed at *Pah Tempe*.

166

 Veyo Resort: Nothing fancy - just a warm pool with clean dressing rooms, a snack bar, and tree-shaded picnic tables next to a stream.

560 VEYO RESORT
750 East Veyo Resort Rd. (801) 574-2744
Veyo, UT 84782 PR

Older community plunge and picnic park with a small running stream. Elevation 4,600 ft. Open end of March to Labor Day.

Natural mineral water flows out of an artesian well at a temperature of 98˚. There is one outdoor swimming pool which is chlorinated and maintains a temperature of 85˚. Bathing suits are required.

Locker rooms, snack bar, volleyball court and picnic area are available on the premises. It is one mile to a store and service station, eight miles to overnight camping and RV hookups, and 12 miles to a motel. No credit cards are accepted.

Directions: From the city of St. George on I-15, go 19 miles north on UT 18 to the town of Veyo and follow signs to the resort.

167

People in NW CA use the ultra hot pools (some listed, some not) to scald pigs & chickens

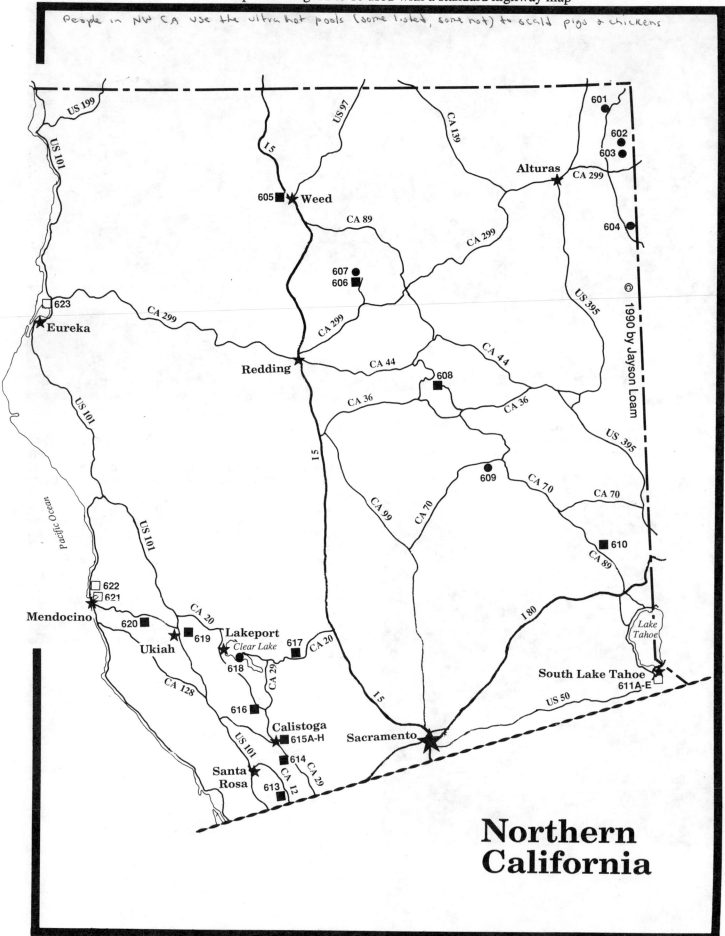

Northern California

MAP AND DIRECTORY SYMBOLS

● Non-commercial mineral water pool

■ Commercial (fee) mineral water pool

□ Gas-heated tap or well water pool

〜〜〜 Paved highway

- - - - Unpaved road

····· Hiking route

PR = Tubs or pools for rent by hour, day or treatment

MH = Rooms, cabins or dormitory spaces for rent by day, week or month

CRV = Camping or vehicle parking spaces, some with hookups,
for rent by day, week, month or year

---

601   FORT BIDWELL HOT SPRING

● **Near the town of Ft. Bidwell**

Two cement pools on private property with a view of Upper Alkali Lake, The Surprise Valley, and surrounding mountains. Elevation 4,700 ft. Open all year with owner's permission. (Owner asks for unspecified donation to help maintain the grounds.)

Natural mineral water is pumped out of a well at 113° and into an 8-foot by-8-foot by-4-foot deep soaking pool kept at 101°, and into a 20-foot by-40-foot swimming pool maintained at 98°. Both pools operate on a flow-through basis, so no chemical treatment is necessary. Inquire of owner as to current clothing policy.

The owner is pleased to have guests, but asks that you contact him for permission to camp on the premises and for directions. All other services are 25 miles away in Cedarville. Contact: Granville Peterson, Box 146, Ft. Bidwell, CA 96112, (916) 279-2367.

---

602   LEONARD'S HOT SPRING   (see map)

● **Near the town of Cedarville**

Abandoned and deteriorated old resort on a barren slope along the east side of Middle Alkali Lake. Elevation 4,500 ft. Open all year.

Natural mineral water flows out of the ground from several springs at a temperature of 150° and cools as it runs toward the lake. A diversion ditch used to carry this water to the resort, but it now flows through a winding ditch fifty yards southeast of the old swimming pool. Volunteers have built shallow soaking pools in the ditch where the water has cooled to approximately 100°. The apparent local custom is clothing optional.

No services are available on the premises. There is an abundance of unmarked level space on which overnight parking is not prohibited. It is nine miles to a service station and all other services.

Source map: USGS *Cedarville*.

---

603   GLEN HOT SPRING   (see map)

● **Near the town of Cedarville**

Undeveloped cluster of hot springs on a barren slope along the east side of Upper Alkali Lake. Elevation 4,600 ft. Open all year.

Natural mineral water flows out of several springs at 150° and cools as it runs toward the lake. Volunteers have built shallow soaking pools where the water has cooled to approximately 100°. The apparent local custom is clothing optional.

No services are available on the premises. There is a limited amount of unmarked open space on which overnight parking is not prohibited. It is ten miles to a service station and all other services.

Source map: USGS *Cedarville*. 10-27-92
MUCH TO HOT!!!

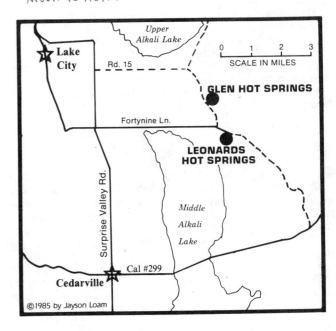

◀ *Leonard's Hot Spring:* This is a typical volunteer-built rock-and-sand soaking pool, plus two of the volunteers who built it.

10-27-92   I was unable to locate this pool, however there was a small one in a drainage ditch, but it wasn't very good. I took a dip bath using a cooking pot for a dipper, perfect bath tub temp. water.

 Eagleville Hot Spring: This pool is not surrounded by a lush forest but it does have the advantage of parking within 25 yards.

604   EAGLEVILLE HOT SPRING

Also has large barrel to sit in, fed by rubber hose

● (**South of the town of Cedarville**

Shallow, primitive soaking pool with a commanding view of Surprise Valley and surrounding mountains. Elevation 4,600 ft. Open all year.

Natural mineral water flows out of a hot spring at 108° and is piped to a volunteer-built, rock-and-sand pool below a highway embankment on the west side of the valley. Surface cooling maintains the water temperature at approximately 104°, depending on wind and weather conditions. The pool is not visible from the road, so the apparent local custom is clothing optional.

There are no services. All services are available within 23 miles at Cedarville.

Directions: From Cedarville, on CA 81, drive south 15 miles to Eagleville. From the Eagleville Post Office continue 7.5 miles south to a turnout on the east side of the road. Walk 25 yards north and then down the embankment to the pool.

Source map: *Modoc National Forest* (hot spring not shown). *10-27-92 / not 7.5 miles but 8, 8.2 miles 300 m North of tiny house located on East side of road Great Hot Springs!*

605   STEWART MINERAL SPRINGS
2222 Stewart Springs Rd.   (916) 938-2222
■ Weed, CA 96094   PR+MH+CRV

A well-kept rustic retreat available for special events or group seminars. Located on a mountain stream in a green canyon northwest of Mt. Shasta. Elevation 3,900 ft. Open all year on a reservation basis only.

Natural mineral water is pumped from a well at 40° and propane heated as needed. There are 12 individual bathtubs and larger tubs in private rooms. Water temperature in each tub is controlled, as desired, by mixing cold and hot mineral water. Tubs are drained and refilled after each use, so no chemical treatment of the water is necessary. The outdoor hydropool is filled with creek water, filtered, chlorinated and heated to 102°. Bathing suits are required in public areas.

Facilities include rooms, restaurant, bar (beer and wine), camping spaces and partial-hookup RV spaces. No credit cards are accepted. It is seven miles to a store, service station and public bus. Special pickup at the bus depot and at the Weed airport is available by arrangement.

Directions: From I-5 north of Weed, take the Edgewood exit and follow signs four miles north on Stewart Springs Road to the resort.

 Big Bend Hot Springs: Hot geothermal water flows through the pools in foreground, cooling as it meanders to the Pit River.

606   BIG BEND HOT SPRINGS
196 Hot Springs Row   (916) 337-6680
■ Big Bend, CA 96011   PR+MH+CRV

The remains of an historical resort being improved and operated by a cooperative self-sufficient Essene Community. Located 50 miles northeast of Redding on the tree-shaded south bank of the Pit River. Elevation 2,000 ft. Open all year.

Natural mineral water flows from three springs at 180°.

(1) Indian Springs. Located ten feet above the level of the nearby Pit River, the flow from this spring cools as it meanders through a series of shallow pools created by volunteers from riverbed rocks. Bathing suits are optional in this area and in the adjoining river.

(2) Main spring. Located on a plateau 50 feet above the river level, this major, controlled flow supplies a greenhouse and a bathhouse containing three bathtubs in separate rooms, plus a steambath room. Just outside the bathhouse is a large fiberglass tub with a view of the river. Bathing suits are optional in these tubs.

(3) Minor spring. Located on the edge of a plateau 50 feet above the Pit River, this smaller flow runs continuously into three interconnected natural stone/cement pools, each large enough for six persons. Faucet-controlled cold creek water is added to each pool to produce whatever temperature is desired by occupants. Each pool has seating at various depths, and all of them have a superb view of the river. Bathing suits are required.

Massage, cabins, RV spaces and overnight camping are available on the premises. Seminar programs are also open to the public. No credit cards are accepted. It is 1/4 mile to a cafe, store and service station.

Directions: From I-5 in Redding, go 35 miles east on CA 299, then turn north 15 miles to the town of Big Bend, which is at the end of the pavement. Look for Big Bend Hot Springs sign 200 yards south of Big Bend store.

607   HUNT HOT SPRING

● **North of the town of Big Bend**

Rock pools on the east bank of Kosk Creek shaded by oak, sycamore and pine trees. Located on private land adjacent to Shasta National Forest. Elevation 2,000 ft. Open all year.

Natural mineral water flows out of rocks above the creek at 136° and into three shallow, rock pools which volunteers have dammed to increase the size and depth. Water temperature is controlled by diverting the hot water running down the hill or adding buckets of cold water from the nearby creek. The apparent local custom is clothing optional.

There are no facilities located on the premises. A store and service station are within two miles at Big Bend.

Note: Big Bend ranger station freely gives directions to the spring and there are no gates or "keep out" signs posted. Since the spring is on private land, you use it at your own risk.

Directions: From I-5 in Redding, go 35 miles east on CA 299, then turn north 15 miles to the town of Big Bend which is at the end of the pavement. North of Big Bend cross the Pit River Bridge and proceed northwest on FS 11. After one mile there is a road to the right signed *Grasshopper Flat*. Go past this road 100 yards and turn left onto a 4WD recommended road. After another 100 yards take the right fork which goes steeply downhill 200 yards to the pools. (Be sure to follow the above directions as some of the roads to the spring indicated on the National Forest map are no longer accurate.)

Source map: *Shasta National Forest;* USGS *Big Bend.*

608   DRAKESBAD GUEST RANCH
c/o California Guest Ranch
■   2150 Main St. #7   (916) 529-1512
    Red Bluff, CA 96080   MH

A rustic mountain ranch/resort with a mineral-water swimming pool, plus horses and guides for riding and hiking. Located in a superb mountain meadow within the boundaries of Lassen Volcanic National Park. Elevation 5,700 ft. Open June 9 to October 1.

Natural mineral water flows out of two springs at temperatures of 85° and 125° and is piped to the pool and to four private-room bathtubs. The swimming pool is maintained in the 80s during the day and over 100° at night by mixing the two hot water flows. Pool flow is shut off after midnight, and chlorine is added to control algae growth; but chlorine content reduces rapidly when flow-through is resumed the following day. Bathing suits are required, except in private bathtub rooms. Pools and bathtubs are available to registered guests only. No day use is permitted.

Facilities include lodge, rooms, cabins, bungalows and dining room (all kerosene lit). Saddle horses and guides are available by the hour. Visa and MasterCard are accepted. It is 20 miles to RV spaces, store and service station. Telephone for reservations.

Directions: From CA 36 in the town of Chester take Warner Valley Road northwest to resort, which is at the end of the road.

Drakesbad Guest Ranch: (above) The private bathtub rooms are in the building at the far end of the pool. (below) The source hot springs are on a slope overlooking the pool.

609 WOODY'S FEATHER RIVER HOT SPRINGS

P.O. Box 7   (916) 283-4115
Twain, CA 95984   PR+MH+RV

Primarily a fishing and hunting resort, this site does have two small soaking pools on the north bank of the Feather River, where you can also pan for gold. The resort is located in the tree-covered upper Feather River Canyon. Elevation 2,700 ft. Open all year.

Natural mineral water flows directly into two cement pools at 99° and 102°. No chemical treatment is added. Clothing is optional in the pools and in the adjoining river.

Facilities include motel rooms, RV spaces, restaurant and bar. No credit cards are accepted. It is three miles to a store and 15 miles to a service station.

Directions: On CA 70, go four miles west from the Quincy-Greenville "Y."

▲ *Woody's Feather River Hot Springs*: Located 30 yards from a highway and a tavern, this is a good place for having informal fun.

▲ *Sierra Hot Springs*: These three pools and adjoining sundeck have their own enclosure. Several other kinds of soaking pools have been installed among the nearby trees.

610 SIERRA HOT SPRINGS

P.O. Box 234   (916) 994-8984
Sierraville, CA 96104   PR+MH+C

A 700-acre rustic resort and spiritual community which is being restored and expanded by a nonprofit organization. Public use of the facilities is welcome on a space-available basis. Elevation 5,000 ft. Open all year.

Natural mineral water flows out of several springs at temperatures up to 112°. On a wooded slope a variety of tubs at several temperatures, use flow-through mineral water without chemical treatment: (a) three cement soaking pools, 110°, 106°, 102°; (b) two white bathtubs, 102°; (c) one redwood hot tub, 102°, and (d) an eight-foot galvenized tub. Clothing is optional in all pool areas.

Massage and camping spaces are available on the premises. No credit cards are accepted. It is two miles to a store, service station, cafe and motel.

Directions: From the intersection of CA 89 and CA 49 in Sierraville, follow CA 49 east to Lemon Canyon Rd., which runs along the north edge of the airport; then turn right on Campbell Hot Springs Rd., which runs along the east edge of the airport and drive into the foothills and to the main office.

611A NEPHELE
1169 Ski Run Blvd.   (916) 544-8130
❑ So. Lake Tahoe, CA 95729   PR

Combination bar, restaurant and rent-a-tub establishment, located between the lake and a ski run.

Four private, enclosed outdoor pools are for rent to the public. Using gas-heated tap water and treated with chlorine, the pools are maintained at 102°. Bar service (but not food) is available at poolside.

A bar and restaurant are available on the premises. There are dinner-and-soak combination discounts. Visa, MasterCard and American Express are accepted. Phone for rates, reservations and directions.

▼   *Nephele*: Dinner reservations and bar service to private outdoor hot pools is available day and night, including during snow season.

611B PACIFICA LODGE
931 Park Ave.   (916) 544-4131
❑ So. Lake Tahoe, CA 95729   MH/P

Large motel with some special rooms containing fiberglass hydropools. Located a few blocks from the beach and from the Nevada state line.

Gas-heated tap water is used in six in-room pools which may be rented overnight or longer for private use. These pools are drained and refilled after each check-out, so no chemical water treatment is necessary.

The outdoor communal swimming pool is maintained at 80° and uses gas-heated tap water treated with chlorine. All pools are for registered guests only. Visa, MasterCard and American Express are accepted. Phone for rates, reservations and directions.

611C TAHOE HACIENDA MOTEL
3820 Hwy 50   (916) 541-3805
❑ So. Lake Tahoe, CA 95705   MH/P

Major motel with a dozen rooms containing hydropools. Located on the south side of Hwy 50.

Gas-heated tap water is used in 12 fiberglass pools in rooms which may be rented for private use overnight or longer. These pools are drained and refilled after each check-out, so no chemical water treatment is needed. Temperature in each pool is adjustable to the guests' preference.

The outdoor communal swimming pool (approximately 80°) is open June through September, and the outdoor communal hydropool (approximately 103°) is open all year. Both outdoor pools require chlorination. Bathing suits are required in outdoor pools. Visa, MasterCard, American Express and Carte Blanche are accepted. Phone for rates, reservations and directions.

611E CHATEAU L'AMOUR
3620 Hwy 50   (916) 544-6969
❑ So. Lake Tahoe, CA 95706   MH/P

Specialized motel with in-room spas, adult movies and appropriate decor, located on the south side of Hwy 50.

Gas-heated tap water is used in fiberglass pools in rooms which may be rented for private use overnight or longer. These pools are drained and refilled after each check-out, so no chemical water treatment is needed. Water temperature in each pool is adjustable to the guest's preference. There are no outdoor communal pools. Visa, MasterCard, American Express, Carte Blanche and Diners Club are accepted. Phone for rates, reservations and directions.

611D PINEWOOD LODGE
3818 Hwy 50   (916) 544-3319
❑ So. Lake Tahoe, CA 95729   MH+PR

Small motel with one separate room containing a hot tub, sauna and shower. Located on the south side of Hwy 50.

·Gas-heated tap water treated with chlorine is used in the redwood tub, and water temperature is maintained at 100°. The tub/sauna room may be rented by the hour or negotiated in connection with regular motel room registration.

Visa, MasterCard and American Express are accepted. Phone for rates, reservations and directions.

613 AGUA CALIENTE MINERAL SPRINGS
17350 Vailetti Dr.   **(707) 996-6822**
Sonoma, CA 95476   **PR**

A summertime plunge and picnic grounds in the middle of the Sonoma Valley. Elevation 100 ft. Open summer months only.

Natural mineral water is pumped from a well at 96° and piped to a swimming pool which averages 86° and to a hydropool which averages 95°. The adjoining diving pool and wading pool, averaging 70°, are filled with unheated tap water; both pools are treated with chlorine and are drained and filled every day. Bathing suits are required.

A seasonal snack bar is available on the premises. No credit cards are accepted. It is less than one mile to a store, service station and all other services.

Directions: From the city of Sonoma, go three miles north on CA 12 and watch for Agua Caliente signs.

 White Sulphur Springs Resort: This chlorine-free outdoor soaking pool is not the only source of relaxation available at this location. A picnic in a quiet redwood grove by a running stream can be a welcome change of pace from the crowds of visitors which flock to the Napa Valley wine country.

614 WHITE SULPHUR SPRINGS RESORT
3100 White Sulphur Springs Rd.   **(707) 963-8588**
St. Helena, CA 94574   **PR+MH**

Historic, 330-acre, older resort located in rustic Sulphur Canyon on the west side of Napa Valley. Elevation 400 ft. Open all year.

Natural mineral water flows out of several springs at various temperatures up to 95° and is piped to one outdoor soaking pool on a flow-through basis requiring no chemical treatment. This pool is available to the public for day use, as well as to registered guests. Bathing suits are required.

Facilities include rooms, cabins, a redwood grove picnic grounds by a running stream and hiking trails. Large meeting rooms with adjoining kitchen are available for weddings, family reunions, retreats, etc. Massage and facials by appointment are available on the premises. Visa and MasterCard are accepted. It is three miles to central St. Helena and all other services.

Future plans include private patio hydropools attached to some of the cabins and private-space hydropools for rent to the public by the hour. Phone ahead for the status of construction.

Directions: From CA 29 in the center of St. Helena, drive west on Spring St. to the resort.

All eight of the following locations are in or near the town of Calistoga, which is on CA 29 in Napa County. Elevation 400 ft. All of them are open all year and are one to ten blocks from a store, cafe, service station, public bus and the RV campground operated by Napa County at the Fairgrounds.

All of them have their own hot wells, and offer soaking and swimming pools containing natural mineral water treated with chlorine. Resorts with pool facilities offer them for day use unless otherwise noted. Soaking tubs in bathhouses are drained and filled after each use, so that no chemical treatment of the water is necessary. Bathing suits are required in all public areas.

▲ *Dr. Wilkinson's Hot Springs*: This indoor tropical-foliage soaking pool is especially popular on nippy winter days and nights.

▼ *Calistoga Spa Hot Springs*: This large covered hydropool is a favorite gathering place when the sun becomes too hot for comfort.

615A   CALISTOGA SPA HOT SPRINGS
■ 1006 Washington St.   (707) 942-6269
   Calistoga, CA 94515   PR+MH

Outdoor soaking pool, 100°; outdoor swimming pool, 83°; and outdoor wading pool, 90°. Covered hydropool, 105°. Indoor men's and women's bathhouses, each containing four individual tubs, two mud baths and three steambaths.

Rooms, massage, blanket wraps, steambaths, aerobic classes and workout rooms are available on the premises. Visa and MasterCard are accepted.

615B   DR. WILKINSON'S HOT SPRINGS
   1507 Lincoln Ave.   (707) 942-4102
■ Calistoga, CA 94515   PR+MH

Two outdoor mineral pools, 82° and 92°; one tropical-foliage indoor mineral pool, 104°. Indoor men's and women's bathhouses, each containing four individual tubs, two mud baths and a steambath.

Rooms, massage, mud baths, blanket wraps and skin care salon are available on the premises. Visa and MasterCard are accepted.

▲ *Indian Springs*: A continuous cloud of geothermal steam evelopes the source springs and pipes on the slope above this·site.

▲ *Hideaway Cottages*: This is the only Calistoga location which does not offer day use pools.

615C   GOLDEN HAVEN HOT SPRINGS
■ **1713 Lake St.**   (707) 942-6793
Calistoga, CA 94515   **PR+MH**

Outdoor redwood hot tub, 103°; enclosed swimming pool, 80°; covered hydropool, 100°.

Rooms, massage, facials, mud bath and European body wrap are available on the premises. Visa and MasterCard are accepted.

▲ *Golden Haven Hot Springs*: These covered pools can be used in all kinds of weather.

615D   HIDEAWAY COTTAGES
■ **1412 Fairway**   (707) 942-4108
Calistoga, CA 94515   **MH**

Outdoor swimming pool, 82°, and hydropool, 104°. Reserved for registered guests; no day use.

Cottages are available. Visa and MasterCard are accepted.

615E   INDIAN SPRINGS
■ **1712 Lincoln Ave.**   (707) 942-4913
Calistoga, CA 94515   **PR+MH**

Outdoor, Olympic-size swimming pool, 85-95°. Open all year. Indoor men's and women's baththouses, each containing five one-person mud or mineral water soaking tubs and a steam room.

Rooms and massage are available on the premises. Visa and MasterCard are accepted.

 Nance's Hot Springs: Mud baths are a famous specialty of this spa at the airport's edge.

615F LE SPA FRANCAIS
1880 Lincoln Ave.   (707) 942-4636
Calistoga, CA 94515   PR+MH

Outdoor swimming pool, 80-85°, and wading pool, 90-95°. Enclosed hydropool, 100-105°. Indoor men's and women's bathhouses, each containing two hydrotherapy tubs, two mud baths, two steam cabinets and a sauna.

Massage, facials, herbal bath, salt scrub and sweat wrap are available on the premises. Facilities include rooms and conference meeting rooms. Visa and MasterCard are accepted.

Roman Spa: In the space below the balcony is an indoor hydropool, a welcome alternative on cold nights or during inclement weather.

615G NANCE'S HOT SPRINGS
1614 Lincoln Ave.   (707) 942-6211
Calistoga, CA 94515   PR+MH

Indoor hydropool, 103°. Indoor men's and women's bathhouses, each containing four individual tubs (up to 110°), three mud baths and two steambaths.

Rooms and massage are available on the premises. Glider rentals are available at the adjoining airport. Visa, MasterCard and American Express are accepted.

615H ROMAN SPA
1300 Washington St.   (707) 942-4441
Calistoga, CA 94515   PR+MH

Outdoor swimming pool, 90°, and hydropool, 104°. Indoor hydropool, 100°. Motel rooms available. Visa and MasterCard accepted.

International Spa, under separate management, offers massage, reflexology, accupressure, coed mud baths, mineral baths, herbal blanket wrap and herbal facials. Visa, MasterCard and American Express are accepted.

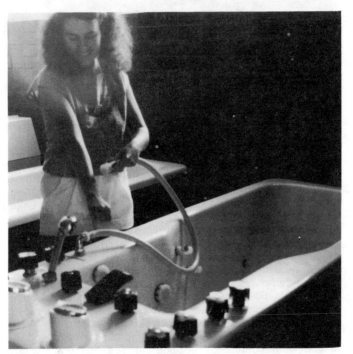

Le Spa Francais: All hydrotherapy tubs are drained and cleaned after each use.

▲ *Harbin Hot Springs*: A soaking pool is being used to demonstrate a special form of Shiatsu Massage which is taught at this location.

▼ Wherever necessary, signs are posted on *Harbin Hot Springs* roads to remind guests where conventional clothing is required.

▲ The theraputic history of *Harbin Hot Springs* dates back to California's gold rush days, and is being continued by the present owners.

▼ Within Harbin's clothing optional policy, children as well as adults are welcome to choose to wear or not wear swim suits.

616   HARBIN HOT SPRINGS

■ P.O. Box 782
Middletown, CA 95461

(707) 987-2477
PR+MH+CRV

Large historical resort being restored and expanded by a nonprofit organization with a major residential program. Located in a rugged foothill canyon south of Clear Lake. Elevation 1,500 ft. Open all year.

Natural mineral water with mild mineral content flows out of the ground at 120° and is piped to several soaking pools and a swimming pool. An enclosed cement pool has an average temperature of 110-115°, an adjoining cement pool has an average temperature of 100-104°, and the swimming pool ranges from 60-70°. All pools operate on a frequent cleaning and flow-through basis, so no chemical treatment is needed. Clothing is optional everywhere within the grounds.

Facilities include day use of pools, rooms, camping and RV spaces, four conference buildings, and a restaurant where vegetarian meals are optional. Massage and massage training in a state-accredited school are available on the premises. Visa and MasterCard are accepted. It is four miles to a store and service station.

Phone for rates, reservations and directions.

617 WILBUR HOT SPRINGS

Wilbur Springs   (916) 473-2306
Williams, CA 95987   PR+MH

A self-styled "Health Sanctuary" 22 miles from the nearest town, with an abundance of hot mineral water and no electricity. The large, multi-temperature soaking pools, the sundecks, and the restored turn-of-the-century hotel are located in the foothills of the western Sacramento Valley. Elevation 1,350 ft. Open all year.

Natural mineral water flows out of several springs at 120°, through a series of large concrete soaking pools under an A-frame structure, and into an outdoor swimming pool. Soaking pool temperatures are approximately 115°, 105° and 95°, with the swimming pool kept warm in the winter and cool in the summer. The water is not chemically treated. Bathing suits are optional in pool areas only, required elsewhere.

Massage, rooms, dormitory and communal kitchen are available on the premises. Visa and MasterCard are accepted. It is 22 miles to a restaurant, store and service station.

Note: Please no drop-in visitors. Phone first for reservations and confirmation of any services or uses.

Directions: From Interstate 5 in Williams, go west on CA 20 to the intersection with CA 16. A few yards west of that intersection, take gravel road heading north and west for approximately five miles, and follow signs.

Soda Bath: You don't have to be a showgirl to bathe in what feels like warm champagne. This effervescent island is one of several geothermally active sites in the Clear Lake area, including an electric power plant.

 Wilbur Hot Springs: The structure above the swimming pool is filled with large soaking pools at various water temperatures.

618 SODA BATH

●   **In Clear Lake, east of the town of Lakeport**

A unique masonry pool built over effervescent hot springs on a little island in Clear Lake. Elevation 1,300 ft. Open all year.

Naturally bubbling mineral water at approximately 100° flows up from the bottom of a well-worn sandstone block pool and mixes with lake water which seeps in through fissures in the walls. Pool temperature is affected by the level of the lake but is usually in the vicinity of 90°. Wearing bathing suits is the apparent local custom.

All services are available in the many towns and shopping centers within a few miles around the edge of Clear Lake.

Directions: From the town of Lakeport, drive three miles south on CA 29, then seven miles east on Soda Bay Rd. to Clear Lake State Park. Boats may be rented just south of the state park on the west shore of Soda Bay. The island is visible from the boat rental dock.

As an alternative, competent swimmers go without a boat direct from the shoreline nearest to the island.

 Vichy Springs: Part of the recent expansion of facilities at this famous site is the tiled soaking pool in the foreground and the creek-spanning bridge in the background.

619   VICHY SPRINGS

2605 Vichy Springs Rd.   (707) 462-9515
Ukiah, CA 95842   PR+MH+RV

Historic 682-acre resort in the Ukiah Valley foothills area of Mendocino County, famous for its naturally carbonated mineral water, which is still being bottled and sold to the public. Elevation 900 ft. Open all year.

Naturally carbonated mineral water flows out of three springs at temperatures ranging from 50°-90° and through traditional redwood pipes to ten enclosed, two-person concrete soaking tubs and four outdoor, two-person tubs. These tubs are drained and filled after each use, so no chemical treatment is necessary. There is one large, communal soaking tub in which the water is treated with bromine and heated to 103°. The Olympic-size swimming pool contains bromine-treated water maintained at approximately 80°. All tubs and pools are available to the public for day use as well as to registered guests.

Facilities include a tree-shaded central lawn ringed by country-style cottages and rooms, overnight parking for self-contained RVs, a shaded picnic area by a trout fishing pond, a running stream and a 30-minute hiking trail to a user-friendly waterfall. Massage and facials by appointment and bed and breakfast are available on the premises. Visa, MasterCard and American Express are accepted. It is five miles to a campground and three miles to the center of Ukiah.

Phone for rates, reservations and directions.

 Orr Hot Springs: Grass and greenery around this warm swimming pool give it the appearance and feel of a quiet oasis.

180

 Sweetwater Gardens: This is one of the authentic Northern California communal hot tubs which helped make the idea popular.

---

621   SWEETWATER GARDENS
955 Ukiah St.   (707) 937-4140
☐ Mendocino, CA 95460   PR+MH

Rustic rent-a-tub establishment featuring natural wood tubs, walls and decking with hanging greenery. Located on the coast of Northern California.

Pools are for rent to the public and use gas-heated tap water treated with bromine. One private enclosure can be rented by the hour. The water temperature is maintained at 104°, and a sauna is included. One private suite can be rented by the hour and also by the night. The water temperature is maintained at 104°, and a sauna is included. One communal hydropool is available at a day-rate charge. The water temperature is maintained at 104°, and a sauna is included.

Special features: There is a private room above the communal pools that is available for overnight rental. Bathing suits are optional everywhere. Massage is available on the premises. Visa and MasterCard are accepted. Phone for rates, reservations and directions.

---

622   MENDOCINO TUBBS
45310 Pacifica Dr.   (707) 961-1809
☐ Caspar, CA 95420   PR+MH

Tranquil, outdoor hot tubs located in the McCornack Center for the Healing Arts, five miles north of the city of Mendocino.

Private-space hot pools using gas-heated well water treated with chlorine, maintained at 104°, and are for rent to the public by the hour. There are three enclosed areas, each including a dressing room, sauna, shower and redwood hot tub. Clothing is optional in private spaces.

Facilities include a cottage with kitchen and bathroom. Massage is available on the premises. No credit cards are accepted. Phone for rates, reservations and directions.

---

623   FINNISH COUNTRY SAUNA & TUBS
5th and J St.   (707) 822-2228
☐ Arcata, CA 95521   PR

A charming, European-style pond surrounded by grass-roofed Finnish sauna cabins, outdoor hot tubs and a cafe in a small northern California coastal town. Open all year.

Pools are for rent to the public and use gas-heated tap water treated with bromine. There are six private, outdoor Jarrah-wood hot tubs rented by the hour and maintained at 104°. Bathing suits are optional in private spaces.

Facilities include two rentable private saunas and a cafe. No credit cards are accepted. Phone for rates, reservations and directions.

 The *Orr Hot Springs* indoor hot tub (behind the stained glass) looks out on a garden with a beautifully tiled outdoor soaking pool.

---

620   ORR HOT SPRINGS
13201 Orr Springs Rd.   (707) 462-6277
■ Ukiah, CA 95482   PR+MH+C

A small, older resort being gradually improved by an active residential community offering friendly informality and colorful flowerbeds. It is located on a wooded creek, 35 miles inland from the ocean. Elevation 800 ft. Open all year on Friday, Saturday, Sunday and Monday for day use. Overnight stays extend from 4 P.M. Thursday until noon Tuesday.

Natural mineral water flows out of several springs at 100° and is piped to a swimming pool, an indoor soaking pool, and four bathtubs in private rooms. The swimming pool averages 70-80°. Some of the water is heated to 105° and pumped to an enclosed redwood tub and to an adjoining outdoor soaking pool. All pools operate on a flow-through basis, so no chemical treatment is added. Clothing is optional everywhere on the grounds.

Facilities include a sauna, communal kitchen, cabins, dormitory and tent spaces along the creek. Massage is available by reservation. Space is limited, so telephone first for any use of the facilities. No credit cards are accepted. It is 13 miles of steep and winding roads to a restaurant, store and service station.

Directions: From Route 101 in Ukiah, take the North State Street exit, go several hundred yards north to Orr Springs Road, and turn west for 13 miles to the resort.

This map was designed to be used with a standard highway map

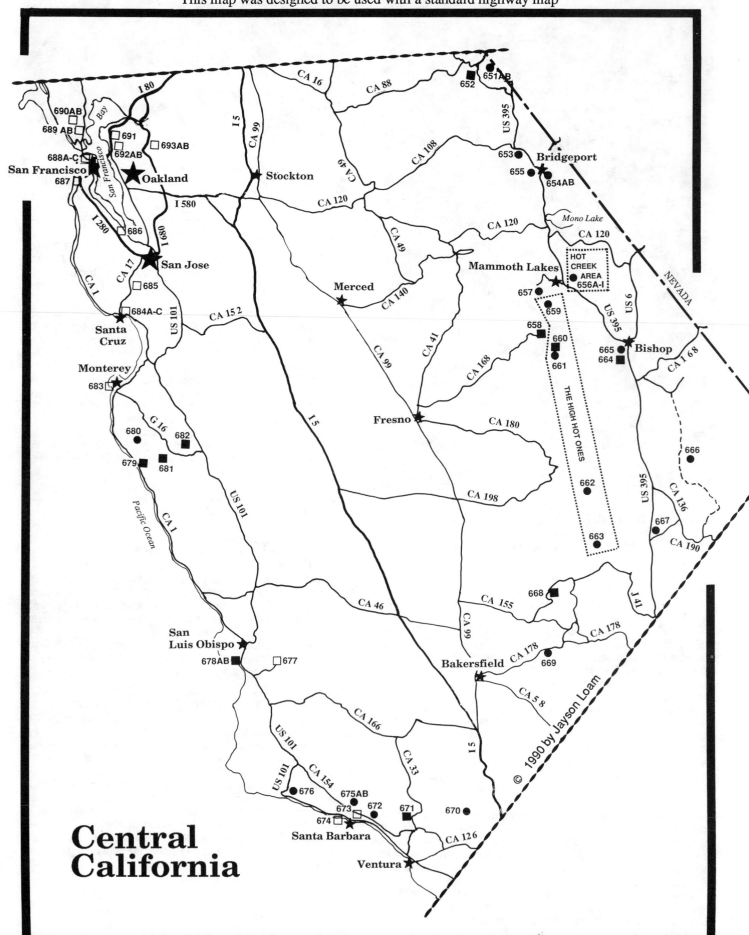

Central California

182

 Riverside Hot Springs: The raft trip leader is demonstrating how to enter a riverside geothermal waterfall while fully dressed.

651A   RIVERSIDE HOT SPRINGS

● **Near the town of Markleeville**

One of two primitive hot springs on a remote section of the East Carson River in Toiyabe National Forest. The only access is by raft or kayak. Elevation 5,000 ft. Open during rafting season, which is approximately May, June and July.

Natural mineral water emerges from several springs at 107° and cools as it flows toward the river. The temperature of the water drops to approximately 104° by the time it reaches some shallow pools near an eight-foot cliff at the edge of the river. The apparent local custom is clothing optional.

There are no services available on the premises. One- and two-day raft trips (Class II rapids) conducted by experienced guides are available locally. For information and/or pre-trip meals and lodging, contact Sorenson's Resort, (916) 694-2203.

These springs are not shown on any Forest Service or USGS map but are well known to raft trip guides.

 These are the *Riverside Hot Springs* soaking pools on the ledge just above that waterfall.

 Hot Showerbath: A 500 yard hike from the East Carson River is needed to reach this head-pounding stream of hot mineral water.

▲ *Grover Hot Springs*: These hot and warm pools make the nearby campground one of the most popular in the state park system.

651B HOT SHOWERBATH

● **Near the town of Markleeville**
The other primitive hot spring on the East Carson River, approximately one mile downstream from Riverside Hot Springs.

Natural mineral water flows out of a spring at 110° and cools to approximately 98° before dropping over a 20-foot bank into a canyon which extends 500 yards west of the river. The apparent local custom is clothing-optional.

See the preceding listing, RIVERSIDE HOT SPRINGS, for information on access and services.

652 GROVER HOT SPRINGS
Box 188   (916) 694-2248
■ Markleeville, CA 96120   PR (free) +CRV

Conventional swimming pool and soaking pool next to a major state campground and picnic area, located in a wooded mountain valley. Elevation 6,000 ft. Open all year.

Natural mineral water flows out of several springs at 147º and into a holding pond from which it is piped to the pool area. The soaking pool, using natural mineral water treated with bromine, is maintained at approximately 103º. The swimming pool, using creek water treated with chlorine, is maintained at 70-80º. A heat exchanger is used to simultaneously cool down the mineral water and warm up the creek water. Admission is on a first-come, first-served basis, and the official capacity limit of 50 persons in the hot pool plus 25 in the cold pool is reached early every day during the summer. Bathing suits are required.

Campground spaces are available by prior reservation, as with all other California state parks. Cross-country skiers are encouraged to camp in the picnic area during the winter and to ski in to use the soaking pool. It is four miles to the nearest restaurant, motel and service station.

Location: On Alpine County Road E4, 4 1/2 miles west of Markleeville. Follow the signs.

Grover Hot Springs: If the pool area is full when you reach the gate, all you can do is stand in line until someone leaves.

▲ *Fales Hot Ditch*: Perhaps the Fales Hot Spring Resort will reopen some day, but the mineral water can be used here in the meantime.

---

653   FALES HOT DITCH

● **North of the town of Bridgeport**

A series of primitive pools on Hot Springs Creek in the sagebrush foothills of the Eastern Sierra. Elevation 7,200 ft. Open all year.

Natural mineral water emerges at 140° from a spring on the property of a nearby resort, now closed, and flows down Hot Springs Creek gradually cooling as it goes. Volunteers have built rock-and-sand soaking pools where the creek temperature is in the 100°105° range. The apparent local custom is clothing optional because the pools are not visible from nearby US 395.

There are no services available at the premises but overnight camping is not prohibited. It is seven miles to a Forest Service campground and 13 miles to all other services in Bridgeport.

Directions: From Bridgeport, drive north on US 395 13 miles to the now closed Fales Hot Spring Resort. Go .1 mile past the resort and turn left on a dirt road which leads toward a private residence. Do not drive over the bridge, but park off the road, walk over the bridge, and then walk 25 yards downstream to the pools.

Warning: This location is unfenced private property. You will not be prosecuted for trespassing, but you will be using the pools at your own risk.

Source map: *Toiyabe National Forest*

185

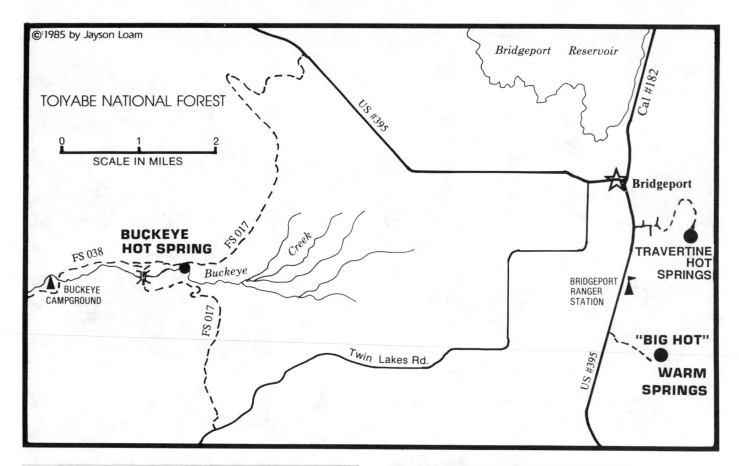

TOIYABE NATIONAL FOREST

Bridgeport Reservoir

BUCKEYE HOT SPRING

Bridgeport

TRAVERTINE HOT SPRINGS

BRIDGEPORT RANGER STATION

BUCKEYE CAMPGROUND

"BIG HOT" WARM SPRINGS

Twin Lakes Rd.

▲ *Travertine Hot Springs*: This round metal tub is the highest in the group of pools.

654A   TRAVERTINE HOT SPRINGS   (see map)

● **Southeast of the town of Bridgeport**

A unique group of colorful soaking pools (picture on front cover) on a series of large travertine ridges with commanding views of the High Sierra. Located two miles from the center of Bridgeport. Elevation 6,700 ft. Open all year.

Natural mineral water flows out of one travertine ridge at 138° and is channeled into a series of volunteer-built, rock-and-sand soaking pools which average temperatures of 118°, 110°, 103°, 96° and 84°. From another ridge, geothermal water emerges at 158° and is channeled to a ground-level metal tub and to a large soaking pool excavated into the travertine formation. The scalding source water receives some initial surface cooling and may be temporarily diverted whenever the soaking pool water reaches the desired temperature. The apparent local custom is clothing optional.

There are no services, but there is level ground on which overnight parking is not prohibited. All other services are available within two miles in Bridgeport.

Directions: From Bridgeport, drive .6 mile south on US 395 and turn east on paved Jack Sawyer Rd. Within the next .3 mile there are three unmarked forks. At the first fork (on the left), keep going straight. At the second fork where the paved road goes off to the right, keep going straight on the dirt road. At the third fork (on the left), bear right on the road which winds up into the hills. Drive .4 mile to fourth fork (on the left, signed *Bridgeport Borrow Pit*). Continue straight ahead for .7 mile to a parking area near the large soaking pool. To reach the series of volunteer-built pools, walk downhill 100 yards southwest.

654B "BIG HOT" WARM SPRINGS (see map)

● **Near the town of Bridgeport**

A cluster of geothermal "glory holes" with a great view of the High Sierra. Elevation 7,000 ft. Open all year, but the unmaintained dirt road is not passable in winter.

As mineral-heavy geothermal water flows over the edge of a spring, it gradually builds up a cone structure by depositing some of its minerals. This location has dozens of such "glory-holes", some of them over ten feet deep and large enough to swim in. Water temperature is approximately 80°, depending on wind and weather conditions. The apparent local custom is clothing optional.

No services are available on the premises. There is a substantial amount of unmarked open space on which overnight parking is not prohibited. The final 200 yards of road go up a steep bank suitable only for walking or 4WD vehicles. Please be sure to close any gates you open. It is four miles to the nearest store, restaurant, motel and service station.

Source map: USGS *Bodie*.

 This spacious volunteer excavation is known as the Upper *Travertine* Big Pool.

▼ These *Travertine* pools (see front cover) are supplied with mineral water by the largest of several geothermal ridges in the area.

 "Big Hot" Warm Springs: At the center of this "glory Hole", where the mineral water emerges from the ground, it is too deep to stand up.

655 BUCKEYE HOT SPRING (see map)

● **Near the town of Bridgeport**

Delightful hot spring in a superb natural setting on the north bank of Buckeye Creek in Toiyabe National Forest. One of the best. Elevation 6,900 ft. Open all year; not accessible by road in winter.

Natural mineral water flows out of the ground at 135°, runs over a large cliff built up by mineral deposits, and drops into the creek. Volunteers have built loosely constructed rock pools along the edge of the creek below the hot waterfall. The pool temperature is controlled by admitting more or less cold water from the creek. The apparent local custom is clothing optional.

There are no services on the premises. There is a parking turnout on the south side of the road on the bluff above the springs. The easiest route to the springs is to take the path down the slope from the turnout. Three hundred yards upstream are several acres of unmarked open space on which overnight parking is not prohibited. It is one mile to a Forest Service campground and nine miles to a restaurant, motel, store and service station in Bridgeport.

Source maps: *Toiyabe National Forests;* USGS *Matterhorn Peak*.

 Buckeye Hot Spring: This soaker is in that magic spot where the cold creek water does a perfect mix with the scalding mineral water.

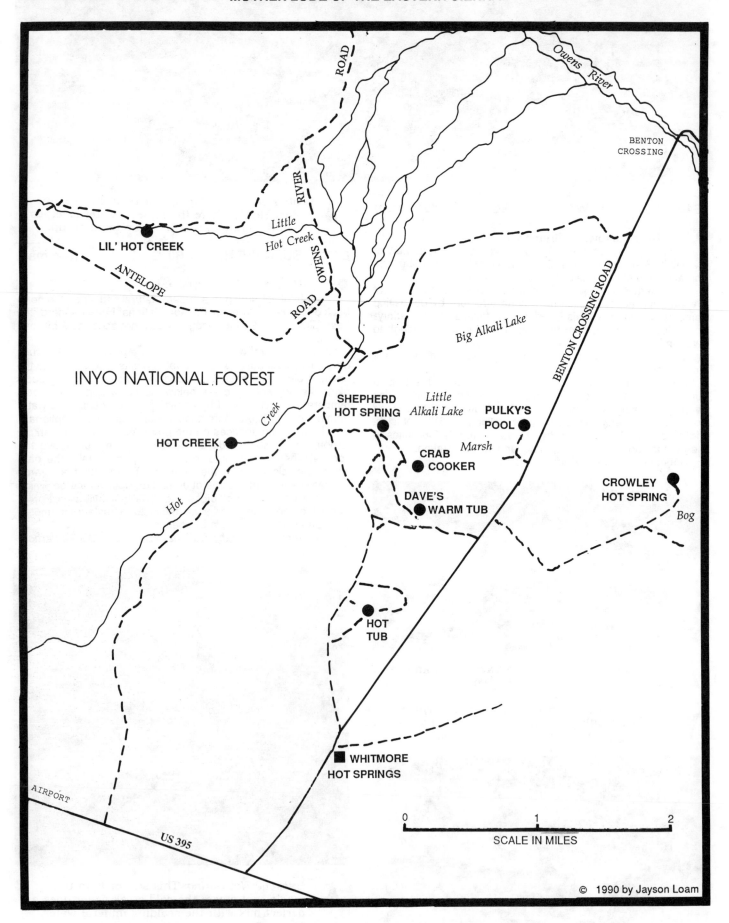

ROAD

Owens River

BENTON CROSSING

RIVER

Little
Hot Creek

LIL' HOT CREEK

ANTELOPE

ROAD OWENS

Big Alkali Lake

BENTON CROSSING ROAD

INYO NATIONAL FOREST

Creek

SHEPHERD
HOT SPRING

Little
Alkali Lake

PULKY'S
POOL

HOT CREEK

CRAB
COOKER

Marsh

CROWLEY
HOT SPRING

Hot

DAVE'S
WARM TUB

Bog

HOT
TUB

WHITMORE
HOT SPRINGS

AIRPORT

US 395

0   1   2

SCALE IN MILES

© 1990 by Jayson Loam

Motorists on US 395 in Mono County see a few signs that they are passing through geologically active territory. The Mono Craters, south of Mono Lake, have exhibited volcanic activity within the last 100 years, and there is a geothermal power plant beside the highway, just east of the famous skiing town of Mammoth Lakes. What the motorists canot see are the numerous hot springs, fumeroles, and glory holes which imply the term "mini-Yellowstone", and which have given Hot Creek its name. They also do not see the dozens of seismometers which have been installed by scientists to monitor this abundance of geologic activity.

In general, the area is open all year, but, at an altitude of 7,000 ft., heavy snows limit winter access to cross-country skiers and hikers. The official Forest Service Observation Site (Hot Creek) is open only during daylight hours and Whitmore Hot Springs is open only during the summer.

The surrounding BLM land is sprinkled with hot springs which flow into bogs, marshes and alkali lakes. Many decades ago, sheepherders started the practice of building crude shallow pools to catch some of that hot water for the purpose of soaking their bodies. Over the years volunteers have used modern materials to build an impressive group of larger pools with ingenious methods for controlling the water temperature. To anyone who has traveled many hours to enjoy just one geothermal soak, this does seem to be the Mother Lode of Hot Springs, complete with a spectacular view of the snow-capped Sierra.

Because these precious resources are so close to roads, they are especially vulnerable to being trashed by uncaring party animals. Please make sure that you remove all of your litter, and any extra you see, so that these springs do not degenerate into unsightly dumps.

Overnight parking is not prohibited in the undeveloped portions of the area. It is ten miles to all other services in the town of Mammoth Lakes.

Source maps: *Inyo National Forest*. USGS *Mt. Morrison*.

Hot Creek: The eddy just below the bridge is the one spot in this snow-melt creek where hot water vents on the bottom add enough heat to make the swirling mix tolerable to humans.

Most Hot Creek fatalities occurred at night so access is now limited to daylight hours.

656A   HOT CREEK   (see map)

● **East of the town of Mammoth Lakes**

Primarily a geologic observation and interpretive site with some limited use by bathers. Open daylight hours only.

Natural mineral water emerges from many fissures as steam or boiling water and several danger areas have been fenced off for safety. Substantial amounts of boiling, geothermal water also flow up from the bottom of the creek. A bend in the creek provides a natural eddy in which the mixing of hot and cold water stays within a range of 50° to 110°. Those who venture into this confluence experience vivid thermal skin effects, but they must be careful to avoid the geothermal vents because of the danger of scalding. Bathing suits are required.

In the past, night use of this location has resulted in many injuries and some fatalities, so the Forest Service closes the area at night. During the winter, when snow blocks the access road, skiers and hikers are still admitted during daylight hours.

Men's and women's dressing rooms are available on the premises. Overnight parking is prohibited.

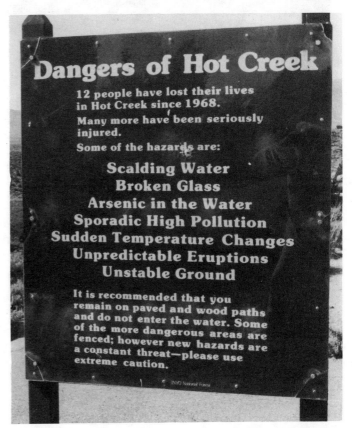

Dangers of Hot Creek

12 people have lost their lives in Hot Creek since 1968. Many more have been seriously injured.

Some of the hazards are:

Scalding Water
Broken Glass
Arsenic in the Water
Sporadic High Pollution
Sudden Temperature Changes
Unpredictable Eruptions
Unstable Ground

It is recommended that you remain on paved and wood paths and do not enter the water. Some of the more dangerous areas are fenced; however new hazards are a constant threat—please use extreme caution.

▲ *Shepherd Hot Spring*: A group of volunteers will probably adopt this tired soaking pool and give it a whole new personality.

▲ *Crab Cooker*: The volunteers who built this pool went high tech, installing a mechanical valve on the hot water supply pipe.

(see map on preceding page)

656B   LIL' HOT CREEK

● **East of the town of Mammoth Lakes**
A very hot flowing creek fed by a 180° geothermal spring. The name *Lil' Hot Creek* has been given to a large, squishy-bottom soaking pool located just below where the flow from several cold springs cools the hot stream to approximately 107°.

Caution: Be sure to reclose any gates you open as you traverse the access road, and do not block the road when you park.

656C   SHEPHERD HOT SPRING

● **East of the town of Mammoth Lakes**
Natural mineral water flows out of a spring at 107° and through a hose to one of the first volunteer-built soaking pools in the area. The pool temperature is controlled by diverting the hot water flow when the desired soaking temperature has been reached. The apparent local custom is clothing optional.

656D   CRAB COOKER

East of the town of Mammoth Lakes
Natural mineral water flows out of a spring at 112° and through a pipe to a rock-and-cement soaking pool with an especially good view of the mountains. The pool temperature is controlled by turning off a valve in the pipe when the desired soaking temperature is reached. The apparent local custom is clothing optional.

▲ *Dave's Warm Tub*: A creative design award should go to the volunteer who found rocks arranged just right to hold this bathtub.

656E   DAVE'S WARM TUB

● **East of the town of Mammoth Lakes**
Natural mineral water flows out of a spring at 89° and through a hose to a very private, single porcelain bathtub in a lush green ravine. The rate of flow is sufficient to maintain a temperature of 89° in the tub, so no method of temperature control is needed. The apparent local custom is clothing optional.

 Pulky's Pool: This recent high-tech volunteer effort incorporated hot and cold running water, plus a drain to simplify cleaning.

Crowley Hot Spring: The volunteers who built this big beauty got an assist from an earthquake which increased the rate of flow.

656F   PULKY'S POOL

● **East of the town of Mammoth Lakes**

Natural mineral water flows out of a spring at 131° and through a pipe to a free-form, rock-and-cement pool. Of recent construction, this pool features a very smooth surface and a drain to facilitate easy cleaning. Temperature is controlled by admitting cold water piped from a nearby pond. The apparent local custom is clothing optional.

Caution: Park 100 yards south and below the nearby plateau and walk to this pool. 4WD vehicles have become stuck in the soft ground.

656G   CROWLEY HOT SPRING

● **East of the town of Mammoth Lakes**

Natural mineral water flows out of a spring and down a small creek channel at 110°, then into a cement pool large enough for 30 people. Construction of such a pool was made possible by the 1983 earthquake which substantially increased the flow of geothermal water in the creek. No temperature control is necessary because surface cooling keeps the pool temperature about 103° most of the year. The apparent local custom is clothing optional.

Caution: The bog near the pool is a form of clay which remains soggy for several weeks after a heavy rain. Even 4WD's have been trapped.

656H   HOT TUB

● **East of the town of Mammoth Lakes**

Natural mineral water flows out of a spring at 110° and through a hose to a large rock-and-cement pool with a superb view of the mountains. The pool temperature is controlled by diverting the hot water inflow whenever the desired soaking temperature has been reached. The apparent local custom is clothing optional.

Hot Tub: Soakers in this low-tech pool will push the supply hose away when the desired pool water temperature has been reached.

191

Red's Meadow Hot Springs: The concrete casing and locked metal doors in the foreground contain the source spring for this site.

Whitmore Hot Springs: In the Hot Creek area, this is the only geothermal site which offers tiled swimming pools and dressing rooms.

6561   WHITMORE HOT SPRINGS   (see map)
P.O. Box 1609   (619) 935-4222
Mammoth Lakes, CA 93546   PR

Large, conventional public swimming pool jointly operated by Mono County and the Town of Mammoth Lakes on land leased from the Los Angeles Department of Water and Power. Open daytime; approximately Memorial Day to Labor Day.

Natural mineral water is pumped from a well at 90° and piped to the swimming pool where it is treated with chlorine. Depending on air temperature and wind conditions, the pool water temperature averages 82°. An adjoining shallow wading pool averages 92°. Bathing suits are required. No credit cards are accepted.

No services are available on the premises, but overnight parking is not prohibited on the large paved parking lot.

---

657   RED'S MEADOW HOT SPRINGS
●   In Red's Meadow Campground near
**   Devil's Postpile National Monument   CRV**

Tin-roof shed with six cement tubs in six small private rooms, on the edge of a mountain meadow campground. Elevation 7,000 ft. Open approximately Memorial Day to September 20.

Natural mineral water flows out of the ground at 100°, into a storage tank, and then by pipe into the bathhouse. Depending on the rate of use, water temperature out of the shower heads will vary from 95-105°. No charge is made for the use of the tubs which are available on a first-come, first-served basis.

A Forest Service campground adjoins the hot springs. A restaurant, store, gas station and motel rooms are available at a nearby pack station which is a stop on the shuttle bus service to Mammoth Lakes. No credit cards are accepted. It is 13 miles to full RV hookups.

Directions: From the town of Mammoth Lakes take CA 203 west to end, then follow signs to Devil's Postpile National Monument and to Red's Meadow Campground.

Source map: *Inyo National Forest.* USGS *Devil's Postpile.*

192

 Mono Hot Springs: This outdoor ground-level fiberglass hydropool is a recent addition to the mineral water facilities.

---

658   MONO HOT SPRINGS

■   (Summer) Mono Hot Springs, CA 93642
(Winter) Lake Shore, CA 93634   PR+CRV+MH

A vacation resort offering fishing, hiking and camping in addition to mineral baths. Located on the south fork of the San Joaquin River near Thomas Edison Lake in the Sierra National Forest. Elevation 6,500 ft. Open May to October.

Natural mineral water flows from a spring at 107°, then is piped to a bathhouse containing five two-person soaking tubs in private rooms. Customers may add cold tap water as desired to control temperature. Tubs are drained and refilled after each use, so no chemical treatment of the water is necessary. The outdoor hydrojet pool is maintained at 103-105° and is treated with chlorine. Bathing suits are required except in private rooms.

Facilities include a cafe, store, service station, cabins, campground and RV park. Massage and sweat wrap are available on the premises. Visa and MasterCard are accepted.

On the south side of the river, directly across from the resort and on National Forest land, is another hot spring supplying two old cement soaking pools which average a temperature of 101°. Bathing suits are advisable in the daytime.

Directions: From the city of Fresno on CA 99, go 80 miles northeast on CA 168. The last 15 miles are steep, winding and rough.

 These unofficial soaking pools are the last remnants of a bathhouse which once existed across the river from *Mono Hot Springs*.

193

*A special report by Dave Bybee, advanced rated
Sierra Club backpacking leader and keeper of the
Club's Special Hot Springs List.*

The High Sierra, referred to by the Sierra Club's founder, John Muir, as the "Range Of Light", contains several unique hot springs which cannot be reached by vehicle or by short hikes. The area is laced with many of the finest backpacking trails in the world, some of them crossing the Great Western Divide at altitudes of more than 12,000 ft. Most of them are open only during the summer months Though few hikers would undertake such long hikes just to soak, making one of these hot springs a planned layover day will add a special treat to your backpacking experience.

The first step toward any of the high hot ones is to buy a National Forest Service map of the area. Also, Forest Service Wilderness Permits are usually required to enter these areas on foot for any overnight stay. Therefore, the address and phone number of the responsible Forest Service office is given at the end of the listing for each location. If the backpacking load is beyond your personal ability, ask the Forest Service office for a list of licensed pack companies. Finally, when you are ready to start your hike, ask that office for last minute information about weather and trail conditions.

If you have not previously hiked in the area we recommend that you buy a copy of *Sierra North* and/or *Sierra South,* published by Wilderness Press, 2440 Bancroft Way, Berkeley, CA 94704, available at most outdoor equipment stores.

▲ This sandy-bottom lower pool is the most popular at *Fish Creek Hot Springs.*

▲ *Fish Creek Hot Springs*: The uppermost pool at this location commands a magnificent view.

659 FISH CREEK HOT SPRINGS

● **South of the Devil's Postpile
National Monument**

A delightful cluster of volunteer-built soaking pools, some with spectacular views of the wilderness. The twelve-mile hike (one way) involves an elevation gain of 1,000 ft. Elevation 7,200 ft.

This location is also called the *Iva Bell Hot Springs* after a baby that legend says was born nearby. In the Iva Bell camp area there are numerous camping sites separated by meadows and stands of pines.

The two main soaking pools are not visible from the main camping area but are to be found 50 yards east, up and behind an obvious bare rock ledge. The most popular pool has a nice sandy bottom and is nestled on the back side of this ledge where a 106º trickle flows out of a fissure slowly enough to maintain a 101º pool temperature in the summertime. A 100º squishy-bottom pool may be reached by following a path 30 yards southeast across a meadow.

From the first pool, another path leads due east for 50 yards to a cozy campsite. From this site, a steep 100-yard path leads up to four more assorted pools, ranging from 101º to 110º. The higher elevation of these pools offers a commanding view west down the canyon to the headwaters of the San Joaquin River.

Source: USGS *Devil's Postpile*
Inyo National Forest
Mammoth Ranger District (619) 934-2505
P.O. Box 146
Mammoth Lakes, CA 93546

660 MUIR TRAIL RANCH

■ **Southeast of Florence Lake**

A small (25 guests maximum), rustic mountain resort with two geothermal soaking pools in addition to horses, hiking trails, log cabins, fishing lessons and family-style meals. From the road end at Florence Lake, the hiking distance is eight miles, but guests ride the ranch-owned *Sierra Queen* ferryboat for three miles across the lake and then ride ranch horses or 4-wheel-drive vehicles the remaining five miles. Elevation 7,700 ft. Open mid-June to October.

Muir Trail Ranch offers its guests High Sierra adventure with rustic comfort, including enclosed, beautiful rock-and-tile flow-through mineral water soaking pools which average 98º and 110º. It is possible that future operations will discontinue individual reservations and replace them with organized groups who supply their own food. Write or phone for current policy, rates and reservations.

Winter: P.O. Box 269
     Ahwahnee, CA 93601
     (209) 966-3195
Summer: P.O. Box 176
     Lakeshore, CA 93634

 Blayney Hot Springs: Here is a classic squishy-bottom soaking pool in a classic mountain meadow in the famous High Sierra.

661 BLAYNEY HOT SPRINGS

● **Southeast of Florence Lake**

One squishy-bottom pool and a small warm lake in a meadow on the South Fork of the San Joaquin River. The eight-mile hike east from the road end at Florence Lake can be reduced three miles by riding the *Sierra Queen* ferryboat across the lake. An elevation gain of 1,000 ft. is involved in the eight-mile (one way) route. Backpackers on the John Muir Trail can make a side-trip to the springs by hiking 1 1/2 miles west on the Florence Lake Trail. Elevation 7,700 ft.

Riding the *Sierra Queen*, which looks like the *African Queen*, can be a lot of fun. It is usually stationed at the west end of the lake, but there is a direct-line phone at the east end. From a point on the Florence Lake Trail, just east of of Muir Trail Ranch, a well-worn trail heads south 1/4 mile to the San Joaquin River. Crossing this river can be hazardous even during late summer. The best campsites and easiest river crossing are located 1/2 mile upstream.

After using the upper crossing to the south side of the San Joaquin River, hike downstream 1/2 mile to the meadow area. The large pool, which is big enough for 12 people, and averages 102º, is at the south edge of the meadow. This pool drains under a thicket of bushes to a small 80º lake big enough to swim in. To reach it without clawing your way through the thorny bushes, follow the south edge of the meadow 50 yards west to the trees, cross the creek outlet of the lake, and walk south 20 yards to a grassy beach area.

Source: USGS *Blackcap Mountain*
Sierra National Forest
Pine Ridge Ranger District (209) 841-3311
P.O. Box 300
Shaver Lake, CA 93664

Kern Hot Spring: Three dedicated hikers celebrate their safe arrival by filling this slightly-crowded soaking pool.

Jordan Hot Spring: This mountain meadow is shared by the Golden Trout Wilderness and a commercial resort, a rare combination.

662   KERN HOT SPRING

● **On the remote upper Kern River**

The most remote and difficult-to-reach hot spring in California, with a spectacular view of the Kern River Canyon. The shortest route from Mineral King (22 miles one way) involves an elevation gain of more than 4,000 feet to Franklin Pass and a 6,000-foot loss down to the Kern River. Elevation 6,900 ft.

Natural mineral water at 111° flows into a cozy, cement soaking pool located at the edge of the river. Pool temperature is controlled by adding buckets of cold river water when needed. There is a campground with pit toilets and a bear cable 100 yards upriver.

There are alternate hiking routes from Whitney Portal (32 miles one way) and from Crescent Meadows (37 miles one way).

Be sure to bring a camera when you visit this hot spring. Being located at the bottom of the Kern River Trench, the largest single geological feature in the High Sierra, the views, including Chagoopa Falls, are spectacular.

Source: USGS *Kern Peak*
Sequoia National Forest
Tule Ranger District (209) 539-2607
32588 Highway 190
Porterville, CA 93257

663   JORDAN HOT SPRING

● **Northwest of the town of Little Lake**

Four cement tubs in private bathhouses on Ninemile Creek in the Southernmost part of the Golden Trout Wilderness. The 5 1/2-mile hike (one way) involves an elevation loss of 2,500 feet. Elevation 6,500 ft.

The two bathhouses on the north side of the creek are on Forest Service land and are available without charge. Unfortunately, the natural mineral water supply is only warmish. The other two bathhouses, on private land, require the payment of a small fee. They have a 121° source so that buckets of cold creek water must be added to obtain a tolerable soaking temperature.

The private land is a small rustic resort which was operated by Kennedy Meadows Pack Trains before the area was declared a Wilderness. You can pack or hike in and stay and eat at the resort for a fee, or you can camp for free at many nice sites on the north side of the creek.

The lodge and five log cabins were built in the 1920s, and many of the primitive improvements are still in operation. A Pelton Wheel generator supplies 12-volt electricity for night lighting. Canals bring water to keep the meadows green all summer and supply cold tap water from a holding tank up the hill. Some of the cold water is used in a burlap-walled, evaporative cooler locker in the central yard, shaded by pines. Cold soda, beer or wine is for sale, a welcome surprise to wilderness backpackers. Meals are prepared on antique, wood-burning cook stoves and served family style. If there is extra food, backpackers may pay a fee to join the registered guests for dinner.

Write or phone for rates and reservations:
Kennedy Meadow Pack Trains
P.O. Box 1300
Weldon, CA 93283
(619) 378-2232 or (805) 259-9062

Source: USGS *Hockett Peak*
Inyo National Forest
Mt. Whitney Ranger District (916) 876-5542
Lone Pine, CA 93545

664   KEOUGH HOT SPRINGS

Route 1, Box 9   **(619) 872-1644**
■ **Bishop, CA 93514**   **PR+RV**

Older hot springs resort in the Sierra foothills. The bathhouse is closed and the swimming pool access is limited. It is advisable to phone for current information. Elevation 4,200 ft. Open all year.

Natural mineral water flows out of the ground at 128° and into the enclosed swimming pool (87-95°) and the wading pool (100°), using flow-through mineral water so that no chlorine needs to be added. Bathing suits are required.

Partial RV hookups are available on the premises. No credit cards are accepted. It is eight miles to the nearest restaurant, motel, service station and store.

Directions: Go seven miles south of Bishop on US 395, then follow signs west from US 395.

 Keough Hot Springs: Three generations of swimmers have received lessons in this historic mineral water pool.

665   KEOUGH HOT DITCH

● **Near Keough Hot Springs**

Runoff from Keough Hot Springs cools as it flows through a series of volunteer-built rock pools in a treeless foothill gully. Elevation 4,100 ft. Open all year

Natural mineral water flows out of the ground at 128° on the property of Keough Hot Springs, then wanders northeast over BLM land for about a mile before joining with a cold water surface stream. Volunteer-built rock dams create several primitive pools of various depths, each one cooler than the preceding one upstream. The apparent local custom is clothing optional.

No services are available on the premises. There is a limited amount of level, unmarked space on which overnight parking is not prohibited. It is one mile to an RV park, and eight miles to a restaurant, store and service station.

Directions: Seven miles south of Bishop on US 395, turn west on Keough Hot Springs Road approximately .6 mile. At the only intersection with a paved road (old US 395), turn north 200 yards to where a cold stream crosses the road. (Note: There is an abundance of level parking space on the north side of the cold stream, but the stream must be forded with care.) Walk an additional 50 yards north to Keough Ditch. Either stream may be followed to where they join, forming a warm swimming pond.

 Keough Hot Ditch: This family has arranged a no-cost Sunday outing which includes mud and warm-water play without soiling any clothes.

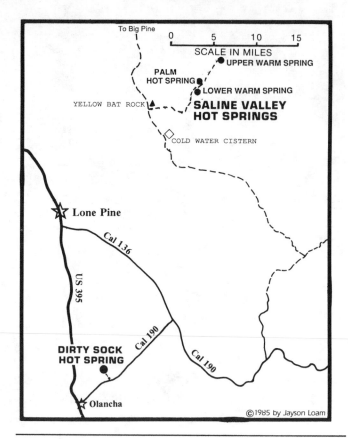

Saline Valley Hot Springs: The only natural shade at this site is a row of low trees along the hot springs run-off channel. This is one of the volunteer-built pipe-supplied soaking pools built at a well-shaded spot.

666   SALINE VALLEY HOT SPRINGS   (see map)

● **Northeast of the town of Olancha**

A sometimes crowded, spring-fed oasis located on a barren slope of BLM land in a remote desert valley northwest of Death Valley. Elevation 2,900 ft. Open all year, but snow chains may be needed in winter on access-road summits.

Natural mineral water flows out of the two main source springs at 107°. Volunteers have installed pipes to carry this water to a variety of man-made, cement-and-rock pools for soaking, shampooing, dish washing, etc. By mutual agreement, no one bathes in the source pools. The rate of flow through the soaking pools is sufficient to eliminate the need for chemical treatment of the water. A third (upper) source spring flows into a natural, squishy-bottom pool which maintains an average temperature of 102°. The apparent local custom in the entire area is clothing optional.

There are no services except crude volunteer-built latrines on the premises, but there is an abundance of level space on which overnight parking is not prohibited. It is more than 50 miles to a store, cafe, service station.

Temperatures regularly soar over the 120° mark in the summer, so this desert location with very little natural shade is preferred in the winter and spring. It becomes very crowded and should be avoided on major holidays and three-day weekends. The peace and quiet of the desert can best be enjoyed during the week.

Directions: The preferred route via Olancha is shown on the map. An alternate route starts at the north end of the town of Big Pine, on US 395. Drive northeast on CA 168 for two miles and turn right (southeast) on Death Valley Road. Drive approximately 15 miles and turn right on Waucoba-Saline Road. Drive 27 miles south to a yellow rock with a bat image on the left side of the road. Turn left (east) for six miles to the springs. Either route may be temporarily washed out by infrequent, but severe flash floods, so it is advisable to inquire about road conditions before making the trip.

Source maps: So. CA Auto Club *Death Valley*. USGS *Waucoba Wash* and *New York Butte*.

▲ Volunteers have built this *Saline Valley Hot Springs* soaking pool out in the open, so it gets plenty of sunshine and a fine view.

▲ Volunteers have piped *Saline Valley Hot Springs* water to separate sinks for dish washing so that there is no pollution of source springs or soaking pools.

▲ This is the squishy-bottom pool fed by the *Saline Valley Hot Spring*s upper warm spring.

◀ At some of the open area soaking pools temporary shade is provided by awnings.

199

Remington Hot Springs: During high water flow in the Kern River this site is flooded, but the concrete construction does not wash away.

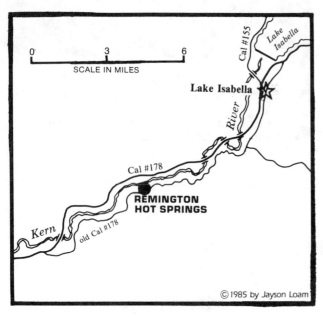

667   DIRTY·SOCK HOT SPRING

● **Near the town of Olancha**

Large, shallow pool, green with algae, in an open desert area. Elevation 3,600 ft. Open all year.

Natural mineral water flows up from the bottom of a circular, cement-edged pool at 90° and flows out at various lower temperatures, depending on wind and air temperature. The murky water gives an uninviting appearance. The apparent local custom is clothing optional.·

No services are available on the premises, and there are no remaining buildings. There are many acres of unmarked level space on which overnight parking is not prohibited. It is five miles to the nearest restaurant, motel, service station and store.

Directions: From the intersection of US 395 and CA 190, go five miles northeast on CA 190. There are no signs on the highway, so look for a narrow, paved road on the northwest side and follow it 300 yards to the spring.

668   CALIFORNIA HOT SPRINGS

■ **P.O. Box 146**   (805) 548-6582
California Hot Springs, CA 93207   **PR+RV**

Historic resort which has been restored and expanded to offer family fun. Located in rolling foothills at the edge of Sequoia National Forest. Elevation 3,100 ft. Open all year except Thanksgiving and Christmas holidays.

Odorless natural mineral water flows out of several artesian wells at a temperature of 126° and is piped to the pool area where there are two large, tiled hydrospas maintained at 100° and 104°. A flow-through system eliminates the need for chemiCA treatment of the water. There is one large swimming pool containing filtered and chlorinated spring water which is maintained at 85° in the summer and 94° in the winter. Bathing suits are required.

The restored main building contains an office, delicatessen, ice cream parlor, pizza stand, gift shop and dressing room facilities. Massage is available on the premises. Full-hookup RV spaces are adjacent to the resort area. Visa and MasterCard are accepted. It is two miles to a motel, store and gas station.

Directions: From CA 99 between Fresno and Bakersfield, take the J22 exit at Earlimart and go east 38 miles to the resort.

669   REMINGTON HOT SPRINGS   (see map)

● **Near the town of Isabella**

A delightful, two-person cement tub in an unspoiled, primitive, riverside setting of rocks and trees. Located in the Kern River Canyon down a steep trail from old Highway 178. Elevation 2,200 ft. Open all year except during high water in the river.

Natural mineral water at 104° emerges from the ground at more than 100 gallons-per-minute. This flow comes directly up through the bottom of a volunteer-built, cement tub and provides a form of hydrojet action, maintaining the pool temperature at 104°. Twenty yards uphill is a drainable, one-person rock-and-cement pool fed by a smaller flow of 96° water. Even though this site has obviously been used for many years, there is almost no unsightly trash. The apparent local custom is clothing optional.

There are no services available on the premises. It is six miles to a motel, restaurant and service station, and two miles to a Forest Service campground.

Directions: From the Miracle Hot Springs Store on old Highway 178, go west 1 1/2 miles to a large turnout with a telephone pole in the middle. Overnight parking is not prohibited. The steep, unmaintained trail leads directly to the riverbank springs, 300 yards below. Keep it beautiful by packing out whatever you pack in.

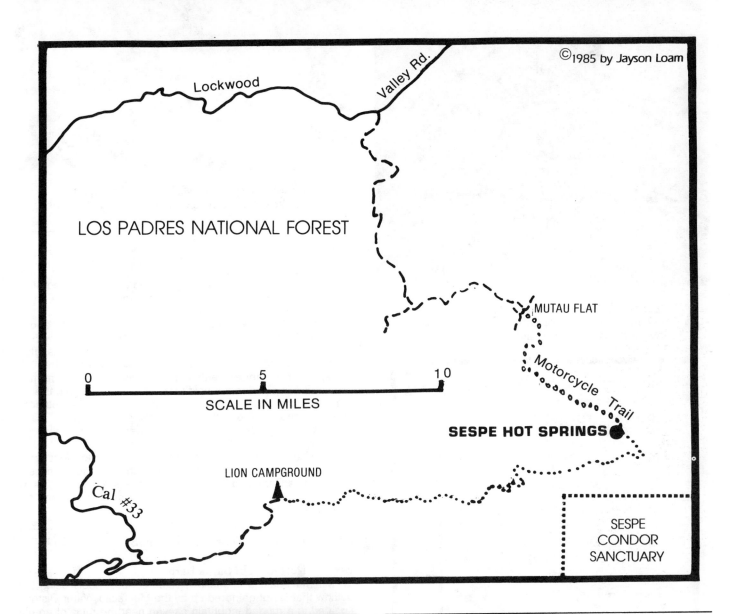

LOS PADRES NATIONAL FOREST

Lockwood

Valley Rd.

MUTAU FLAT

Motorcycle Trail

0   5   10

SCALE IN MILES

SESPE HOT SPRINGS ●

LION CAMPGROUND

Cal #33

SESPE CONDOR SANCTUARY

---

670   SESPE HOT SPRINGS   (see map)

●   **Near the Sespe Condor Sanctuary**

A remote, undeveloped hot spring located in rugged, desert mountains subject to some flash flooding. Elevation 2,800 ft. Open all year, subject to Forest Service closures.

Natural mineral water flows out of the side of a mountain at 185°, cooling as it flows through a series of shallow, volunteer-built soaking pools. A sauna-shack steambath has also been built over the spring mouth. The apparent local custom is clothing optional.

There are no services on the premises. Access is via a nine-mile motorcycle trail from Mutau Flat, or via a 17-mile hiking trail from Lion Campground. A Forest Service permit is required to enter the area at any time. Be sure to inquire about fire-season closures, flood warnings, and the adequacy of your preparations for packing in and packing out.

California Hot Springs: This long-closed therapeutic spa site has been fully converted to recreational use of mineral water.

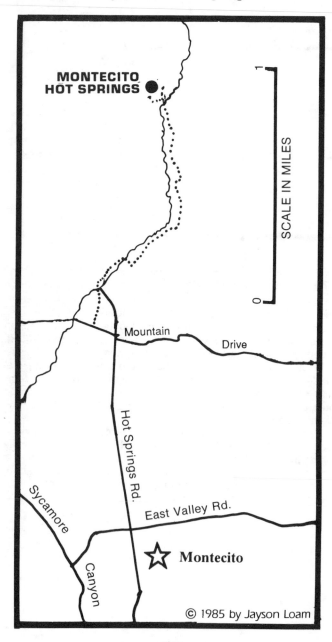

Montecito Hot Springs: Only small seeps were left for soaking pools after the water company piped away the main hot spring flow.

Wheeler Hot Springs: White interior paint makes it easy to clean the wooden hot tubs.

671   WHEELER HOT SPRINGS
P.O. Box 250   (805) 646-8131
Ojai, CA 93023   PR

An historic, geothermal spa equipped with modern hot tubs in a rocky, wooded canyon in the Las Padres National Forest. Elevation 1,600 ft. Open all year.

Natural mineral water flows out of the ground at 101° and is piped to four private, indoor rooms, each equipped with a hydrojet hot tub and a cold tub. The mineral water is gas-heated to maintain a temperature of 104° on a flow-through basis, so no chemical treatment is necessary. Water from a cold spring is piped to the cold tubs on a flow-through basis so that no chemical treatment is necessary. The outdoor swimming pool, filled with chlorine-treated cold spring water and warmed by solar heat to 78°, is open from June through October.

Facilities include a gourmet restaurant. Massage, reflexology and polarity work are available on the premises. Visa, MasterCard and American Express are accepted. It is seven miles to central Ojai and all other services. Phone for rates, reservations and directions.

672   MONTECITO HOT SPRINGS   (see map)

● **Northeast of Santa Barbara**
Minimal soaking in shallow, volunteer-built pools using the outflow that is not gathered up by the Montecito Water District. Located in a rugged mountain canyon near the ruins of an old resort. Elevation 1,500 ft. Open all year.

Water District pipes carry away most of the geothermal water, but there are still two surface seeps which flow at 113°, and have been channeled by volunteers into rock, sand and plastic pools where the water cools to a tolerable temperature. The hiking trail to the area is so popular that bathing suits are advisable.

There are no services available on the premises. It is less than five miles to a service station, restaurant and store.

Directions: From US 101 east of Santa Barbara, exit north on Olive Mill Road, which becomes Hot Springs Road after intersecting with Alston Drive. Continue north to Mountain Drive and turn west 1/4 mile to the trailhead, which is marked by a Montecito Trails Foundation sign on the north side of the road. It is not possible to legally park any closer to the springs.

The first few hundred yards of the trail cross and parallel some driveways, so watch for the Montecito Trails Foundation signs. Shortly after leaving the last of the residences, the trail veers right across the canyon bottom and intersects with the old road which used to serve the now-defunct Hot Springs Club. Pass by a power-line service road which veers left and continue on up the east side of the canyon to the resort ruins. Follow the Water District pipes beyond the ruins to the first flowing seep. To reach the second seep, watch for a faint trail leading down into the canyon just beyond the ruins. Follow it south along the canyon bottom to the first side canyon on the west side and go up that canyon to the seep and pool.

Source maps: Los Padres National Forest; USGS Quad: Santa Barbara; Santa Barbara area street map.

MONTECITO HOT SPRINGS ●

SCALE IN MILES

Mountain   Drive

Hot Springs Rd.

Sycamore

East Valley Rd.

Canyon

☆ **Montecito**

© 1985 by Jayson Loam

673 THE HOURGLASS

213 W. Cota   (805) 963-1436
Santa Barbara, CA 93101   PR

Basic private-space, rent-a-tub facility located on a residential street near downtown Santa Barbara.

Three private rooms with pools and eight private outdoor enclosures are for rent to the public. Gas-heated tap water treated with chlorine is maintained at 104°.

A juice bar is available on the premises. Visa and MasterCard are accepted. Phone for rates, reservations and directions.

674 CLUB TAN

6576 Trigo Rd.   (805) 968-3384
Isla Vista, CA 93117   PR

Clean, inviting, rent-a-tub establishment. Located in a residential neighborhood adjoining the UC Santa Barbara campus.

Eight private enclosed pools are for rent to the public. The roofless enclosures are tree shaded. The pools use gas-heated tap water treated with chlorine; water temperature is maintained between 102-104° and can be adjusted on request.

An indoor tanning booth is available on the premises. No credit cards are accepted. Phone for rates, reservations and directions.

675A BIG CALIENTE HOT SPRINGS
(see map on following page)
●   **Near the city of Santa Barbara**

An improved, noncommercial hot spring located in a sparsely wooded canyon reached via ten miles of gravel road. Elevation 1,500 ft. Open all year, subject to fire closure.

Natural mineral water flows out of a bluff at 115°, then through a faucet-controlled pipe to a six-foot by ten-foot concrete pool. Water temperature in the pool is determined by the inflow of hot water. There is general compliance with an official NO NUDE BATHING sign.

There are government-built rest rooms and changing rooms nearby, and a year-round running stream 20 yards away. There are no other services available on the premises. A Forest Service campground is within five miles, and it is 25 miles to a restaurant, store and service station.
Source map: *Los Padres National Forest.*

▲ *Big Caliente Hot Springs*: According to local legend, the long drive to this spring is what spurred the invention of the redwood hot tub.

675B LITTLE CALIENTE HOT SPRINGS
(see map on following page)
●   **Near the city of Santa Barbara**

A small, volunteer-built pool in a rocky canyon at the end of a wooded Forest Service road. Elevation 1,600 ft. Open all year, subject to fire-season closures.

Natural mineral water flows out of a spring at 105° and into a rock-and-cement soaking pool. An adjoining wooden sunning platform has been built by volunteers. Continual flow-through of geothermal water keeps the pool temperature constant. The apparent local custom is clothing optional.

No services are available on the premises. It is 1/4 mile to a campground and 27 miles to all other services.
Source map: *Los Padres National Forest.*

▲ *Little Caliente Hot Springs*: Fire season or winter storms sometimes force the Forest Service to temporarily close this site.

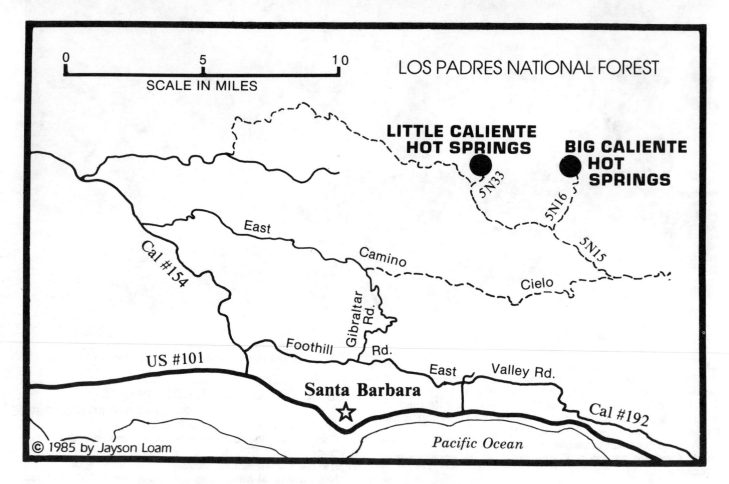

LOS PADRES NATIONAL FOREST

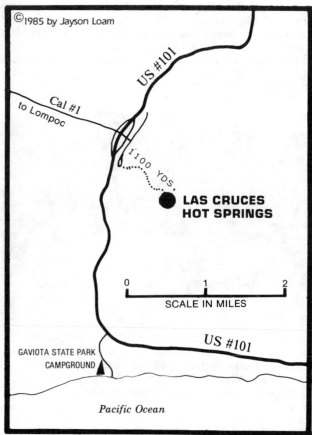

676   LAS CRUCES HOT SPRINGS   (see map)

● **Near Gaviota State Park**

Two primitive, mud-bottom pools on a tree-shaded slope a few miles from the ocean. Elevation 500 ft. Open all year.

Natural mineral water emerges from the ground at 96° directly into a small soaking pool and then flows into a larger pool which averages 90°. Both of these volunteer-built pools have dirt sides and cloudy water. The apparent local custom is clothing optional.

There are no services available on the premises, and overnight parking is prohibited in the parking area at the bottom of the trail. It is three miles to a campground with RV hookups and six miles to all other services.

677   MUSTANG WATER SLIDE AT LOPEZ LAKE

☐   Near the town of Arroyo Grande   PR

Recreation concession, including hot pools, on the grounds of a county park in hills north of Lopez Lake. Elevation 700 ft. Open seven days per week, June 1 to September 15; weekends starting approximately April 1; closed approximately November 1.

Gas-heated well water, chlorine-treated, is used in soaking pools which are available without extra charge to those who have paid by the hour to use the two adjoining 600-foot waterslides. Water temperature in the four cement-and-tile hot pools varies from 90-102°. Bathing suits are required at all times.

A snack bar is available on the premises. RV and camping spaces are available in the county park. It is ten miles to a motel, restaurant, store and service station.

Directions: From the city of Arroyo Grande on US 101, follow Lopez Lake signs northeast and around the lake to County Recreation Area main gate. Pay use fee and follow signs to water slide.

Sycamore Hot Springs: This couple is enjoying a social soak in a hot tub on the hillside. One of the stairs up to the hot tubs can be seen above this lawn-bordered swimming pool.

The newest motel units at *Sycamore Hot Springs* have acrylic soaking pools on the balcony rather than redwood hot tubs.

678A   AVILA HOT SPRINGS SPA & RV PARK

250 Avila Rd.   (805) 595-2359
San Luis Obispo, CA 93401   PR+CRV

Combination hot spring resort and RV park located in a foothill hollow at a freeway exit. Elevation 40 ft. Open all year.

Natural mineral water is pumped out of a well at 130° and piped to various pools. There are six indoor, tiled Roman tubs in which the water temperature is determined by the amount of hot mineral water and cold tap water admitted. These tubs are drained and refilled after each use so that no chemical treatment is needed. There is an outdoor swimming pool (88°) and an outdoor soaking pool (107°) which use natural mineral water treated with chlorine. Bathing suits are required except in private tub rooms.

Massage, snack bar, RV and camping spaces and a small store are available on the premises. It is three miles to a motel, restaurant and service station.

Directions: From US 101 four miles south of San Luis Obispo, take the Avila Beach exit and go north one block to resort entrance.

678B   SYCAMORE HOT SPRINGS

1215 Avila Beach Dr.   (805) 595-7302
San Luis Obispo, CA 93401   PR+MH

Establishing an innovative new example for other hot springs to follow, this delightful resort offers dozens of secluded redwood hot tubs out under the oak trees and a private redwood hot tub on the balcony of every motel room. There are no separate men's and women's bathhouses. Located on a wooded rural hillside two miles from the ocean. Elevation 40 ft. Open all year, 24 hours per day.

Natural mineral water is pumped from a well at 110° and piped to the tubs on the hillside and on the motel balconies. Each tub has a hot mineral-water faucet and a cold tap-water faucet, so the temperature in each tub is under the control of the customer. Each tub also has its own jet pump, filter and automatic chlorinator. One of the outdoor tubs is 12 feet in diameter, capable of holding more than 40 persons. The swimming pool is filled with tap water treated with chlorine and maintained at 89° by a heat exchanger. Bathing suits are required except in motel tubs and those outdoor tubs which are screened by vines and shrubbery.

Facilities include motel rooms with hot tubs on the balcony, a one-bedroom cottage with its own hot tub in a private enclosure, dressing rooms and a sand volleyball court. Several varieties of massage and reflexology are available on the premises. A half-hour soak in one of the outdoor tubs is included in each appointment. On request, directions to a nearby clothing-optional state beach will be given. American Express, MasterCard and Visa are accepted. Phone for rates and reservations.

Directions: From US 101 eight miles south of San Luis Obispo, take the Avila Beach exit, then go one mile west on Avila Beach Dr. and watch for resort sign on south side of road.

679 ESALEN INSTITUTE

■ **Big Sur, CA 93920**

(408) 667-3000
PR+MH

Primarily an educational/experiential center rather than a hotspring resort. Located on CA 1, 45 miles south of Monterey and 50 miles north of San Simeon. Elevation 100 ft. Open all year.

Esalen is a pioneer in the growth center movement, specializing in residential programs which focus on education, philosophy and the physiCA and behavioral sciences. Access to the grounds is permitted only to workshop participants and people registered for room and board, which is occasionally available on short notice. Phone or write for a catalog of programs being offered; attendance is by prior registration and confirmation only.

Natural mineral water flows out of the ground at 120° and into a bathhouse built on a cliff face, 50 feet above a rocky ocean beach. Within the bathhouse, which is open toward the ocean, are four concrete soaking pools and eight individual tubs. There are also two adjoining outdoor soaking pools. Water temperature is determined within each tub by admitting controlled amounts of hot mineral water and cold well water. This flow-through process, plus frequent cleaning of the pools, makes chemical treatment of the water unnecessary. Clothing is optional in and around the bathhouse.

Facilities include housing and a dining room for registered guests. Massage is available on the premises. Visa, MasterCard and American Express are accepted. It is 11 miles to a restaurant, store and service station.

680 SYKES HOT SPRING   (see map)

● **Near the village of Big Sur**

Remote, undeveloped hot spring on the Big Sur River in the Ventana Wilderness portion of the Los Padres National Forest. Elevation 1,110 ft. May be submerged during high water in the river.

Natural mineral water flows out of the ground at 104° from under a fallen tree and into a main, volunteer-built soaking pool near the source, and into five more small soaking pools nearby. This location is an 11-mile hike on the Pine Ridge Trail and a Wilderness Permit must be obtained from the Forest Service before entering the area. However, this spring is near one of the most popular hiking routes in the wilderness, so the distance is no assurance of quiet or privacy during the summer months.

The access trail appears on USGS *Ventana Cones* and *Partington Ridge*, but the hot spring is not shown. The Forest Service issues a trail map to those holding Wilderness Permits and, on request, will mark the hot-spring location on that map.

There are no services available at the location. When you obtain your Wilderness Permit, check your preparations, including water supply, with the ranger.

▲ *Esalen Institute*: The unique ocean-cliff location of this spring is complemented by natural-stone construction of the pools.

▲ *Sykes Hot Spring*: This famous soaking pool under a fallen tree is not big enough to accomodate all of the hikers on a busy day.

206

681   TASSAJARA BUDDHIST MEDITATION CENTER

■
Tassajara Springs　　　　(415) 431-3771
Carmel Valley, CA 93924　　　　**PR+MH**

Primarily a Buddhist Monastery with limited accommodations available to the public from May 1 to Labor Day. Located in wooded mountains southeast of Monterey. Elevation 1,500 ft.

Please, no drop-in visitors. Prior reservations and confirmation required for all uses. Guests are expected to respect the spirit of a monastic community.

Natural mineral water flows out of the ground at 110° into two large, enclosed, soaking pools which average 108°. This water, which is not chemically treated, cools as it flows into nearby streambed soaking areas. The outdoor swimming pool is maintained at approximately 70°. There are also men's and women's steambaths. Bathing suits are required at swimming pool only.

Rooms and meals are included as part of confirmed reservation arrangements. The use of meditation facilities is also included. No credit cards are accepted. It is 20 miles to a store, cafe and service station.

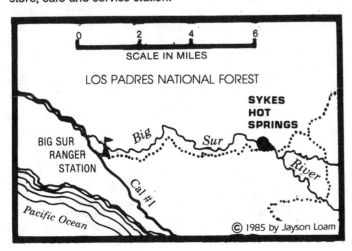

 Different Soaks: The open-roof garden by the wall gives an outdoors feel while retaining the comfort of an indoors installation.

682   PARAISO HOT SPRINGS

■
　　　　　　　　　　　　(408) 678-2882
Soledad, CA 93960　　　　**PR+MH+CRV**

A quiet resort for adults, with several acres of tree-shaded grass areas, located on the west slopes of the Salinas Valley. Elevation 1,200 ft. Open all year.

Natural mineral water flows out of the ground at 115° and is piped to the pools. There are two outdoor swimming pools averaging 75° and 95° and an indoor soaking pool with a temperature of 108°. All pools are treated with chlorine. Bathing suits are required. No cut-offs permitted.

Cottages, RV spaces, overnight camping and a cocktail bar are available on the premises. No credit cards are accepted. It is eight miles to a restaurant and service station.

Directions: From US 101, exit on Arroyo Seco Road, one mile south of Soledad. Go one mile west to stop sign, then turn onto Paraiso Springs Rd. Continue uphill for six miles to resort at end of road.

683   DIFFERENT SOAKS

❑
1157 Forest Ave.　　　　(408) 646-8293
Pacific Grove, CA 93950　　　　**PR**

Unusually spacious hot-pool rental and retail spa sales establishment located in a suburb of Monterey.

Five pools in private rooms are for rent to the public. One room has a tub large enough for ten persons, and rooms can be combined for larger groups. Gas-heated tap water treated with bromine is heated to 103°. Each room has a shower, dressing space, music speaker and a landscaped, open-roof garden along one wall.

No credit cards are accepted. Phone for rates, reservations and directions.

Kiva Retreat: A policy of clothing optional means that parents and children have freedom of choice, even in the soaking pools.

Lupin Naturist Club: This hydropool is located on the edge of a canyon, which gives the impression of being in a tree house.

684B KIVA RETREAT

702 Water St. (408) 429-1142
Santa Cruz, CA 95060 PR

Trees, grass and flowers lend a parklike setting to this unusual, clothing-optional, hot-pool rental establishment. Located near the city center.

A single day rate gives entry to the communal grass area, two large hot tubs, a cold-tub plunge and a large sauna. Adjoining indoor dressing and social rooms are also available. Pools use gas-heated tap water and are treated with chlorine and ozone. Two private enclosures, rented by the hour, have water maintained at 104˚. Bathing suits are optional everywhere except in the front entry.

Massage is available on the premises. No credit cards are accepted. Phone for rates, reservations and directions.

684A HEARTWOOD SPA

3150A Mission Dr. (408) 462-2192
Santa Cruz, CA 95065 PR

A clothing-optional, tree-shaded hot tub rental establishment located on a suburban side street.

A wooden hot tub, cold tub, sauna and communal sunning areas are available for a day-rate charge. One private enclosure, with a water temperature of 105˚, can be rented by the hour. All pools use gas-heated tap water treated with chlorine. Bathing suits are optional everywhere except the front desk.

Massage is available on the premises. The total facility may be chartered for, private parties before and after regular business hours. No credit cards are accepted. Phone for rates, reservations and directions. (Open on Sunday evenings for women only.)

684C WELL WITHIN

112 Elm St. (408) 458-9355
Santa Cruz, CA 95060 PR

Beautiful hot pool and sauna rooms overlooking a Japanese bamboo garden, located in the heart of downtown Santa Cruz.

Private-space hot pools using bromine-treated tap water are for rent to the public by the hour. There are four indoor fiberglass pools with a view of the garden. Temperatures are maintained at 104˚. Two of the rooms also have saunas. Herbal tea and large towels are provided.

Massage is available on the premises. No credit cards are accepted. Phone for rates, reservations and directions.

685 LUPIN NATURIST CLUB

P.O. Box 1274 (408) 353-2250
Los Gatos, CA 95031 PR+MH+CRV

A clothing-optional resort where both sexes are equal and the differences are accepted as natural. Located on 120 acres of tree-shaded tranquility in the Santa Cruz mountains. Elevation 200 ft. Open all year.

Gas-heated well water, bromine treated, is used in two outdoor fiberglass tubs available to all members and registered guests. Water temperature is maintained at 102-104˚. Bromine-treated well water is also used in two outdoor swimming pools, one of which is heated and covered with a plastic dome in the winter. Bathing suits are prohibited in all pools. Clothing is optional elsewhere on the grounds.

Lodge rooms, RV and camping spaces, and restaurant meals are available on the premises. Visa and MasterCard are accepted. It is seven miles to a store and service station.

Note: This is a private club, not open to the public for drop-in visits. Phone first for information, guest passes and directions.

▲ *Heartwood Spa*: Massage customers arrive 15 minutes before their appointment to enjoy a soak in the outdoor garden communal pool.

▲ *Watercourse Way*: The Japanese decor of this suburban location calls for artistic prints rather than television sets with VCR's.

▲ *Well Within*: A Japanese garden, and tea in Japanese cups, contribute to the feeling of quiet serenity at this downtown location.

---

686   WATERCOURSE WAY
☐   165 Channing Way   (415) 329-8827
      Palo Alto, CA 94301   PR

An innovative bathing center with a sushi bar, offering a variety of enjoyable rooms and experiences. The beautiful oriental decor creates a comfortable and interesting environment.

Pools, for rent to the public, use gas-heated tap water treated with bromine. Nine individually decorated private rooms each have a different combination of hot pool, cold pool, sauna and steambath. Water temperature in the pools is approximately 103°. To accommodate larger groups, two rooms can be joined.

A flotation tank for private rental, massage and sushi bar are available on the premises. Visa and MasterCard are accepted. Phone for rates, reservations and directions.

687 TROPICAL GARDENS
❑ 200 San Pedro Rd. (415) 755-8827
Colma, CA 94105 PR

Recreation-oriented rent-a-tub establishment sharing quarters with a racquetball facility and health club. Located a few blocks south of Daly City.

Ten private rooms with pools use gas-heated tap water treated with chlorine. Water temperature is maintained at 102-104˚. A sauna is included in seven of the rooms.

Other facilities include racquetball and handball courts, a tanning studio, Nautilus conditioning, swimming pool and locker rooms. Massage is available by appointment. No credit cards are accepted. Phone for rates, reservations and directions.

688A THE HOT TUBS
❑ 2200 Van Ness Ave. (415) 441-TUBS
San Francisco, CA 94109 PR

One of the few stress-reduction establishments offering tile tubs and decks in a chrome and glass urban environment. Located on a main street just west of downtown.

Pools in 20 private rooms are for rent to the public. Gas-heated tap water treated with chlorine is maintained at 105˚. A sauna is included.

Massage and a juice bar are available on the premises. No credit cards are accepted. Phone for rates, reservations and directions.

688C GRAND CENTRAL SAUNA & HOT TUB CO.
❑ 15 Fell St. (415) 431-1370
San Francisco, CA 94102 PR

The first one of a chain of urban locations established by Grand Central, a pioneer in the private room rent-a-tub business.

Pools in 26 private rooms, each with a sauna, are for rent to the public. The pools use gas-heated tap water treated with chlorine and are maintained between 102-104˚.

Credit cards are not accepted. Reservations are not accepted. Phone for rates and directions.

688B FAMILY SAUNA SHOP
❑ 2308 Clement (415) 221-2208
San Francisco, CA 94121 PR

One of the pioneer stress-reduction centers in San Francisco. Located in the Richmond District.

Two private rooms with pools, for rent to the public, use gas-heated tap water treated with chlorine. Water temperature is 108˚.

Four private saunas are available for rent. Massage is available on the premises. Visa and MasterCard are accepted. Phone for rates, reservations and directions.

689A F. JOSEPH SMITH'S MASSAGE THERAPY
❑ 158 Almonte Blvd. (415) 383-8260
Mill Valley, CA 94941 PR

Informal therapy establishment with redwood hot tubs, located in a Marin County suburb.

Pools using gas-heated tap water teated with bromine are for rent to the public. Two private enclosures, with water temperatures ranging from 104-108˚, can be rented by the hour. One of the tubs is available for communal use. Bathing suits are optional everywhere except the front office.

A private sauna is available for rent. Massage, facials, manicures and pedicures are available on the premises. No credit cards are accepted. Phone for rates, reservations and directions.

210

689B TRAVELODGE—MILL VALLEY
❑ 707 Redwood Hwy (415) 383-0340
Mill Valley, CA 94941 PR+MH

A conventional motel with one enclosed redwood hot tub filled with chlorine-treated, gas-heated tap water, for rent to the public by the hour. The water temperature is 102˚. Use of the sauna is included. The communal swimming pool is available to registered guests only. Bathing suits are required in the pool and optional in the private enclosure.

Motel rooms are available. Visa and MasterCard are accepted. Phone for rates, reservations and directions.

690A SHIBUI GARDENS
❑ 19 Tamalpais Ave. (415) 457-0283
San Anselmo, CA 94960 PR

An inviting blend of Marin County natural redwood hot tubs and Japanese landscaping. Located on a suburban side-street.

Three privately enclosed hot tubs using bromine-treated, gas-heated tap water are for rent by the hour. Water temperatures range from 102-105˚. One communal cold pool is also available to customers at no extra charge. Bathing suits are optional inside pool and sauna spaces.

A private indoor sauna is for rent on the premises. Massage is available. Phone for rates, reservations, credit cards and directions.

690B REALAX/C.A.L.M. INC.
❑ #10B School St. Plaza (415) 453-5276
Fairfax, CA 94930 PR

One of the first rent-a-tub facilities in the San Francisco Bay area. Located in a Marin County suburb and recently renovated by new ownership.

Mahogany pools for rent to the public use gas-heated tap water magnetically polarized, treated with chlorine and maintained at 105˚. There are two soaking tubs in private enclosures, plus a large communal hot tub and a cold plunge with Japanese volcanic minerals. There is also a private sauna, a communal sauna and a clothing-optional sundeck.

Massage is available by appointment, and vitamins are sold at discount prices. Visa and MasterCard are accepted. Phone for rates, reservations and directions.

Realax/C.A.L.M. Inc.: An authentic Marin County communal hot tub still in daily use.

691 ALBANY SAUNA AND HOT TUBS

1002 Solano Ave.   (415) 525-6262
Albany, CA 94706   PR

One of the first of a dozen rent-a-tub establishments in the Bay Area. Located a few blocks west of San Pablo Ave.

Three privately enclosed pools, for rent to the public, use gas-heated tap water, treated with chlorine. Water temperature is maintained at approximately 105˚.

Four private rock-steam saunas are available for rent. Masage, juice bar, and skin care products are available on the premises. Visa and MasterCard are accepted. Phone for rates, reservations and directions.

692A GRAND CENTRAL SAUNA & HOT TUB CO.

1915 University Ave.   (415) 843-4343
Berkeley, CA 94704   PR

One of a chain of urban locations established by Grand Central, a pioneer in the private room rent-a-tub business.

Sixteen private rooms with pools, for rent to the public, use gas-heated tap water treated with chlorine. Water temperature varies between 102-108˚. A sauna is included.

A juice bar is available on the premises. No credit cards are accepted. Reservations are not accepted. Phone for rates and directions.

692B THE BERKELEY SAUNA

1947 Milvia St.   (415) 845-2341
Berkeley, CA 94704   PR

A stress-reduction establishment located a few yards north of University Avenue.

Three private rooms with gas-heated tap water pools are available for rent to the public. The bromine-treated water is maintained at temperatures from 104-106˚.

Three private saunas are also for rent. Massage is available on the premises. Visa and MasterCard are accepted. Phone for rates, reservations and directions.

 Shibui Gardens: The classic outdoor garden redwood tub experience, in an atmosphere of friendly informality, is a *Shibui* tradition.

693A SUNSHINE SPA

1948 Contra Costa Blvd. (415) 685-7822
Pleasant Hill, CA 94523   PR

Funky, fun-loving, rent-a-tub establishment located in the Pleasant Hill Plaza, 15 miles east of Oakland.

Pools using gas-heated tap water treated with bromine are for rent to the public. There are seven private rooms, each with an in-ground hot tub, sauna, shower, massage table and mural wall. Pool temperatures range from 90-102˚.

Massage is available on the premises. Visa and MasterCard are accepted. Phone for rates, reservations and directions.

693B AMERICAN FAMILY HOT TUB

88 Trelany Lane   (415) 827-2299
Pleasant Hill, CA 94523   PR

Suburban rent-a-tub establishment located a few yards west of Contra Costa Blvd.

Twelve private outdoor pools are for rent by the hour. Gas-heated tap water treated with chlorine is maintained at 102-104˚.

A juice bar and massage are available on the premises. Visa and MasterCard are accepted. Phone for rates, reservations and directions.

This map was designed to be used with a standard highway map

Southern California

NEVADA

751AB

CA 178

US 395

752 753A-D
Tecopa

CA 127

I 15

© 1990 by Jayson Loam

CA 58

US 395

I 40

CA 138

I 15

769

CA 247

768

CA 330

San Bernardino

767

CA 38

CA 62

764A-Z
765A-P
766A-P

778

776

770

Los Angeles

CA 91

CA 215

763

Palm Springs

762

I 10

771

772

773AB

CA 111

755A-D

774

761

San Juan Capistrano

I 15

CA 79

CA 86

Salton Sea

S 22

756

CA 78

775

I 5

Pacific Ocean

CA 78

757

S 2

El Centro

I 8

754

760

759

I 8

San Diego

758

MEXICO

Colorado River

ARIZONA

212

MAP AND DIRECTORY SYMBOLS

● Non-commercial mineral water pool

■ Commercial (fee) mineral water pool

☐ Gas-heated tap or well water pool

～～ Paved highway

– – – Unpaved road

······ Hiking route

PR = Tubs or pools for rent by hour, day or treatment

MH = Rooms, cabins or dormitory spaces for rent by day, week or month

CRV = Camping or vehicle parking spaces, some with hookups, for rent by day, week, month or year

Furnace Creek Inn: Most of Death Valley is indeed a barren wasteland, but this palm-shaded poolside sun deck is a very nice vantage point from which to contemplate the desert. Some of the palms date back to when 20-mule teams served the borax mines.

750   SILVER VALLEY SUN CLUB
48382 Silver Valley Rd.   (619) 257-4239
☐   Newberry Springs, CA 92365   PR+MH+CRV

Southern California's first clothing-optional lake resort, located on a paved road in the high desert 26 miles east of Barstow. Sunshine 355 days per year. Elevation 1800 ft. Open all year.

Electric-heated well water, treated with bromine, is used in an outdoor hydropool which is maintained at a temperature of 104º. Clothing is optional everywhere on the ground, but bathing suits are prohibited in the lake, pool and showers.

Facilities include a 2 1/2 acre lake, air-conditioned clubhouse, restaurant, snack bar, rental rooms, RV hookups, tent sites and exercise equipment. Volleyball, shuffleboard, horseshoes, children's games, theme parties and bingo are available on the premises. Visa and MasterCard are accepted. It is seven miles to a service station and store, 25 miles to a motel.

This is a commercial resort, affiliated with the American Sunbathing Association, open to the public. Phone for hours, rates, reservations and directions.

751A   FURNACE CREEK INN
Box 1   (619) 786-2345
■   Death Valley, CA 92328   MH

An historic resort built around a lush oasis on a barren hillside overlooking Death Valley. Elevation, sea level. Open all year.

Natural mineral water flows out of a spring at 89°, into two outdoor pools, and through a large, palm-shaded arroyo. The swimming pool maintains a temperature of approximately 85°, and the flow-through rate is so great that no chemical treatment of the water is necessary. Bromine-treated, heated mineral water is used in the outdoor hydropool where the temperature is regulated by poolside controls in the 100-105° range. Bathing suits are required. Pools are for the use of registered guests only.

Facilities include two saunas, lighted tennis courts, rooms, restaurant and bar. Visa, MasterCard, American Express, Diners Club and Carte Blanche are accepted.

Note: Runover water from the spring and pool cools as it flows through a ditch down the slope below this resort. Volunteers have dug out shallow soaking pools along the ditch, which is on BLM land. Bathing suits are advisable in the daytime at this location.

213

751B FURNACE CREEK RANCH

Box 1
Death Valley, CA 92328

(619) 786-2345
PR+MH

A large, ranch-style resort in a green oasis setting. Located in the center of Death Valley, one mile west of Furnace Creek Inn. Elevation 178 ft. below sea level. Open all year.

Natural mineral water is piped from the 89° spring serving the Inn to a swimming pool at the Ranch. The rate of flow-through is so great that a temperature of approximately 85° is maintained and no chemical treatment is necessary. Pool use is open to the public as well as to registered guests. Bathing suits are required.

Facilities include rooms, restaurant, bar, store, service station, overnight camping spaces, RV hookups, golf course and lighted tennis courts. Visa, MasterCard, American Express, Diners Club and Carte Blanche are accepted.

▲ *Shoshone Motel and Trailer Park*: This traditional swimming pool has no hydrojets but does have a sparkling warm waterfall.

◄ *Furnace Creek Ranch*: This valley floor oasis is made possible by the same mineral water spring which serves Furnace Creek Inn. This is one of the largest swimming pools with enough flow-through to be chlorine-free.

752 SHOSHONE MOTEL AND TRAILER PARK

Box 143
Shoshone, CA 92348

(619) 852-4367
PR+MH+CRV

Older resort located on CA 127 in desert foothills near the southern entrance to Death Valley. Elevation 1,600 ft. Open all year.

Natural mineral water flows out of a spring at 93° and is piped to an outdoor swimming pool. The rate of flow-through is so great that a temperature of 92° is maintained and no chemical treatment of the water is necessary. Pool use is available to the public as well as to registered guests. Bathing suits are required.

Facilities include rooms, restaurant, bar, store, service station, RV hookups and overnight camping spaces. Visa and MasterCard are accepted.

 Bathing suits are officially prohibited in these *Tecopa Hot Springs* private pool rooms, but who will tattle if you bathe clothed?

 Tecopa Hot Springs: The new hydropool building (right) overlooks the RV section of the resort and surrounding desert.

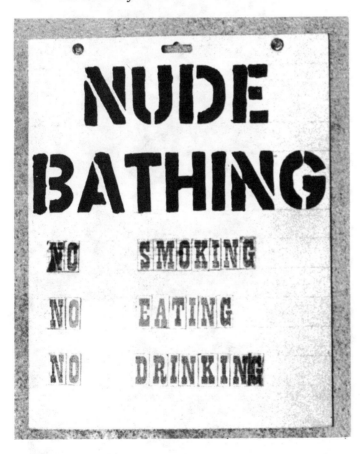

753A   TECOPA HOT SPRINGS RESORT

Box 420   (619) 852-4373
Tecopa, CA 92389   MH+CRV

Newer motel, restaurant and RV park, located on the Tecopa loop of CA 127 in desert foothills near the Dumont sand dunes. Elevation 1,400 ft. Open all year.

Natural mineral water flows from an artesian well at 108° and is piped to seven hydropools in private rooms. Continuous flow-through maintains a temperature of approximately 107°, and no chemical treatment of the water is necessary. Posted signs require nude bathing in these pools, which are for the use of registered guests only.

Facilities include rooms, laundromat, store, RV hookups and overnight camping spaces. It is one mile to a service station. Visa and MasterCard are accepted.

753B CRYSTAL CROSS DESERT CLAY CENTER

Box 336   (619) 852-4422
Tecopa, CA 92389   PR+MH

Small motel and health spa located on the Tecopa loop off CA 127. Elevation 1,400 ft. Open all year.

Natural mineral water flows out of an artesian well at 118° and is piped to several pools. Two indoor hydropools in private rooms are maintained at 104° on a flow-through basis requiring no chemical treatment of the water. Three outdoor clay baths where you can fully submerge yourself in the clay are maintained at 80°. An outdoor swimming pool is maintained at 90°. A minimum of chlorine is used in the clay baths and swimming pool. Bathing suits are required, except in private rooms.

Day use of spas and pools by the public is available. Bus tours are welcome. No credit cards are accepted. It is one mile to a restaurant, store and other services.

753C TECOPA HIDE-A-WAY

Box 101   (619) 852-4438
Tecopa, CA 92389   PR+CRV

Small RV park located on the Tecopa loop off CA 127. Elevation 1,400 ft. Open all year.

Natural mineral water flows out of an artesian well at 118° and is piped to two indoor soaking pools where the temperature is controlled between 100-108°, depending on the season. The rate of flow-through is so great that no chemical treatment of the water is necessary. The pools are available to the public as well as to registered guests.

Facilities include RV hookups and camping spaces. No credit cards are accepted. It is one mile to a motel, restaurant, store and service station.

753D TECOPA HOT SPRINGS
(OPERATED BY INYO COUNTY)

Tecopa, CA 92389   PR (free) +CRV

A county-operated trailer park, bathhouse and campground located on the Tecopa loop off CA 127. Elevation 1,400 ft. Open all year.

Natural mineral water flows out of a spring at 108° and is piped to separate men's and women's bathhouses. Each one has two soaking pools maintained at 100° and 105°, plus an enclosed outdoor sunbathing area. Posted signs require nude bathing and also prohibits mixed bathing.

RV hookups and overnight spaces are available on the premises. No credit cards are accepted. It is two miles to a store and service station.

 Highline South Hot Well: The mineral-well water flows sparkling clear from the pipe but rapidly grows algae in the small pool.

754 HIGHLINE SOUTH HOT WELL

Near the town of Holtville

A cement soaking pool by an artesian well, located just off the I-8 right-of-way on the east edge of Holtville. Elevation sea level. Open all year.

Natural mineral water flows out of an artesian well at 125° and splashes on the edge of a six-foot by six-foot cement cistern. Pool water temperature is controlled by diverting the hot flow after the water in the pool is as hot as desired. Because it takes so little hot water to maintain a pool temperature of more than 100° there is very little self-cleaning action and algae growth is rapid.

There are no services available on the premises and overnight parking is prohibited. However, a primitive BLM campground with a 14 day limit is located 20 yards north of the well.

Directions: At the east end of Holtville, take the Van Der Linden exit from I-8. Go north taking the first right turn onto a frontage road (Evan Hughes Hwy). Within the next few hundred yards you will cross over the Highline Canal and go past the Holdridge Road Intersection. Watch for a large parking area on your right directly opposite the BLM *Hot Springs Campground* sign on the north side of the road. The hot well and pool are visible at the west side of the parking area.

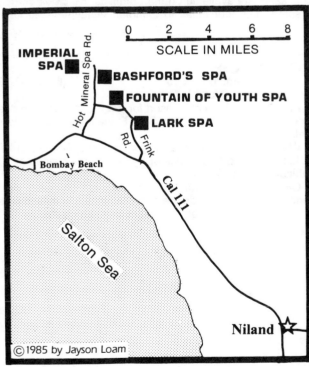

Fountain of Youth Spa: This location is especially popular with "snowbirds," those who bring their trailers south every winter.

755A   FOUNTAIN OF YOUTH SPA (see map)
Rte. 1, Box 12 (619) 348-1340
Niland, CA 92257 PR+CRV

The largest and newest of the RV parks in this area, located on a desert slope overlooking the Salton Sea. Elevation, sea level. Open all year.

Natural mineral water flows out of an artesian well at 137° and into several cooling tanks, from which it is piped to two pool areas, one of which is reserved for adults. The two outdoor swimming pools range in temperature from 85-90°. The five outdoor hydropools have a variety of temperatures from 100-107°. The water in all pools is treated with chlorine. The pools are available only to registered day campers and overnight campers. Bathing suits are required.

The facilities include a laundromat, store, RV hookups, overnight camping spaces and recreation rooms. Services include massage, physical therapy, and beauty and barber shop. No credit cards accepted.

It is four miles to a motel, restaurant and service station.

217

Bashford's Hot Mineral Spa: These oversize bathtubs not only soothe aching muscles but also serve as comfortable social centers.

(see map on preceding page)

755B BASHFORD'S HOT MINERAL SPA

HCO 1, Box 26   (619) 348-1315
Niland, CA 92257   CRV

Primarily an RV winter resort for adults, located on a desert slope overlooking the Salton Sea. Elevation 50 ft. below sea level. Open October 1 to May 30.

Natural mineral water flows out of an artesian well at 145° and into two cooling tanks from which it is piped to an outdoor swimming pool maintained at 84° and to an outdoor hydropool maintained at 102°. The water in both pools is chlorine-treated. Mineral water is also piped to six, outdoor soaking tubs with temperatures from 101-105°. These tubs are drained and refilled after each use so that no chemical treatment is needed. Bathing suits are required.

RV hookups, overnight spaces and a laundry room are available on the premises. No credit cards are accepted. It is seven miles to a motel, restaurant and service station.

755C IMPERIAL SEA VIEW HOT SPRINGS

HCO 1, Box 20   (619) 348-1204
Niland, CA 92257   CRV

The original "Old Spa" location, with the first hot well drilled in this area. Recently expanded hot-water facilities, located on a desert slope overlooking the Salton Sea. Elevation 50 ft. below sea level. Open all year.

Natural mineral water flows out of an artesian well at 165° and into a large holding and cooling tank from which it is piped to seven outdoor pools. Five hydropools are maintained at a variety of temperatures from 96-104°. One mineral-water soaking pool is maintained at 96° and an adjoining fresh-water pool is maintained at 88°. All pools are treated with chlorine. Bathing suits are required.

RV hookups, overnight camping spaces, a store and mobile home sales are available on the premises. No credit cards are accepted. It is four miles to a motel, restaurant and service station.

755D LARK SPA

Star Rte. 1, Box 10   (619) 348-1384
Niland, CA 92257   CRV

Primarily an RV winter resort for adults, located on a desert slope overlooking the Salton Sea. Elevation 50 ft. below sea level. Open all year.

Well water and mineral water, gas heated and chlorine treated, are used in an outdoor hydropool maintained at 102°. Bathing suits are required.

Overnight spaces and RV hookups are available on the premises. No credit cards are accepted. It is one mile to a store and four miles to a motel, restaurant and service station.

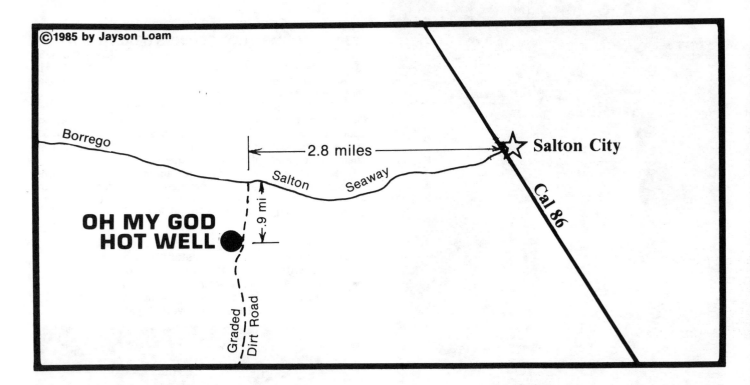

Borrego

← 2.8 miles →

Salton   Seaway

Salton City

Cal 86

OH MY GOD
HOT WELL ●

↕ .9 mi

Graded
Dirt Road

▲ *Oh My God Hot Well*: An easy access road and unlimited free parking, help make this one of the most cosmopolitan non-commercial sites.

---

756   OH MY GOD HOT WELL   (see map)

● **Near the town of Salton City**

A few very popular, rock-and-sand pools built around a free-flowing hot well on an unposted piece of private, desert land west of the Salton Sea.

Natural mineral water flows from the rusted pipe of an abandoned well at 108°. Volunteers have built a series of shallow connecting pools, making the first one small enough to to maintain a temperature of approximately 104°. The others are considerably cooler, depending on air temperature and wind conditions. A graded gravel road passes within a few yards of the pools, so there is often a wide variety of visitors. The apparent local custom is clothing optional, which sometimes means that a few skinnydippers are surrounded by many clothed spectators.

There are no services available on the premises but there is an abundance of level space on which overnight parking is not prohibited. If you want to build a fire, bring your own wood; and windbreak materials might also come in handy. It is four miles to a store, restaurant, service station and other services..

219

758 JACUMBA HOT SPRINGS HEALTH SPA

■ Box 466   (619) 766-4333
    Jacumba, CA 92034   MH

An older motel spa located just off I-8, 80 miles east of San Diego. Elevation 2,800 ft. Open all year.

Natural mineral water flows out of a spring at 97° and is then piped to an indoor hydropool and an outdoor swimming pool. Continuous flow-through maintains a temperature of 95° in the hydropool and 85° in the swimming pool, with no chemical treatment of the water required.

Facilities include rooms, restaurant, bar and sauna. Massage is available on the premises. Visa, MasterCard and American Express are accepted. It is one block to a store and service station and 1/2 mile to RV hookups.

◄
▼
Agua Caliente County Park: The outdoor pool is popular with youngsters, but a bit cool for parents. Within the warmer indoor pool, pumps create a whirlpool action around a central island at a speed which provides good exercise for those who walk "upstream".

757 AGUA CALIENTE COUNTY PARK

■ For reservations call   (619) 565-3600
                                 PR+CRV

A county-operated, desert campground located in a wildlife refuge area near the Anza Borrego Desert. No pets are permitted at any time! Elevation 1,300 ft. Open September through May.

Natural mineral water flows out of several springs at 96° and is then piped to two pools where it is filtered and chlorinated. An outdoor pool with a water temperature usually between 80-90° is available for children. A large indoor hydropool (adults only) uses chlorine-treated mineral water and is solar-and-gas-heated to 102°. Pool facilities are available to the public for day use, as well as for those occupying campground spaces.

Facilities include RV hookups and overnight camping spaces. No credit cards are accepted. It is ten miles to a restaurant, store and gas station, and 35 miles to a motel. There is a nearby airstrip—Agua Caliente.

 Swallows/Sun Island Nudist Resort: This communal hydropool is available to non-resident members as well as to residents.

 Murietta Hot Springs Resort and Health Spa: Mud baths are part of the health and beauty programs at this recently renovated resort.

---

759   SWALLOWS/SUN ISLAND NUDIST RESORT

☐ 1631 Harbison Canyon Rd.   (619) 445-3754
El Cajon, CA 92021   PR+MH+CRV

A large, well-equipped, traditional nudist park located in a tree-shaded canyon 15 miles east of San Diego. Elevation 500 ft. Open all year.

Gas-heated well water, chlorine treated, is used in an outdoor swimming pool with a temperature range of 75-80° and in an outdoor hydropool with water temperature maintained at 104°. Bathing suits are not permitted in pools, and clothing is prohibited everywhere, weather permitting.

Facilities include rooms, restaurant, tennis and volleyball courts, RV hookups and overnight camping. Visa and MasterCard are accepted. It is one mile to a store and eight miles to a service station.

Note: This is a membership organization not open to the public for drop-in visits, but prospective members may be issued a guest pass by prior arrangement. Resort rules prohibit guns, cameras, drugs and erotic behavior. Telephone or write for information and directions.

---

760   THE TUBS

☐ 7220 El Cajon Blvd.   (619) 698-7727
San Diego, CA 92115   PR

San Diego's original, rent-a-tub establishment, located on a main suburban street near San Diego State University.

Eleven spa suites for rent to the public use gas-heated tap water which is treated with chlorine and maintained at 102°. Saunas are included in all rooms. The VIP Suite, large enough for 12 persons, has a bathroom and steambath in addition to a sauna.

A juice bar is available on the premises. Visa and MasterCard are accepted. Phone for rates, reservations and directions.

---

761   MURIETTA HOT SPRINGS RESORT AND HEALTH SPA

■ 39405 Murietta Hot Springs Rd.   (714) 677-7451
Murietta, CA 92362   PR+MH

A full-service resort and European health spa located two miles east of I-15 on Murietta Hot Springs Rd., 90 miles south of Los Angeles and 60 miles north of San Diego. Elevation 800 ft. Open all year.

Natural mineral water flows out of a spring at 140° and is piped to a variety of pools and tubs. The outdoor Olympic-size swimming pool is treated with chlorine and uses a combination of mineral water and cold well water to maintain a temperature of 85°. A similar combination of water is used to maintain a temperature of 102° in the outdoor Roman spa and 85° in an outdoor exercise pool. Natural mineral water is also piped to 36 indoor, one-person soaking tubs which are drained and refilled after each use so that no chemical treatment is necessary. There are separate mud-bath sections for men and women, each containing nine tubs. Bathing suits are required everywhere except in the mud baths, where they are not permitted. Spa facilities are available to the public as well as to registered guests.

Facilities include 242 rooms, various health programs, two restaurants (including the Spring Garden featuring natural, healthful, spa cuisine), beauty shop, tennis courts, a store and overnight parking. Massages, facials, herbal body glow treatments, energizing body wraps, manicures and pedicures are available on the premises. Visa, MasterCard and American Express are accepted. It is five miles to RV hookups and a service station.

Phone for rates, reservations and additional information.

221

Palm Springs Spa Hotel: These communal outdoor pools supplement the individual tile tubs in the men's and women's bathhouses.

762 PALM SPRINGS SPA HOTEL

100 N. Indian Ave.   (619) 325-1461
Palm Springs, CA 92262   PR+MH

A major destination resort with an elaborate mineral-water spa located in downtown Palm Springs. Elevation 500 ft. Open all year.

Natural mineral water flows out of historic Indian wells on the property at a temperature of 106°. The spa has separate men's and women's sections, each containing 14 tile tubs with mineral-water temperature separately controllable up to 104°. These tubs are drained and refilled after each use so that no chemical treatment of the water is necessary. Each spa also has vapor-inhalation rooms, a steambath and a dry sauna. Bathing suits are required in the outdoor pool area, optional in the bathhouse.

Services and facilities on the premises include massage, barber and beauty shop, rooms, restaurant, bar, stores, travel agent, airport pickup and group conference rooms. Visa, MasterCard, American Express and Diners Club are accepted. Pool and spa facilities are available to the public as well as to registered guests.

Directions: Take the Indian Ave. exit from I-10 and drive south five miles to the resort.

763 TREEHOUSE TOO

1466 N. Palm Canyon Dr.   (619) 322-9431
Palm Springs, CA 92262   PR+MH

A refurbished Palm Springs resort hotel offering a policy of clothing optional. Affiliated with Treehouse Fun Ranch Nudist Resort. Located on a main street and on the Palm Springs bus line. Elevation 1,500 ft. Open all year.

Gas-heated tap water treated with chlorine is used in two outdoor pools. The hydrojet pool is maintained at 104°, and the swimming pool is maintained at 80°. Pools and other facilities are available only to registered guests. Clothing is prohibited in the pools, optional elsewhere.

Facilities include rooms, kitchen suites, non-smoking rooms, sunning lawns and lounge chairs, outdoor summer cool misting system, recreation lounge, BBQ and picnic area. Facilities are available for day use on a limited basis. Services include complimentary continental breakfast, afternoon snacks and beverages, and free transfer from Palm Springs Airport. Visa, MasterCard and American Express are accepted. Restaurants, stores and service stations are within walking distance, and it is one mile to downtown Palm Springs.

Phone for rates, reservations and directions.

All of the establishments listed below are in or near the city of Desert Hot Springs, at an elevation of 1,200 ft. and are open all year.

Unless otherwise noted, all of them pump natural mineral water from their own wells and offer at least one chlorine-treated swimming pool and one hydropool, where bathing suits are required. Locations which offer daytime spa use, or in-room pools, or tap water in their pools, are noted. It is one mile or less to a store, restaurant or service station. For additional information about accomodations and the general area, contact DESERT HOT SPRINGS TOURISM AUTHORITY, 11-711 West Drive, Desert Hot Springs, CA 92240. (619) 329-6411 or 1 (800) FIND DHS.

Directions: Take the Desert Hot Springs exit from I-10 north of Palm Springs, and phone for further directions to a specific location.

764A   **AMBASSADOR ARMS SPA MOTEL**
12921 Tamar Dr.   (619) 329-1909
■   Desert Hot Springs, CA 92240   MH
Visa and MasterCard accepted.

764B   **ATLAS-HI LODGE**
13336 Avenida Hermosa   (619) 329-5446
☐   Desert Hot Springs, CA 92240   MH
Visa and MasterCard are accepted.

764C   **BEST WESTERN PONCE DE LEON HOTEL**
11000 Palm Dr.   (in-room pools)   (619) 329-6484
■   Desert Hot Springs, CA 92240   PR+MH
Open to public for day-rate use. Restaurant on the premises. Visa, MasterCard, American Express, Carte Blanche, Discover and Diners Club are accepted.

764D   **BLUE WATER SPA**
66729 Eighth St.   (619) 329-6912
■   Desert Hot Springs, CA 92240   MH
No credit cards are accepted.

764E   **CACTUS LODGE**
68061 Calle Azteca   (619) 329-0584
■   Desert Hot Springs, CA 92240   MH
Visa and MasterCard are accepted.

764F   **CACTUS SPRINGS LODGE**
68075 Club Circle Dr.   (619) 329-5776
■   Desert Hot Springs, CA 92240   MH
Visa and MasterCard are accepted.

764G   **CARAVAN MOTEL**
66810 Fourth St.   (619) 329-7124
■   Desert Hot Springs, CA 92240   PR+MH
Open to public for day-rate spa use. Visa and MasterCard are accepted.

764H   **DAVID'S SPA MOTEL**
11220 Palm Dr.   (619) 329-6202
☐   Desert Hot Springs, CA 92240   MH
Visa and MasterCard are accepted.

Best Western Ponce De Leon Hotel: The rooms of most Desert Hot Springs hotels are built around a central patio containing the pools. This hotel also has several in-room pools.

223

▲ *Desert Hot Springs Spa:* The central patio at this hotel is so large it has its own shopping center along one of the sides.

764I DESERT HOT SPRINGS SPA
10805 Palm Dr.   (619) 329-6495
■ Desert Hot Springs, CA 92240   PR+MH
Open to public for day-rate spa use. Restaurant and bar on the premises. Visa, MasterCard, American Express, Carte Blanche and Diners Club are accepted.

764J DESERT SPRINGS INN
12697 Eliseo Rd.   (619) 251-1668
■ Desert Hot Springs, CA 92240   MH
No credit cards are accepted.

764K FOUNTAIN OF HEALTH
66705 E. Sixth St.   (619) 329-6015
■ Desert Hot Springs, CA 92240   PR+MH
Open to public for day-rate spa use. Visa and MasterCard are accepted.

764L EL REPOSA SPA
66334 W. Fifth St.   (619) 329-6632
❏ Desert Hot Springs, CA 92240   PR+MH
Open to public for day-rate spa use. Visa, MasterCard and American Express are accepted.

764M GREEN BRIAR INN
66445 Second St.   (619) 329-5109
❏ Desert Hot Springs, CA 92240   MH
No hydropool. No credit cards are accepted.

764N HACIENDA RIVIERA SPA
67375 Hacienda Ave.   (619) 329-7010
■ Desert Hot Springs, CA 92240   PR
Spa only—no rooms. No credit cards are accepted.

764O HIGHLANDER LODGE
68187 Club Circle Dr.   (619) 329-7123
❏ Desert Hot Springs, CA 92240   MH
Visa and MasterCard are accepted.

764P KISMET LODGE
13340 Mountain View   (619) 329-6451
■ Desert Hot Springs, CA 92240   MH
Visa and MasterCard are accepted.

764Q LAS PRIMAVERAS RESORT AND SPA
66659 Sixth St.   (619) 251-1677
■ Desert Hot Springs, CA 92240   MH
Visa and MasterCard are accepted.

764R LIDO PALMS SPA MOTEL
12801 Tamar Dr.   (619) 329-6033
■ Desert Hot Springs, CA 92240   MH
No credit cards are accepted.

764S LINDA VISTA LODGE
67200 Hacienda Ave.   (619) 329-6401
■ Desert Hot Springs, CA 92240   MH
Visa and MasterCard are accepted.

764T LORANE MANOR
67751 Hacienda Ave.   (619) 329-9090
■ Desert Hot Springs, CA 92240   MH
No credit cards are accepted.

764U MA-HA-YAH LODGE
68111 Calle Las Tiendas   (619) 329-5420
■ Desert Hot Springs, CA 92240   MH
No credit cards are accepted.

764V MARY ANN MANOR
12890 Quinta Way   (619) 329-6051
■ Desert Hot Springs, CA 92240   MH
No credit cards are accepted.

764W J & M MCGUIRE'S INN
13355 Palm Dr.   (619) 329-5539
■ Desert Hot Springs, CA 92240   MH
Visa and MasterCard are accepted.

764X MECCA
12885 Eliseo Rd.   (619) 329-6932
■ Desert Hot Springs, CA 92240   MH
No credit cards are accepted.

764Y MIRACLE MANOR
12589 Reposo Way   (619) 329-6641
■ Desert Hot Springs, CA 92240   MH
Visa and MasterCard are accepted.

764Z MISSION LAKES COUNTRY CLUB INN
8484 Clubhouse Blvd.   (619) 329-6481
❏ Desert Hot Springs, CA 92240   MH
Visa and MasterCard are accepted.

765A THE MOORS SPA MOTEL
12637 Reposo Way   (619) 329-7121
■ Desert Hot Springs, CA 92240   MH
No credit cards are accepted.

765B OASIS INN
12561 Palm Dr.   (619) 329-5258
❏ Desert Hot Springs, Ca 92240   MH
Visa and MasterCard are accepted.

765C PYRAMID SPA MOTEL
66563 E. Fifth St.   (619) 329-5652
❏ Desert Hot Springs, CA 92240   MH
Visa and MasterCard are accepted.

765D ROYAL FOX INN
14500 Palm Dr.   (619) 329-4481
■ Desert Hot Springs, CA 92240 MH (in-room pools)
Restaurant on the premises. Visa, MasterCard and
American Express are accepted.

765E SAHARA MOTEL
66700 E. Fifth St.   (619) 329-6666
■ Desert Hot Springs, CA 92240   MH
Visa and MasterCard are accepted.

765F SANDPIPER INN & SPA
12800 Foxdale Dr.   (619) 329-6455
■ Desert Hot Springs, CA 92240   MH
Visa and MasterCard are accepted.

765G SKYLINER SPA
12840 Inaja St.   (619) 329-3031
■ Desert Hot Springs, CA 92240   MH
No credit cards are accepted.

765H STARDUST MOTEL
66634 Fifth St.   (619) 329-5443
■ Desert Hot Springs, CA 92240   MH
Visa and MasterCard are accepted.

765J SUNSET INN
67585 Hacienda Ave.   (619) 329-4488
■ Desert Hot Springs, CA 92240   PR+MH
Open to public for day-rate spa use. Restaurant and bar on
the premises. Visa, American Express and MasterCard are
accepted.

765K TAMARIX SPA MOTEL
66185 Acoma   (619) 329-6615
❏ Desert Hot Springs, CA 92240   MH
Visa and MasterCard are accepted.

765L TRADE WINDS SPA
11021 Sunset Ave.   (619) 329-9102
■ Desert Hot Springs, CA 92240   MH
Visa and MasterCard are accepted.

765M TRAMVIEW LODGE
11149 Sunset Ave.   (619) 329-6751
■ Desert Hot Springs, CA 92240   MH
No credit cards are accepted.

765N TROPICAL MOTEL & SPA
12692 Palm Dr.   (619) 329-6610
■ Desert Hot Springs, CA 92240   MH
Visa and MasterCard are accepted.

765O WALDORF HEALTH RESORT
11190 Mesquite Ave.
■ Desert Hot Springs, CA 92240   MH
Visa and MasterCard are accepted.

765P WHITE HOUSE SPA
11285 Mesquite Ave.   (619) 329-7125
■ Desert Hot Springs, CA 92240   MH
Visa and MasterCard are accepted.

All of the establishments listed below are in or near the city of Desert Hot Springs at an elevation of 1,200 ft. and are open all year.

Unless otherwise noted, all of them pump natural mineral water from their own wells and provide at least one chlorine treated hydropool, where bathing suits are required. A store, restaurant and service station are within five miles of all locations

Directions: Take the Desert Hot Springs exit from I-10, north of Palm Springs, and phone for further directions to a specific location.

766A   AMERICAN ADVENTURE
70405 Dillon Rd.   (619) 329-5371
■ Desert Hot Springs, CA 92240   CRV

A family-oriented, membership recreation resort, not open to the public for drop-in visits but willing to issue guest passes to prospective members. Facilities include one swimming pool, three hydropools and a sauna. No credit cards are accepted.

766B   CORKHILL RV AND MOBILE HOME PARK
17989 Corkhill Rd.   (619) 329-5976
■ Desert Hot Springs, CA 92240   CRV

Older RV park with all pools enclosed and covered. There is one swimming pool, one hydropool, one soaking pool and two cold pools. No credit cards are accepted.

766C   DESERT HOT SPRINGS TRAILER PARK
66434 W. Fifth   (619) 329-6041
■ Desert Hot Springs, CA 92240   CRV

Older trailer park within the city limits. No credit cards are accepted.

Sky Valley Park: This easternmost Dillon Road resort has acquired a reputation for beautiful landscaping and customer comfort.

766D   DESERT SPRINGS SPA AND RV PARK
17325 Johnson Rd.   (619) 329-1384
■ Desert Hot Springs, CA 92240   CRV

Older mobile home and RV park with overnighters welcome. Outdoor swimming pool. No credit cards are accepted.

766E   DESERT VIEW ADULT MOBILE PARK
18555 Roberts Rd.   (619) 329-7079
■ Desert Hot Springs, CA 92240   CRV

Strictly a mobile home park with no RV's and no overnighters. Outdoor swimming pool and two indoor hydropools. No credit cards are accepted.

766F   GOLDEN LANTERN MOBILE VILLAGE
17300 Corkhill Rd.   (619) 329-6633
■ Desert Hot Springs, CA 92240   CRV

Recently renovated pool area with one outdoor swimming pool and three enclosed soaking pools. Mobile home spaces, RV hookups and overnight spaces available. New and used mobile homes are for sale. There is a restaurant, store and service station next door. No credit cards are accepted.

766G   HOLMES HOT SPRINGS MOBILE PARK
69530 Dillon Rd.   (619) 329-7934
■ Desert Hot Springs, CA 92240   CRV

Older RV park with one outdoor swimming pool and one outdoor soaking pool. RV hookups and overnight spaces available. No credit cards are accepted.

766H   MAGIC WATERS MOBILE HOME PARK
17551 Mt. View Rd.   (619) 329-2600
■ Desert Hot Springs, CA 92240   CRV

Well-kept, mobile home park. Hot mineral water is used in an outdoor swimming pool and an indoor hydropool. Mobile spaces, RV hookups and overnight spaces available. No credit cards are accepted.

766I   MOUNTAIN VIEW MOBILE HOME PARK
15525 Mt. View Rd.   (619) 329-5870
■ Desert Hot Springs, CA 92240   CRV

Modern, mobile home park with one outdoor swimming pool and one semi-enclosed hydropool. Mobile home spaces, RV hookups and overnight spaces available. No credit cards are accepted.

766J   PALM DRIVE TRAILER COURT
14881 Palm Dr.   (619) 329-8341
■ Desert hot Springs, CA 92240   CRV

Older trailer court with one soaking pool and one hydropool, open 24 hours. Mobile home spaces, RV hookups and overnight spaces available. No credit cards are accepted.

766K   ROYAL FOX RV PARK
14500 Palm Dr.   (619) 329-4481
■ Desert Hot Springs, CA 92240   CRV

Large, new RV facility operated as part of the Royal Fox Inn complex. A swimming pool, two hydropools and two saunas are available to registered guests in the RV park as well as to motel guests. RV hookups are equipped with instant telephone connections through the motel switchboard.

Visa, MasterCard and American Express are accepted.

▲ *Sam's Family Spa:* These four chlorine-free pools offer a range of temperatures from 108° to 95°. Customers can choose to soak briefly in hot water and then move to the 95° pool for an hour of lolling and socializing.

766L SAM'S FAMILY SPA

■ 70875 Dillon Rd. (619) 329-6457
Desert Hot Springs, CA 92240 PR+MH+CRV

One of the largest, multi-service resorts in the area with all facilities open to the public for day use as well as to registered guests. The outdoor swimming pool uses chlorinated mineral water, but the children's wading pool and four covered hydropools use flow-through mineral water which requires no chemical treatment.

Facilities include a coed sauna, motel rooms, restaurant, RV hookups, overnight spaces, store, laundromat, children's playground and gymnasium. No credit cards are accepted.

766M SANDS RV COUNTRY CLUB

❑ 16400 Bubbling Wells Rd. (619) 251-1030
Desert Hot Springs, CA 92240 CRV

Large, new RV resort with a golf course that is open to the public. Gas-heated tap water, chlorine treated, is used in the outdoor swimming pool and the outdoor hydropool. Facilities include a coed sauna, golf course, RV hookups and overnight spaces. Visa and MasterCard are accepted.

766N SKY VALLEY PARK

■ 74565 Dillon Rd. (619) 329-7415
Desert Hot Springs, CA 92240 CRV

Large, modern, landscaped mobile home and RV park. There are two outdoor swimming pools, one outdoor hydropool, two enclosed hydropools and one indoor hydropool. Facilities include men's and women's saunas, mobile home spaces, RV hookups and overnight spaces. No credit cards are accepted.

▲ *Palm Drive Trailer Court:* This is one of the locations which provides daily exercise classes in the pool for the residents.

766O SKY VALLEY EAST

■ 74711 Dillon Rd. (619) 329-2909
Desert Hot Springs, CA 92240 CRV

Large, new addition to Sky Valley Park. One swimming pool, an outdoor hydropool and an enclosed hydropool are on a separate patio reserved for adults. An adjoining patio contains an outdoor swimming pool and an outdoor hydropool designed for family use.

Facilities include men's and women's saunas, mobile home spaces, RV hookups and overnight spaces. No credit cards are accepted.

766P WAGNER MOBILE HOME PARK

■ 18801 Roberts Rd. (619) 329-6043
Desert Hot Springs, CA 92240 CRV

Older mobile park with one outdoor swimming pool, one indoor hydropool and two indoor cold pools. Mobile home spaces and RV hookups are available. No overnighters. No credit cards are accepted.

Deep Creek Hot Springs: One of the ten most beautiful hot spring locations in the West, worth every step of the gentle seven-mile trail or the steep two-mile trail.

767   PAN HOT SPRINGS

420 E. North Shore Blvd.   (714) 585-2757
Big Bear City, CA 92314   PR

Historic indoor and outdoor swimming pools, with adjoining health club, located in the Big Bear recreation area. Elevation 6,700 ft. Open weekends in May and then every day through September 15.

Natural mineral water is pumped from a well at 90° and piped to an indoor pool which maintains a temperature of 85°. It then flows on through to the outdoor pool, which maintains a temperature of 78°. Both pools are treated with chlorine. Bathing suits are required.

Facilities include dressing rooms, health club, arcade games and a snack bar. All other services are available within five miles. No credit cards are accepted. Phone for rates, reservations and directions.

768   DEEP CREEK HOT SPRINGS (see map)

● Near the town of Hesperia

Beautiful, remote springs on the south bank of Deep Creek at the bottom of a spectacular canyon in the San Bernardino National Forest. Elevation 3,000 ft. Open all year.

Natural mineral water flows out of several rock fissures at 108° and directly into volunteer-built, rock-and-sandbag pools on the edge of Deep Creek, which flows all year. Water temperature in any one pool will depend on the amount of creek water admitted. The apparent local custom is clothing optional.

There are no services, and overnight camping is prohibited in the canyon near the springs. It is seven miles by an all-year trail to an overnight parking area. There is also a steep 2 1/2 mile trail down the north side of the canyon from Bowen Ranch, where a fee is charged for admission to the ranch and for overnight parking. From either parking area it is ten miles to a store, restaurant, service station, and all other services. Note: The trail from Bowen Ranch ends on the north bank of Deep Creek, which runs so high during spring run-off that it is not safe to try to ford the creek.

Source maps: *San Berardino National Forest*. USGS *Lake Arrowhead*.

769   TREEHOUSE FUN RANCH

17809 Glen Helen Rd.   (714) 887-7056
Devore, CA 92407   PR+MH+CRV

A high-profile, event-oriented nudist resort located in a desert foothills canyon, 15 miles north of San Bernardino. Elevation 2,500 ft. Open all year.

Gas-heated spring water treated with chlorine, is used in an outdoor hydrojet pool and in an indoor therapy spa, both of which are maintained at 104°. Similar water is used in a large, unheated outdoor swimming pool. Clothing is prohibited in the pool, sauna and spas, and optional elsewhere.

Facilities include trailer rentals, RV hookups, camping spaces, BBQ pits, sauna, club house, restaurant, cocktail bar, mini-market, tennis and volleyball courts, children's area and pool, game room, and "Frontier Town." Special events include Mr. & Ms. Nude International U.S. Pageants, International Chili Society District Cook-offs, and demonstrations by the Buff Divers, a nude sky-diving team. Visa, MasterCard and American Express are accepted. It is two miles to a service station and all other services, and eight miles to San Bernardino.

Note: This is a membership organization not open to the public for drop-in visits, but a guest pass may be issued for prospective members by prior arrangements. Phone or write for information and directions.

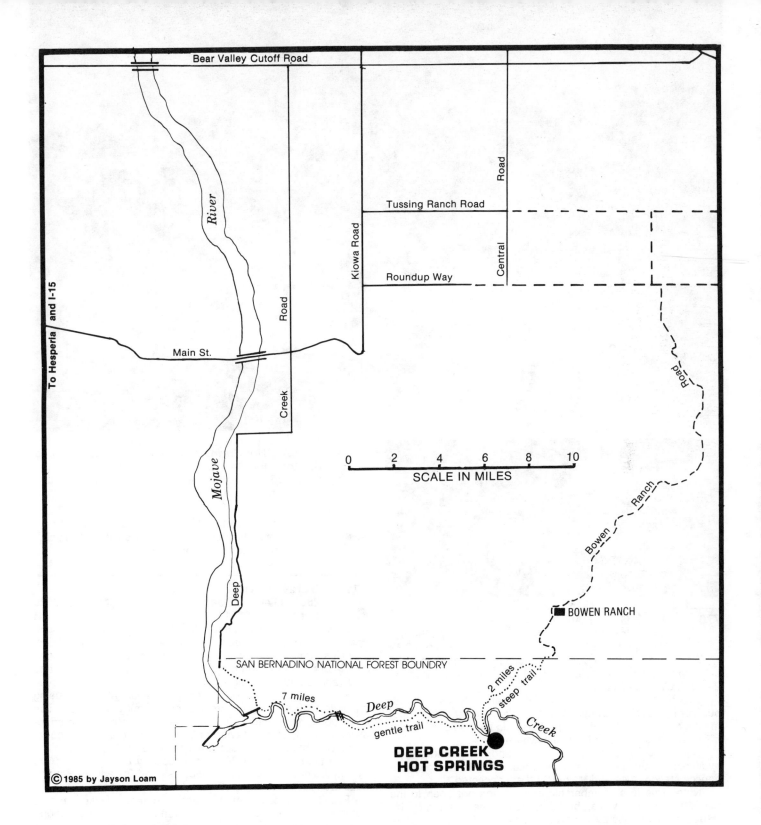

229

POOL RULES
1. This Pool is for Soaking Only.
2. Jumping, Diving, Splashing, Running or Horseplay is ABSOLUTELY PROHIBITED.
3. Parents are RESPONSIBLE for the BEHAVIOR & SAFETY of their CHILDREN at all times.
4. No Lifeguard on Duty at this Pool.

Glen Ivy Hot Springs: A sparkling fountain sets the tone for this lovely shallow pool which was designed just for those who want to float lazily about on air mattresses.

Glen Ivy's famous red clay is to be smeared on with vigor, then allowed to dry, so it will crack, tickle and clean out the pores.

770   OLIVE DELL RANCH

Rte. 1, Box 393   (714) 825-6619
Colton, CA 92324   PR+MH+CRV

A pioneer, Southern California nudist park located on a dry and sunny hilltop 60 miles east of Los Angeles. Elevation 2,000 ft. Open all year.

Gas-heated well water, chlorine treated, is used in an outdoor hydropool maintained at 105° and in a swimming pool maintained at 75°. Clothing is prohibited in the pools and in the main recreation area, optional elsewhere.

Cabins, cafe, overnight camping and RV hookups are available on the premises. It is three miles to a store and service station. Visa and MasterCard are accepted.

Note: This is a membership organization not open to the public for drop-in visits, but prospective members may be issued a guest pass by prior arrangement. Telephone or write for information and directions.

771   GLEN IVY HOT SPRINGS

25000 Glen Ivy Road   (714) 277-3529
Corona, CA 91719   PR

Large, well-equipped, beautifully landscaped day-use resort spa located on the dry east side of the Santa Ana mountains, 70 miles from Los Angeles. Elevation 1,300 ft. Open all year.

Natural mineral water is pumped from two wells at 90° and 110° and piped to a wide variety of pools. There are seven sunken hydrojet tubs with temperatures of 104-106°, using continuous flow-through, unchlorinated mineral water. The other pools have automatic filters and chlorinators. An outdoor swimming pool is maintained at 85°, a covered soaking pool at 103°, two outdoor hydropools at 101° and 104°, a shallow outdoor floating pool at 90° and a red clay bath pool at 100°. The hydrojet pools are in a patio reserved for adults. Bathing suits are required.

Facilities include men's and women's locker rooms equipped with hair blowers, a suntanning table, coed sauna and two snack bars. Massage, herbal blanket wraps and salt glow rub are available on the premises. Visa and MasterCard are accepted.

During the summer months some evening musical events are planned. The entire resort is available for private group charter during evening hours.

Directions: Eight miles south of Corona on I-15, take the Temescal Canyon Rd. exit. Go one mile south to Glen Ivy Rd., turn west and go one mile to resort at end of road.

230

Two of the many *Glen Ivy* soaking pools are enclosed as protection during bad weather. The sunken roman tubs (below) have hydrojets.

Glen Eden Sun Club: The showers, restaurant and recreation room are to the left of the pools, the game courts uphill to the right.

772 GLEN EDEN SUN CLUB
P.O. Box 641   (714) 734-4650
❑   Corona, CA 91720   PR+CRV

Large, well-equipped, traditional nudist park located on the dry side of the Santa Ana mountains, 70 miles from Los Angeles. Elevation 1,200 ft. Open all year.

Gas-heated well water is used in an outdoor hydropool maintained at 105° and indoor soaking pool maintained at 85°. The solar-heated swimming pool averages 75° from May to November. All pools have automatic filters and chlorinators. Bathing suits are prohibited in the pools. There is no requirement of full nudity regardless of weather conditions, but posted signs state that individual dress is expected to conform to that of the majority at any given time.

Facilities include tennis and volleyball courts, sauna, restaurant, RV hookups, overnight camping spaces and recreation rooms. Visa and MasterCard are accepted. It is eight miles to a motel, store and service station.

Note: This is a membership organization not open to the public for drop-in visits, but prospective members may be issued a guest pass by prior arrangement. Telephone or write for information and directions.

773A LAKE ELSINORE HOT SPRINGS MOTEL
316 N. Main   (714) 674-9997
■   Lake Elsinore, CA 92330   PR+MH

Older motel and spa located several blocks north of downtown Lake Elsinore. Elevation 1,300 ft. Open all year.

Natural sulphur water flows out of an artesian well at 100° and is piped to three pools and to the bathtubs in all rooms. The outdoor swimming pool is maintained at 104°. All pools are chlorine treated and are available to the public as well as to registered guests. Bathing suits are required.

Facilities include a sauna and a recreation room. Rooms and massage are available on the premises. Visa and MasterCard are accepted. It is five blocks to a restaurant, store and service station.

773B HAN'S MOTEL AND MINERAL SPA
215 W. Graham   (714) 674-3551
■   Lake Elsinore, CA 92330   PR+MH

An older motel in downtown Lake Elsinore. Elevation 1,300 ft. Open all year.

Natural mineral water flows out of an artesian well at 120° and is piped to two pools and to the bathtubs in every room. The outdoor swimming pool is maintained at 86°, and the indoor hydropool is maintained at 105°. The water in both pools is chlorine treated and bathing suits are required.

Rooms are available on the premises. Visa and MasterCard are accepted. It is two blocks to a restaurant, store and service station.

▲
▶ *San Juan Capistrano Hot Springs*: These well-water hot tubs under the trees are about as close to a natural hot spring as you can get within an easy driving radius from the city.

---

774   SAN JUAN CAPISTRANO HOT SPRINGS
■ P.O. Box 58   (714) 728-0400
  San Juan Capistrano, CA 92693   PR+CRV

A unique combination of outdoor redwood hot tubs, natural mineral water and a pastoral setting under the trees. Located on the Ortega Highway (CA 74), 13 miles east of San Juan Capistrano. Elevation 800 ft. Open 24 hours all year.

Natural mineral water flows out of several springs at 120˚ and is piped to 25 widely scattered redwood, tile/plaster or acrylic tubs rented by the hour, each with its own automatic chlorinator and jets. Water temperature in each tub is controlled by using faucets to admit the desired proportions of hot mineral water and cold well water. The large outdoor swimming pool is filled with well water, treated with chlorine, and geothermally heated by a heat exchanger to 85˚. Bathing suits are required.

Facilities include night lighting, men's and women's dressing rooms, grassy picnic areas, volleyball court, overnight camping, RV spaces and an authentic (rentable) tepee tent. Visa and MasterCard are accepted. It is seven miles to a restaurant and store, 12 miles to a motel and service station.

 Family Hot Tubs: If your legs become sore at Disneyland, get your hydrotherapy here.

---

775   FAMILY HOT TUBS
❑   2784 W. Ball Rd.   (714) 761-8325
        Anaheim, CA 92804   PR
    Modern, suburban pool-rental facility near Disneyland and Knott's Berry Farm.
    Private-space hot pools, using gas-heated tap water, are treated with chlorine. There are six indoor fiberglass pools with water temperatures maintained at 101-104°. Three of the rooms have a sauna.
    Each room has a skylight, shower, hair dryer, phone, stereo system and towels. TV and VCR are available. Visa and MasterCard are accepted. Phone for rates, reservations and directions.

---

776   **BEVERLY HOT SPRINGS**
■   308 N. Oxford Ave.   (213) 734-7000
        Los Angeles, CA 90004   PR
    A modern, Korean-style, indoor spa built over a hot water artesian well a few miles west of downtown Los Angeles. Elevation 300 ft. Open all year.
    From a well drilled in the early 1900's, mineral water flows out at a temperature of 105° and is piped to large, tiled soaking pools equipped with hydrojets in the women's section (first floor) and the men's section (second floor). Each section also has a pool of cooled mineral water. All pools operate on a continuous flow-through basis so that no chemical treatment of the water is necessary. Bathing suits are not required in pool rooms.
    Facilities include a dry sauna and a steam sauna in each section, plus a restaurant and beauty salon. Shiatsu massage, cream massage and body scrub are available on the premises. Visa and MasterCard are accepted. Phone for rates, reservations and directions.

---

777   HOT TUB FEVER
❑   3131 Olympic Blvd.   (213) 829-7576
        Santa Monica, CA 90404   PR
    The first rent-a-tub facility in the Los Angeles area, located near the boundary between the cities of Santa Monica and Los Angeles.
    Thirteen pools in private rooms, with audio and video cassette players included, are for rent to the public. Pools use gas-heated tap water, treated with chlorine. Temperatures ranging between 98-102° are adjustable on request. Saunas are included in all rooms. Each of the two largest rooms also has a bathroom, fireplace, videocassette unit and steambath.
    Massage is available by appointment. Visa and MasterCard are accepted. Phone for rates, reservations and directions.

---

778   ELYSIUM INSTITUTE
❑   814 Robinson Rd.   (213) 455-1000
        Topanga, CA 90290   PR+CRV
    Tree-shaded, rolling lawns are part of a ten-acre, clothing-optional growth center located in smog-free Topanga Canyon, 30 miles west of Los Angeles. Elevation 1,000 ft. Open all year.
    Gas-heated tap water, chlorine treated, is used in a large outdoor hydropool maintained at a temperature of 105°. Chlorine-treated tap water is also used in a solar-heated swimming pool. Clothing is optional everywhere on the grounds.
    Massage, sauna, tennis, volleyball, recreation room and educational/experimental workshops and seminars are available on the premises. There is also a seasonal snack bar on weekends. Visa and MasterCard are accepted. It is two miles to a store, cafe and service station, and seven miles to a motel room.
    Note: This is a membership organization, but nonmemebers are welcome to attend all seminars and all visitor-orientation days. Phone or write for a copy of the *Elysium Journal of the Senses (JOTS)*, which describes all programs and the procedures for obtaining an introductory guest pass.

 Elysium Institute: Some soaking in this king-sized hydrojet pool is often included in the seminars and workshops offered here.

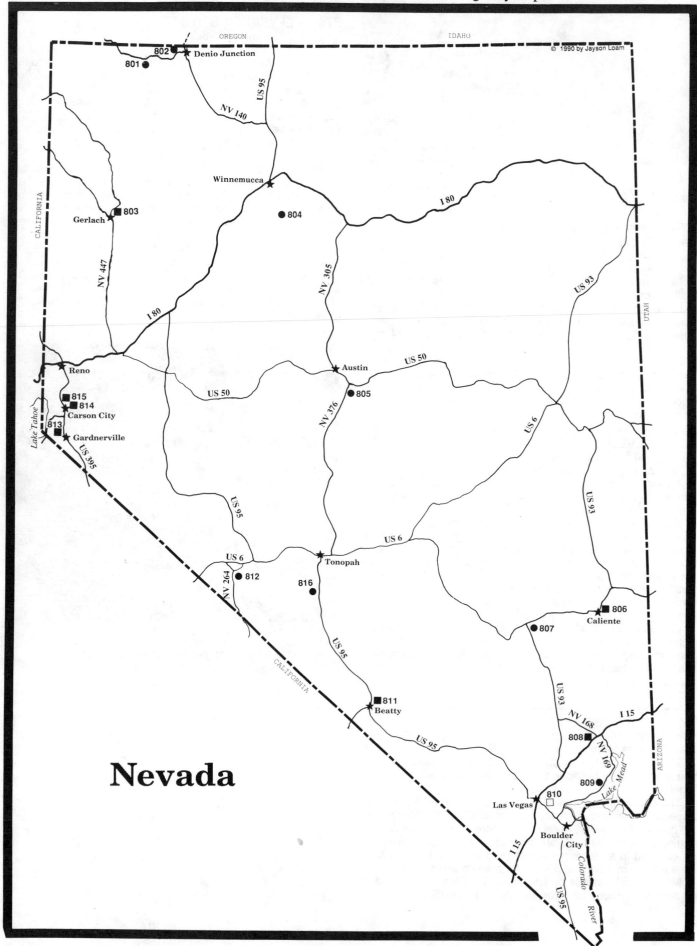

Nevada

801   VIRGIN VALLEY WARM SPRING

● **In the Sheldon Wildlife Refuge**

A charming, gravel-bottomed warm pond, with an old adobe bathhouse in a small campground. Located in the high desert foothills near the Nevada-Oregon border. Elevation 5,100 ft. Open all year, subject to snow blockage on road.

Natural mineral water emerges up through the pond bottom (and is piped from other nearby springs) at 88°. The rate of flow maintains pond temperature at approximately 85°, depending on air temperature and wind speed. No chemical treatment is necessary. Bathing suits are required.

A continuous spring-fed shower at 88° is available in the bathhouse, and the campground is equipped with chemical toilets.

Directions: On NV 140, 24 miles west of Denio Junction and ten miles east of the Cedarville Road Junction, watch for a road sign *Virgin Valley, Royal Peacock Mine*. Go south on the gravel road 2.5 miles to campground.

Virgin Valley Warm Spring: This is not the place for a hot soak but it is a lovely oasis surrounded by miles of wasteland.

235

Bog Hot Spring: A long hot spring ditch makes it possible for each soaker to find a place where the water temperature is just right.

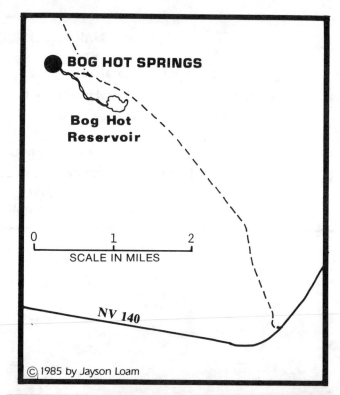

BOG HOT SPRINGS

Bog Hot Reservoir

0   1   2
SCALE IN MILES

NV 140

© 1985 by Jayson Loam

802   BOG HOT SPRINGS

● **Near the town of Denio**

A large sand-bottom ditch carrying hot mineral water to an irrigation pond. Located on brush-covered flat land just below the Nevada-Oregon border. Elevation 4,300 ft. Open all year.

Natural mineral water flows out of several springs at 122°, is gathered into a single man-made channel, and gradually cools as it travels toward the reservoir. A dam with spillway pipe has been built at the point where the temperature is approximately 100°, depending on air temperature and wind speed. Around the dam, brush has been cleared away for easy access and nearby parking, but it is possible to soak in the ditch farther upstream if a warmer water temperature is desired. Clothing optional is probably the custom at this remote location.

There are no services available, but there is an abundance of level space on which overnight parking is not prohibited.

It is seven miles to a restaurant, store and service station, and 18 miles to a motel and RV hookups.

Directions: From Denio Junction, go west on NV 140 for 9.1 miles, then northwest 3.6 miles on a gravel road to the ditch.

803   GERLACH HOT SPRINGS
In the town of Gerlach   (702) 557-2220
■   PR+C

Newly constructed, large soaking pool intended to replace a popular, but dangerous, old free-flowing, very hot spring. Located on the edge of Gerlach, surrounded by desert foothills. Elevation 3,700. Open all year.

Natural mineral water at boiling temperature is piped from a capped artesian well to an adjoining cement-lined soaking pool. Water temperature in the soaking pool is maintained at approximately 100° by adding cold tap water as needed. A continuous flow-through process requires no chemical treatment of the water. Bathing suits are required.

Men's and women's dressing rooms are available on the premises, as are overnight camping spaces. No credit cards are accepted. A motel, restaurant, store and service station are within six blocks.

Directions: From the old train station in Gerlach, go 1/2 mile north on NV 447 to location on east side of highway.

Gerlach Hot Springs: After a delay due to technical problems, construction of this community-owned pool is nearing completion.

804   KYLE HOT SPRINGS

● **Near the town of Winnemucca**

Very funky soaking pit and steambath built from scrap wood over a high sulphur hot spring on a barren mountainside. Elevation 4,500 ft. Open all year.

Natural mineral water flows out of the ground at 106° into a covered soaking pit. High sulphur content gives the water a milky appearance and some sulphur dioxide odor. Another small shack has been built over a nearby steam vent, providing a limited steambath effect. Clothing optional is probably the custom at this remote location.

There are no services available, but there is a limited amount of level space on which overnight parking is not prohibited. It is 18 miles to a store, restaurant and service station.

Directions: From Interstate 80, exit in Mill City onto NV 400 and go 16 miles south. Watch for *Kyle Hot Springs* sign, then go 11.2 miles east on a gravel road to the springs.

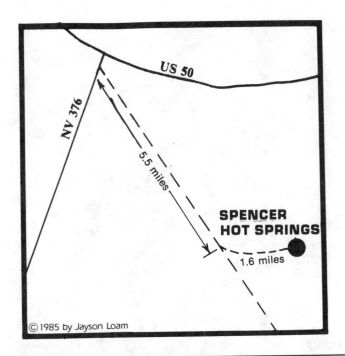

© 1985 by Jayson Loam

Spencer Hot Springs: At this location thoughtful volunteers have provided picnic benches as well as several soaking pools.

805   SPENCER HOT SPRINGS   (see map)

● **Near the town of Austin**

A group of volunteer-built soaking pools on a knoll with a view of barren hills and snow-capped mountains. Elevation 5,700 ft. Open all year.

Natural mineral water flows out of several springs at 122°, then through a shallow channel down the slope of the knoll. Volunteers have dug a small soaking pool next to this channel and also installed several enamel bathtubs. Water temperature in the pools and tubs is controlled by admitting only as much of the hot water as desired. Clothing optional is probably the custom at this remote location.

There are no services available. A man-made swimming pool was bulldozed and filled several years ago after an injury lawsuit against the Bureau of Land Management was filed and won. There is a limited amount of level space on which overnight parking is not prohibited.

Directions: From the intersection of US 50 and NV 376, go 100 yards south on NV 376, then go 5.5 miles southeast on a gravel road. Bear left on a dirt road which leads up the hot-spring knoll.

806   CALIENTE HOT SPRINGS MOTEL

Box 216   (702) 726-3777
Caliente, NV 89008   PR+MH+RV

Primarily a motel, with some hot-water facilities. Located on the edge of Caliente in beautiful Rainbow Canyon, 150 miles north of Las Vegas. Elevation 4,400 ft. Open all year.

Natural mineral water flows from a spring at 115° and is piped to soaking pools. There are three indoor, family-size, tiled soaking pools in which hot mineral water and cold tap water may be mixed as desired by the customer. No chemical treatment is necessary because soaking pools are drained, cleaned and refilled after each use. Soaking pools may be rented by the public on an hourly basis; free to motel guests.

Rooms and RV spaces are available on the premises, and a hot mineral-water soak is included in the room rent. Visa and MasterCard are accepted. A restaurant, store and service station are within two blocks.

Directions: From the center of Caliente, go 1/2 mile north on US 93. Watch for signs and entrance road on east side of highway.

807   ASH SPRINGS

● **At the intersection of US 9 and NV 375**

Tree-lined channels of warm geothermal water, surrounded by barren desert foothills. Elevation 4,000 ft. Open all year.

Hundreds of gallons per minute of natural mineral water flows out of several springs on BLM land at 91° and gradually cools as it runs off though large sandy ditches. In the more secluded areas, clothing optional is the apparent local custom.

Within a few hundred yards, the BLM flow merges with the outflow of additional springs on adjoining private land, where it forms a classic "Ye Olde Swimming Hole." Depending upon the current ownership and management of the private land, it might be open to the public, available only to private club members, or closed. Do not enter the private land until you are sure you are not trespassing.

There are no facilities on the BLM land, but there is plenty of level area on which overnight parking is not prohibited. A service station, restaurant, store and campground are available in the commercial areas of the nearby highway intersection.

237

808   WARM SPRINGS RESORT

■   **Moapa, NV 89025**   **(702) 865-27870**
                                              PR+CRV

A large RV oasis in the desert, with acres of grass and dozens of palm trees, blessed with a warm-water flow of 3,000,000 gallons per day. Located 50 miles north of Las Vegas. Elevation 1,800 ft. Open all year.

Natural mineral water flows out of several springs at 90° and runs through the grounds in a series of gravel-bottom pools and tree-lined channels. A large outdoor swimming pool uses mineral water on a flow-through basis, maintaining a temperature near 90°. The outdoor hydropool uses mineral water heated to approximately 101° and chlorine-treated. Bathing suits are required in both pools.

Facilities include a club house and men's and women's locker rooms. Pool use is available on a day-rate basis. RV hookups and camping spaces are available only to members of a coast-to-coast campers' organization. Prospective members may arrange a two-day trial visit. Phone first for confirmed reservation. No credit cards are accepted.

There are no services available on the premises. It is nine miles to a store, restaurant, service station, etc.

Directions: From I-15, take NV 168 north for seven miles, then follow signs two miles west to resort.

809   ROGERS WARM SPRING

●   **Near the town of Overton**

A refreshing warm pond and shady picnic oasis on the barren north shore of Lake Mead in the Lake Mead National Recreation Area. Elevation 1,600 ft. Open all year.

Natural mineral water at approximately 90° flows directly up through a gravel bottom into a 100-foot-diameter pool at a sufficient rate to maintain the entire three-foot-deep pool at approximately 85°. Hundreds of gallons per minute flow over a cement and rock spillway in a series of small waterfalls. Bathing suits would be advisable at this location in the daytime.

There are no services available, and overnight parking (after 10 P.M.) is prohibited. It is ten miles to a store, restaurant and service station, and five miles to a campground.

Directions: From the intersection of US 93 and NV 147 in the city of Henderson, go northeast on Lake Mead Drive. At the intersection with Northshore Road (NV 167), follow Northshore Road northeast toward Overton. Rogers Warm Spring is four miles beyond the Echo Bay Marina turnoff.

 Warm Springs Resort: This always-warm swimming pool is too large to ever get crowded, even when the park is full.

238

810 SPRING FEVER

3434 Boulder Hwy.   (702) 457-5044
Las Vegas, NV 89005   PR

Modern rent-a-tub establishment located near downtown Las Vegas. Elevation 2,500 ft. Open all year, 24 hours.

Twenty-four pools in private rooms are for rent to the public. Gas-heated tap water treated with chlorine is maintained at temperatures of 94-98° in the summer and 100-102° in the winter. Sauna and toilets are included in each room. Pools are rented on a first-come, first-served basis—no reservations.

A juice bar is on the premises. Visa and MasterCard are accepted. Phone for rates, reservations and directions.

811 BAILEY'S HOT SPRINGS

Box 387   (702) 553-2395
Beatty, NV 89003   PR+CRV

Primarily a restaurant, bar and RV park with three large, indoor hot mineral water soaking pools. Located in the high desert country just east of Death Valley National Monument. Elevation 2,900 ft. Open all year.

Natural mineral water emerges from a capped artesian well at 160°, then is piped into three large, gravel-bottom indoor soaking pools which used to be railroad water reservoirs. Flow rates are controlled to maintain different temperatures in the three pools, approximately 101°, 105° and 108°. The rate of flow is sufficient to permit customers to use soap and shampoo in the pools, and no chemical treatment is necessary.

A restaurant, bar, overnight camping and RV hookups are available on the premises. Visa and MasterCard are accepted. It is six miles to a store and service station.

Directions: From the only traffic signal in Beatty, go three miles north on US 95. Watch for large sign on east side of road.

▲ *Rogers Warm Spring*: An ideal place to go for a picnic and turn the kids loose for a few hours to explore the rocks and splash everywhere in the warm, shallow pool.

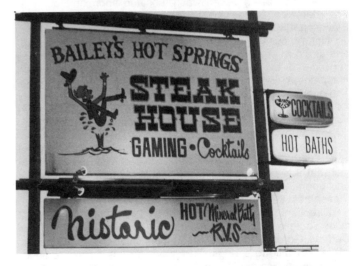

▲ *Bailey's Hot Springs*: Only in Nevada is it possible to find such an inviting combination of geothermal water, good food and gambling.

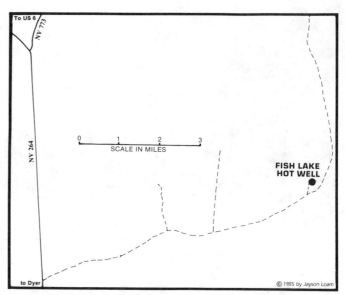

Fish Lake Hot Well: There isn't much scenery to be seen at this location in the daytime, but at night the silence and the brightness of the stars is no less than awe-inspiring.

---

812   FISH LAKE HOT WELL   (see map)

● **Near the town of Dyer**
An inviting, cement-lined soaking pool on the edge of a truly remote barren desert wash. Located approximately half-way between Reno and Las Vegas in Fish Lake Valley. Elevation 4,800 ft. Open all year.

Natural mineral water emerges from a well casing at 105° and at a rate of more than 50 gallons per minute. The casing is surrounded by a six-foot by six-foot cement sump which maintains a water depth of four feet above a gravel bottom. The overflow goes to a nearby shallow pond as a water supply for cattle. Wood pallets have been placed around the cement pool to prevent cattle damage. Clothing optional is probably the custom at this remote location.

There are no services, but there is an abundance of level space where overnight parking is not prohibited. Despite the fact that it is possible to drive within a few feet of the pool, it has been kept surprisingly clear of cans and broken glass. Please help keep it clean.

Directions: From the junction of NV 246 and NV 773, go 5.7 miles south on NV 264 and watch for sign *Middle Creek Trail Canyon*. Go east on gravel road seven miles to fork, then bear left for 0.1 mile to springs. The gravel road is subject to flash-flood damage, so should not be attempted at night.

Source maps: USGS *Davis Mountain and Rhyolite Ridge* (well not shown on map).

Walley's Hot Spring Resort: The design of this modern health club does not include medicinal single-person soaking tubs.

---

813   WALLEY'S HOT SPRING RESORT
Box 26   **(702) 782-8155**
■ **Genoa, NV 89411**   **PR+MH**

A self-styled "upscale destination resort" which attempts to present a nineteenth century resort image. Located 50 miles south of Reno at the foot of the Sierra. Elevation 4,700 ft. Open all year.

Natural mineral water from the original springs bubbles up through the sandy bottom of a large hot pond at 110°, gradually cooling to less than 100° at the overflow spillway. This pond is posted with NO SWIMMING signs. Natural mineral water also flows from several wells at temperatures up to 160° and is then piped to the bathhouse and to six outdoor cement pools where the temperatures are maintained from 96-104°. The cement swimming pool uses bromine-treated creek water and averages 80°. Bathing suits are required in the outdoor pools but are not proper dress in the dining rooms.

The main building is a two-story health club with separate men's and women's sections each containing a sauna, steambath and weight training equipment. Massage is also available in each section. Facilities include rooms, dining-rooms and bars. Visa, MasterCard and American Express are accepted. It is seven miles to a store, service station and RV hookups.

Directions: From Minden on US 395, go 1/2 mile north to Muller Lane, turn west and go three miles to Foothill Rd., then 1/2 mile north to resort.

814 CARSON HOT SPRINGS
1500 Hot Springs Road   **(702)882-9863**
■ **Carson City, NV 89701**   **PR+RV**

Older hot springs plunge with swimming pool and nine large private rooms, each containing a sunken tub large enough for eight persons. Located in the northeast outskirts of Carson City. Elevation 4,300 ft. Open all year.

Natural mineral water flows out of the ground at 126˚. Air spray and evaporative cooling are used to lower this water temperature when pools are drained and refilled during each day. No chemical or city water is added. The outdoor swimming pool temperature is maintained at 98˚ in the summer and 102˚ in the winter. Individual room pool temperatures can be controlled as desired, from 95-110˚. Bathing suits are required in the swimming pool, optional in the private rooms.

Massage, restaurant and no-hookup RV parking are available on the premises. No credit cards are accepted. It is one mile to a store and service station.

Directions: From US 395 at the north end of Carson City, go east on Hot Springs Road one mile to plunge.

815 BOWERS MANSION
4005 US 395 North   **(702)849-1825**
■ **Carson City, NV 89701**   **PR**

A Washoe County Park with extensive picnic, playground and parking facilities, in addition to a large modern swimming pool. Elevation 5,100 ft. Open Memorial Day to Labor Day.

Natural mineral water pumped from wells at 116˚ is combined with cold well water as needed. The swimming pool and children's wading pool are maintained at 80˚. Both pools are treated with bromine. Bathing suits are required. There is a charge for using the facilities.

There are no services available on the premises. Tours of the mansion are conducted from Mother's Day to the end of October. It is four miles to a restaurant, motel, service station and RV hookups.

Directions: Go ten miles north of Carson City on US 395. Watch for signs and turn west on side road 1 1/2 miles to location.

816 SILVER PEAK HOT SPRING

● **Near the town of Goldfield**

Two brick-lined soaking tubs at the edge of a salt flat with mountains in the distance. Elevation 5,000 ft. Open all year.

Natural mineral water flows out of the ground through a flow pipe at 115˚. On one edge of the source spring volunteers have used bricks to build two large (4-6 person) soaking pools in which the temperature is controlled by diverting or admitting hot water whenever desired. The apparent local custom is clothing optional.

There are no services available on the premises but there is abundant level ground on which overnight parking is not prohibited. It is 11 miles to a store, service station, motel, etc.

Directions: From the town of Goldfield (27 miles south of Tonapah), drive north on US 95 for four miles and look for a sign "To Silver Peak" on the west side of the highway. Turn west and drive 6.8 miles on a paved road to a power sub-station. Go to a turn-in just past the sub-station and turn left to the spring.

10-30-92 - Don't go out of your way for this one. Very trashed, garbage everywhere, & the pools are lined w/ algae. O.K. for a dipper bath because the H₂0 is perfect. Not as idyllic as the above photo.

▲ *Carson Hot Springs*: This outdoor pool invites swimmers to jump beyond the incoming water.

▲ *Silver Peak Hot Spring*: This mother and two daughters have found the wide open spaces

241

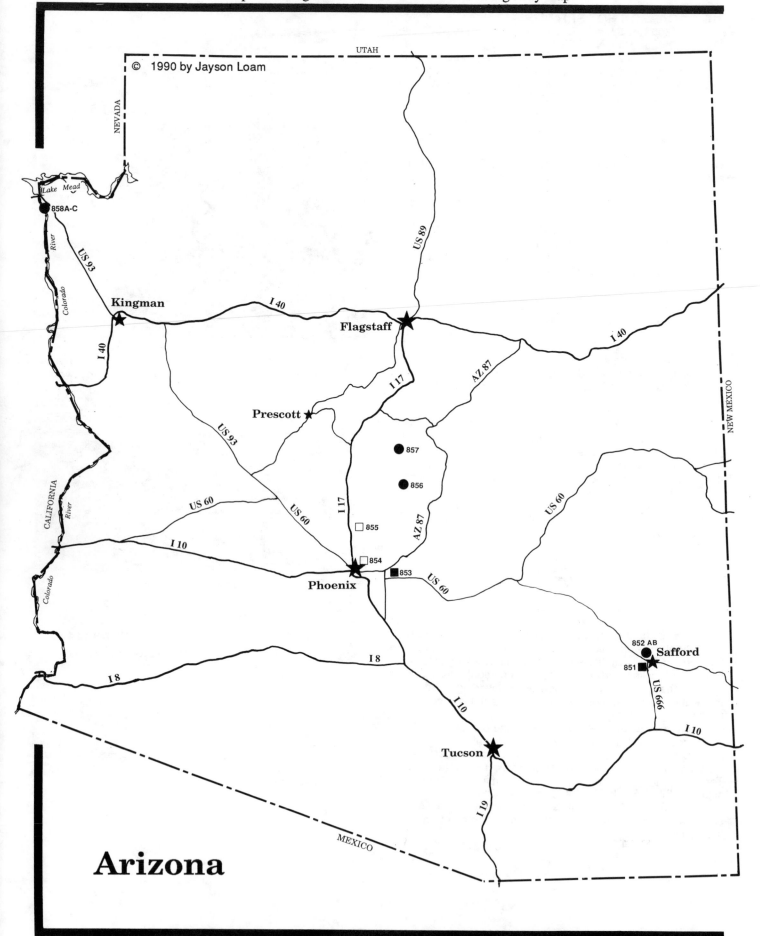

© 1990 by Jayson Loam

UTAH

NEVADA

Lake Mead

● 858A-C

River

Colorado

US 93

I 40

Kingman ★

I 40

I 40

US 89

Flagstaff ★

I 17

AZ 87

NEW MEXICO

US 93

Prescott ★

● 857

● 856

US 60

US 60

I 117

□ 855

AZ 87

US 60

CALIFORNIA

River

I 10

□ 854

Colorado

■ 853

US 60

Phoenix ★

852 AB

● Safford

I 8

851 ■ ★

US 666

I 10

I 8

I 10

I 10

Tucson ★

I 19

MEXICO

Arizona

MAP AND DIRECTORY SYMBOLS

● Non-commercial mineral water pool

■ Commercial (fee) mineral water pool

□ Gas-heated tap or well water pool

—— Paved highway

– – – Unpaved road

· · · · Hiking route

PR = Tubs or pools for rent by hour, day or treatment

MH = Rooms, cabins or dormitory spaces for rent by day, week or month

CRV = Camping or vehicle parking spaces, some with hookups, for rent by day, week, month or year

---

851 KACHINA MINERAL SPRINGS SPA

■

Rte. 2, Box 987   (602) 428-7212

Safford, AZ 85546   PR

Therapy-oriented bathhouse located in the suburbs south of Safford. Elevation 3,000 ft. Open all year.

Natural mineral water flows out of an artesian well at 108° and is piped into private-room soaking tubs. There are six large, tiled sunken tubs. They are drained, cleaned and refilled after each customer so that no chemical treatment is necessary. A free hot-pool soak comes with each therapy service, but private-pool use may also be rented. No credit cards are accepted. Phone for rates and reservations.

Directions: From the intersection of US 70 and US 666 in Safford, go six miles south on US 666, then turn right on Cactus Rd. for 1/4 mile.

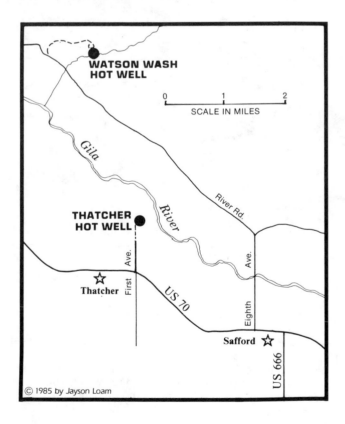

852A WATSON WASH HOT WELL   (see map)

●   Near the town of Safford

A delightful little sand-bottom pool surrounded by willows in a primitive setting. This is also a favorite party spot for local youths, so it is slightly tainted with broken bottles and other party trash. Elevation 3,000 ft. Open all year, subject to flash floods.

Natural mineral water flows out of a well casing at 102° and directly into a volunteer-built, shallow pool large enough for four people. Clothing optional is probably the custom at this remote location.

There are no services available on the premises. On the plateau above the wash there is unlimited level space on which overnight parking is not prohibited. It is six miles to a store, cafe, service station and other services.

Directions: From US 70 in Safford, go north on Eighth Ave. across the river to the highway "Y." Bear left on River Road for 4.7 miles, then turn right on a rough gravel road for one mile to the bluff directly above the hot well in the wash.

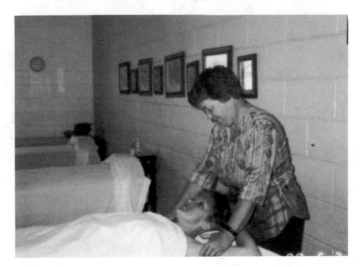

Kachina Mineral Springs Spa: Mrs. Lilly works personally with each therapy customer.

243

Watson Wash Hot Well: Volunteers don't waste time on building a fancy soaking pool because each year's flash floods would sweep it away.

Thatcher Hot Well: Mineral water flows faster from this large well casing than from many natural crack-in-the-rocks hot springs.

It is easy to dig a pool in the Gila River mud flats near *Thatcher Hot Well*, but it will be destroyed every time the river rises.

852B   THATCHER HOT WELL
(see map on preceding page)

● **Near the town of Thatcher**

A substantial flow of hot mineral water out of a riverbank well on the edge of a small town. Elevation 2,900 ft. Open all year, subject to flash floods.

Natural mineral water flows out of a large well casing at 112°, then runs across mud flats toward the current channel occupied by the Gila River. Volunteers dig shallow soaking pools in the mud adjoining the flow of 112° water, controlling the pool water temperature by limiting the amount of hot water admitted. Bring your own shovel; the volunteer-built pools are very temporary. It is possible to drive within five yards of the hot well, so bathing suits are advisable in the daytime.

There are no services available on the premises. There is a limited amount of adjoining space on which overnight parking is not prohibited. It is one mile to a store, cafe, service station and other services.

Buckhorn Mineral Wells: The traditional separation of men's and women's bathhouses is extended to include a men's entrance.

853   BUCKHORN MINERAL WELLS
5900 Main St.   **(602) 832-1111**
Mesa, AZ 85205   **PR+MH**

An historic, older motel-spa which still offers many traditional hot-mineral-water treatment services. Elevation 1,200 ft. Open all year.

Natural mineral water is pumped from two wells at 130° and 140°, then run through a cooling tower. Facilities include separate men's and women's departments, each containing 12 small, individual rooms with cement tubs. A whirlpool pump is mounted on the side of each tub. The temperature of the tub water may be varied by controlling the proportions of hot and cold water admitted. Tubs are drained, cleaned and refilled after each use so that no chemical treatment is required.

Massage, sweat-wrap therapy and motel rooms are available on the premises. Stores and restaurants are located across the street. Service stations and RV spaces are available within one-half mile.

No credit cards are accepted. Phone for rates, reservations and directions.

The tubs at Buckhorn Mineral Baths are equipped with external portable jet pumps, an invention which led directly to modern hot pools with multiple built-in hydrojets.

854   TUBBIE'S
24 West Camelback Rd.   **(602) 263-6055**
Phoenix, AZ 85013   **PR**

Basic, private-room, rent-a-tub facility, located in a shopping center near downtown Phoenix.

Six private rooms, each containing a fiberglass hot pool and changing room, use gas-heated tap water treated with bromine. The water temperature is maintained between 100-105° and will be adjusted on request. One party room large enough for 12 persons is available.

Massage and tanning beds are on the premises. MasterCard, Visa, Discover and American Express are accepted. Phone for rates, reservations and directions.

Tubbie's: Bromine is becoming the preferred water treatment in rent-a-tub establishments. It won't boil off and is easier on the skin.

 Sheep Bridge Hot Spring: The bridge is a government project built for the sole purpose of herding sheep between grazing areas.

856   SHEEP BRIDGE HOT SPRING

● **Southeast of Prescott**

Three large, cattle-watering tubs on a ledge above the Verde River, with a view of a three-million-dollar sheep bridge. Elevation 1,400 ft. Open all year.

Natural mineral water flows out of a spring at 99° and is piped to three large metal tubs in which the water gradually cools as it flows through them in series. The apparent local custom is clothing optional.

There are no services available on the premises. A level camping area is 75 yards upstream. It is 50 miles to all other services in Black Canyon City.

Directions: It is possible to reach this spring via a very difficult 4WD route from Carefree. However, the following is the recommended route: From I-17 north of Black Canyon City, take the Bloody Basin off-ramp and drive southeast on FS 269 for 37 miles. This road crosses several stream beds which are usually dry. The first 16 miles to Summit (elevation 4,500 ft.) is a good gravel road. The remaining 21 miles is a poor dirt road, but it is passable by a high-clearance 2WD vehicle. From a parking area at the bridge, walk 75 yards upstream to the soaking tubs.

To locate the campground, drive .3 mile back up from the bridge and look on the north side of the road for the remains of a building foundation. A steep path (4WD only!) leads 150 yards down to a level camping area by the river. The soaking tubs are 75 yards downstream from this area.

Source maps: *Mazatzal Wilderness, Tonto National Forest;* USGS quads, *Brooklyn Park, Bloody Basin, Chalk Mountain.*

Verde Hot Springs: The crowds are smaller at this beautiful location since the nearest parking has been moved more than a mile away.

Nov. 8, 1992   Excellent

857   VERDE HOT SPRINGS   (see map)

● **Near the town of Camp Verde**

The surprisingly clean remains of an historic resort which burned down years ago. Located on the west bank of the Verde River in a beautiful, high, desert canyon. Elevation 2,800 ft. Open all year, subject to river level and bad-weather road hazards.

Natural mineral water flows out of several riverbank springs at 104° and into small, indoor cement soaking pools. A larger, outdoor cement pool is built over another spring and averages 98°. Twenty feet below, at low water level, are several more springs which feed volunteer-built, rock-and-sand pools. Fifty feet upstream from the large cement pool is a 104° pool in a riverbank cave. The apparent local custom is clothing optional. Conscientious visitors have done a superb job of packing out all trash. Please respect this tradition.

There are no services available on the premises, and it is more than 20 miles to the nearest store, service station, and market. Parking and camping are permitted only in a Forest Service campground one mile south of the Childs Power Plant. Therefore, it is a 1 1/2 mile hike to the river ford at Verde Hot Springs. Check with the ranger station in Camp Verde regarding road conditions and river level before attempting to reach this site.

Source maps: *Coconino National Forest.* USGS *Verde Hot Springs.*

Not much pool space. Inside pool is small but warm 104° outside pool in above photo is warm, more space than inside pool. Cross the river 100 yds upstream of the campground and follow the path north,

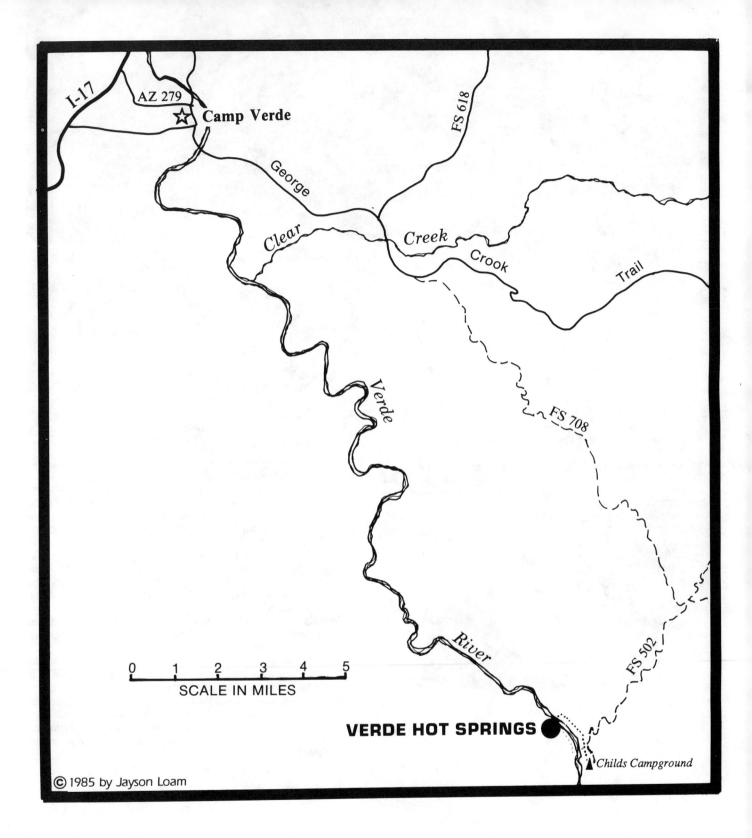

I-17

AZ 279

☆ **Camp Verde**

FS 618

George

Clear

Creek

Crook

Trail

Verde

FS 708

River

FS 502

0 1 2 3 4 5
SCALE IN MILES

VERDE HOT SPRINGS ●

▲ *Childs Campground*

▼ The *Shangri La Resort* hot pool has a roof for protection from the heat of Arizona's sun, especialy during the summer season.

▲ *Shangri La Resort*: Bathing suits are prohibited in the pools because they serve no useful purpose and lint clogs the filters.

855   SHANGRI LA RESORT

☐ Box 4343 New River Rte.   (602) 465-9416
Phoenix, AZ 85027   PR+MH+CRV

Primarily a membership naturist resort located in a scenic high desert valley 30 miles north of Phoenix. Elevation 1,900 ft. Open all year.

Gas-heated well water, chlorine treated, is used in all pools. A large, shaded, fiberglass hot pool is maintained at 104°. The adjoining swimming pool averages 75-80°. Bathing suits are prohibited in both pools, and clothing is optional everywhere else on the grounds.

Facilities include a large club house, volleyball court, tennis courts, sauna and steamroom. Lodge rooms, camping spaces and RV hookups are also available.

A seasonal snack shack is open on most weekends. No credit cards are accepted. It is three miles to a restaurant and five miles to a store and service station.

Note: Being a membership club, Shangri La is not open to the public on a drop-in basis. However, a limited number of guest passes may be issued to qualified visitors. Write or telephone well in advance to make arrangements to visit and to obtain directions.

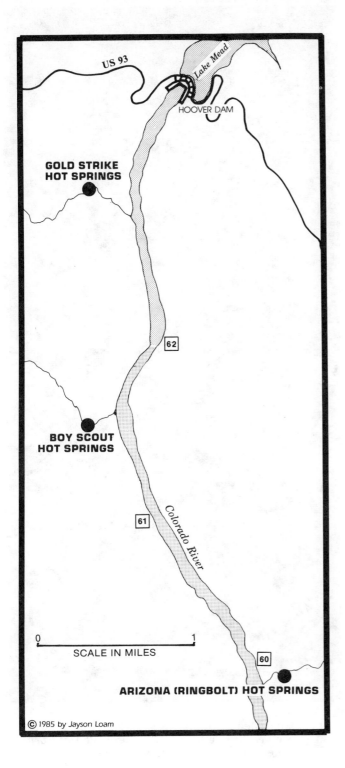

Over many centuries flash floods have carved hundreds of spectacular canyons leading into the Colorado River. In three of these canyons, downstream from Hoover Dam, natural mineral water flows out of rocky sidewalls at temperatures up to 125º, then gradually cools as it tumbles over a series of waterfalls between sandy-bottom pools. The water is sparkling clear, with no odor and a pleasant taste. In all of these canyons, volunteers continue to build rock and sand pools, even though most of them are washed away every year by the rainy season flash floods. Elevation 800 ft. Open all year.

Land routes to these springs range from difficult to impossible, requiring a minimum of several hours of strenuous hiking and climbing. Information and safety instructions can be obtained at the Visitors Center maintained by the Lake Mead National Recreation Area, three miles east of Boulder City on US 93.

Most visitors rent an outboard-powered boat at Willow Beach Resort, which is located eight miles downriver from the springs. Willow Beach also has a ramp for launching your own boat, as well as a restaurant, store, motel and RV spaces. The access road to Willow Beach connects with US 93, 13 miles south of Hoover Dam on the Arizona side of the river.

Rafters and kayakers can obtain a special permit from the Lake Mead National Recreation Area to put-in just below Hoover Dam, float to the various hot springs, and take-out at Willow Beach.

Note: The amount of water being released from Hoover Dam is controlled by the Bureau of Reclamation, and may change from hour to hour, which substantially affects the water level in the river. Therefore, it is important that you secure your boat or raft in a manner which will withstand such changes.

858A   RINGBOLT (ARIZONA) HOT SPRINGS
(see map on preceding page)

● **Near Hoover Dam**

This is the most popular of the three hot springs because it is closest to Willow Beach and downstream from the turbulent water of Ringbolt Rapids. It is 1/8 mile downriver from mile marker 60, and a small warning buoy can be seen on a large submerged rock near the beach at the bottom of this canyon. There is no visible stream at the beach because the hot water disappears into the sand a hundred yards before reaching the river.

The long narrow canyon is beautiful, easy to hike, and includes a ranger-installed metal ladder at the one major waterfall. Source springs in the upper canyon flow at 106°, and volunteers have built a nearby series of rock-and-sand soaking pools, each with a slightly lower temperature than the one above. The geothermal water is cooled down to approximately 95° by the time it flows over the 25-foot waterfall. There is a large amount of camping space in the lower canyon and on a dry sandy plateau just south of the canyon mouth.

▲ *Ringbolt (Arizona) Hot Springs*: This soaking pool was formed by building a rock dam across a narrow portion of the flood-carved canyon.

▲ Lake Mead National Recreation Area Rangers replace this ladder at the *Ringbolt Hot Springs* waterfall whenever it is washed out.

250

858B BOY SCOUT HOT SPRINGS
(see map on preceding page)
● **Near Hoover Dam**

A large cave can be seen in the riverbank just upstream from this canyon. There is no visible runoff at the landing beach because the hot-spring water-flow disappears under the canyon sand one-hundred yards up the wide lower canyon. There are a series of pools and waterfalls in the narrow upper canyon, reached by means of some strenuous scrambling. Water temperature in the lowest pools is over 90˚ and reaches 104˚ in the higher pools. There is plenty of room for a large group to camp in the wide lower canyon.

Boy Scout Hot Springs: The upper part of this canyon has some beautiful large soaking pools, but reaching them requires scrambling over rocks in the narrow lower canyon.

858C GOLD STRIKE HOT SPRINGS
(see map on preceding page)
● **Near Hoover Dam**

The beach at the bottom of this canyon is within sight of the warning cable stretched across the river just below the dam. One hundred yards up-canyon from the beach, natural mineral water flows out of cliff seeps at 109˚ into a beautiful, large, and volunteer-built soaking pool which maintains a temperature of 99˚. The hike up from the beach traverses several waterfalls which are a problem only after a rainstorm. Space for overnight camping at the beach is limited.

Gold Strike Hot Springs: This seep is only one of the mineral water flows in this canyon, which has several substantial hot waterfalls in the portion near the river.

251

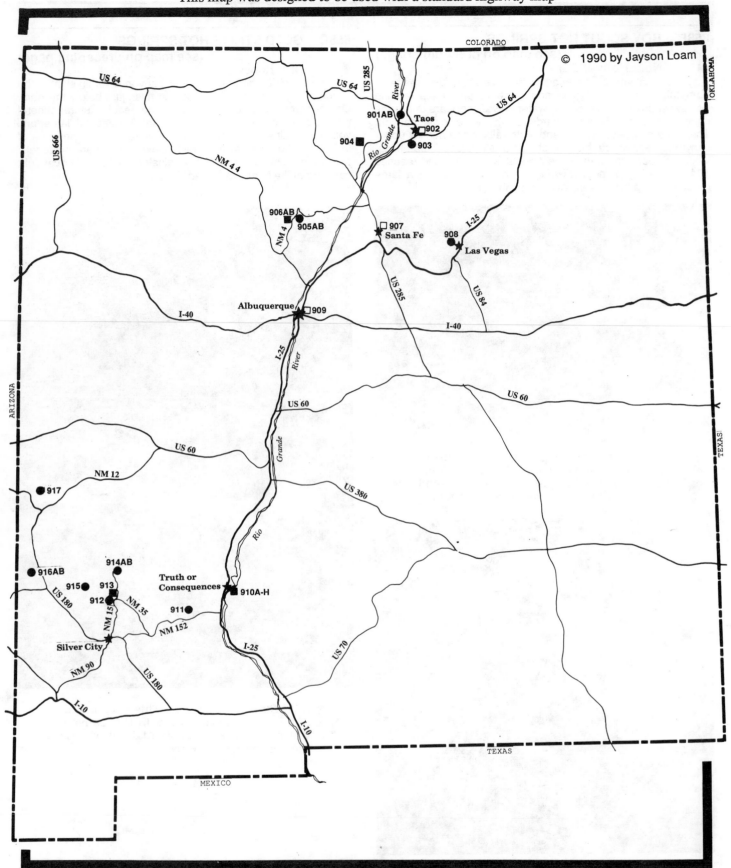

COLORADO

© 1990 by Jayson Loam

OKLAHOMA

US 64

US 64   US 285

US 64

US 666

Rio Grande River

901AB
Taos
902
904
903

NM 44

NM 44

906AB
905AB

907
Santa Fe

908
Las Vegas

I-25

ARIZONA

US 285

US 84

I-40
Albuquerque   909

I-25

I-40

Rio Grande River

US 60

US 60

NM 12

917

US 380

Rio Grande River

916AB
914AB
915   913
912
911

Truth or
Consequences
910A-H

NM 15

NM 35

NM 152

US 70

Silver City

NM 90

US 180

I-25

US 180

I-10

I-10

TEXAS

MEXICO

TEXAS

New Mexico

252

901A BLACK ROCK HOT SPRINGS
(see map on following page)

● **West of the town of Arroyo Hondo**

Rugged, but friendly, sand-bottom rock pool located on the west bank of the Rio Grande Gorge, just a few feet above river level. Elevation 6,500 ft. Open all year.

Natural mineral water flows up through the bottom at a rate sufficient to maintain pool temperature at 97°, except when high water in the river floods the pool. The apparent local custom is clothing optional.

There are no services available. It is three miles to a store, cafe, service station, etc., and nine miles to RV hookups.

Directions: There is a small parking area at the end of the first switchback on the gravel road that winds up the west face of the gorge. Follow the trail downstream from that parking area.

Black Rock Hot Springs: The jagged rocks look somewhat forbidding, but this crystal clear pool has a lovely soft sand bottom.

253

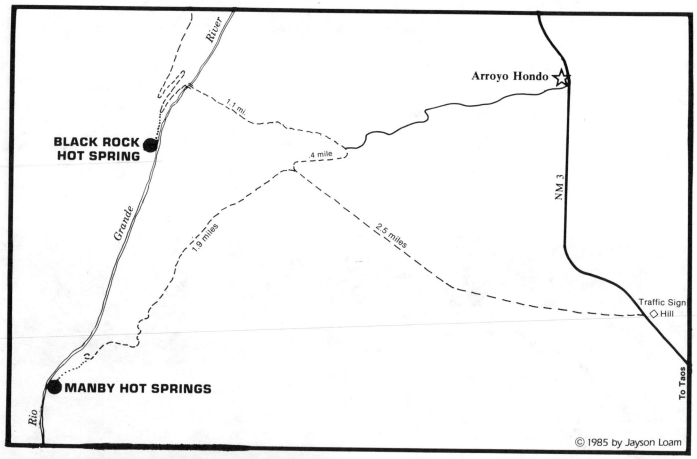

BLACK ROCK
HOT SPRING

MANBY HOT SPRINGS

Arroyo Hondo

1.1 mi.

.4 mile

1.9 miles

2.5 miles

River

Grande

Rio

NM 3

Traffic Sign
◇ Hill

To Taos

 Manby Hot Springs: For those who like stimulating dips in cold river water during a hot soak, this is a very convenient spot.

901B   MANBY HOT SPRINGS   (see map)

● **Southwest of the town of Arroyo Hondo**

Two primitive soaking pools in the ruins of an old stagecoach stop on the east bank of the Rio Grande Gorge. Elevation 6,500 ft. Open all year.

Natural mineral water flows out of the ground at 97° directly into two rock pools large enough for five or six people. The lower pool is only slightly above low water in the river, so the temperature depends on the amount of cold water seeping into the volunteer-built rock pool. The apparent local custom is clothing optional.

There are no services on the premises. There is a limited amount of nearby level space in which overnight parking is not prohibited. It is four miles to a store, cafe, service station, etc., and ten miles to RV hookups.

Directions: Drive southwest from Arroyo Hondo to the parking area at the end of the gravel road, then hike down the grade of the old stagecoach road to the springs.

Source maps: USGS *Arroyo Hondo*.

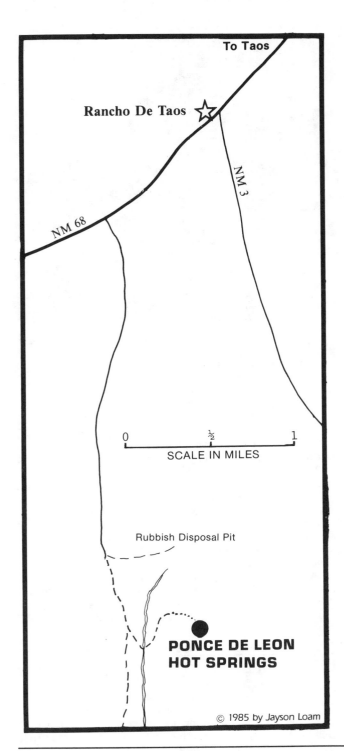

SCALE IN MILES

0 ½ 1

© 1985 by Jayson Loam

903   PONCE DE LEON HOT SPRINGS   (see map)

● **South of the town of Rancho de Taos**

The dynamited and bulldozed remains of a once-elaborate resort located in the desert foothills south of Taos. Elevation 6,900 ft. Open all year.

Natural mineral water flows out of the ground at the rate of 50 gallons per minute and at a temperature of 90°. This flow meanders through the ruins, supplying two badly littered small pools that are used by visitors willing to wade through empty beer cans and broken glass. This appears to be a heavy-duty party place, so clothing is advisable day and night.

There are no services available and very limited parking space. It is three miles to a store, cafe, service station, etc., and six miles to RV hookups.

▲ *Ponce De Leon Hot Springs:* The far wall of the swimming pool was dynamited to discourage party-time use, especially at night.

902   TAOS WATER GARDEN
Pueblo Alegre Mall #5   (505) 758-1669
☐   Taos, NM 87571   PR

Innovative combination of private indoor and communal outdoor hot tubs located two blocks south of Taos Plaza.

Hydropools using gas-heated tap water treated with bromine are for rent to the public. Water temperature is maintained at 99-102°. There are four private tub rooms, each with a shower and music selection. There is also a large, outdoor communal pool surrounded by crystals and flowers. Bathing suits are optional in all pool areas.

Special features include "happi-coats" (kimonos), robes, slippers, shampoo, hair blowers, towels and private lockers. Massage, refreshments and an art gallery are available on the premises. Visa, MasterCard and American Express are accepted. Phone for rates, reservations and directions.

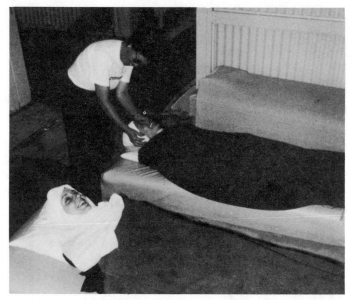

Ojo Caliente Resort: The bathhouse staff keeps customers comfortable while they are tightly wound in a traditional sweat wrap.

---

904   OJO CALIENTE RESORT
■   **Box 468**   **(505) 583-2233**
    Ojo Caliente, NM 87549   **PR+MH+CRV**

An older resort and bathhouse located in the foothills of Carson National Forest, 46 miles north of Santa Fe. Elevation 6,300 ft. Open all year.

Natural mineral water flows out of five different springs with different temperatures and different mineral contents. There are separate men's and women's bathhouses, each containing a large soaking pool at 113° and individual tubs with temperatures up to 105°.

Massage, sweat wrap, herbal facials, dining room, rooms, RV hookups, horseback riding, campground and picnic area are available on the premises. Visa and MasterCard are accepted. It is 25 miles to a public bus, and pick-up service is available for registered guests. Phone for details.

Directions: From Santa Fe, go 46 miles north on US 285. Watch for signs.

905A   SPENCE HOT SPRING   **(see map)**

●   **North of the town of Jemez Springs**

A unique, sand-bottom pool on a steep hillside with a spectacular view of surrounding mountains. Located in the Santa Fe National Forest on the east side of the Jemez River. Elevation 6,000 ft. Open all year.

Natural mineral water (106°) flows up through the sandy bottom into a rock-bordered pool large enough for ten people. The rate of flow-through is enough to keep the pool clean and averaging 104°. Several years ago the spring had a posted Forest Service rule requiring bathing suits on Thursday, Friday and Saturday, with suits optional on Sunday, Monday, Tuesday and Wednesday. Now the apparent local custom is clothing optional every day.

There are no services available. It is seven miles to a store, motel and service station, less than five miles to a campground, and 17 miles to RV hookups.

Directions: From the town of Jemez Springs, go seven miles north on NM 4 to a large parking area on the east side of the highway. The trail includes a log spanning the Jemez River and a steep slope up to the springs.

Source map: *Santa Fe National Forest*.

Spence Hot Spring: This spot is so beautiful and relaxing that students can do homework while sunbathing between soaks in the pool.

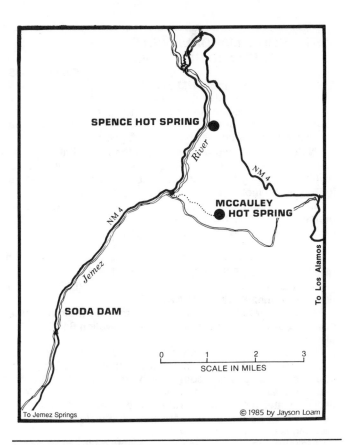

905B MCCAULEY HOT SPRING   (see map)

● **North of the town of Jemez Springs**

Very large, warm pool in a gorgeous mountain clearing. Elevation 7,300 ft. Open approximately mid-April through October.

Natural mineral water flows out of the ground at 90° directly into a two-foot-deep pond, 40 feet in diameter. The rate of flow is sufficient to hold the temperature at approximately 85°. The apparent local custom is clothing optional.

There are no services on the premises. However, the guppies and neon tetras that live in the pool will entertain you by nibbling on your body hair. It is six miles to a store, cafe, service station, etc., five miles to a campground, and 17 miles to RV hookups.

Directions: From Jemez Springs, go 5.2 miles north on NM 4 to Battleship Rock picnic area. From the firepit gazebo, hike 1 1/4 miles up USFS trail 137 to spring and campsite. This trail is moderately strenuous, especially at this altitude.

McCauley Hot Spring: The retaining dam which holds this pool has lasted more than 50 years since it was built by the good old CCC.

The open side of *Spence Hot Spring* has a magnificent view of forested slopes below.

257

906A BODHI MANDALA ZEN CENTER
MOTEL AND HOT SPRINGS

Box 8   **(505) 829-3854**
Jemez Springs, NM 87205   **PR+MH**

A four-unit motel with primitive, riverbank hot pools, operated by the Bodhi Mandala Zen Center. Located in the town of Jemez Springs. Elevation 6,200 ft. Open all year, subject to weather conditions. Phone for current information.

Natural mineral water flows out of the ground at 169°, then into four rock-and-sand soaking pools where natural cooling results in varying temperatures. Use of the pools is reserved for registered motel guests only. Bathing suits are required.

Massage and therapeutic reflexology are available on the premises. It is one block to a store, cafe and service station. Phone for rates, reservations and directions.

906B JEMEZ SPRINGS BATH HOUSE

Box 105   **(505) 829-3303**
Jemez Springs, NM 87205   **PR**

An older, traditional bathhouse located on the main street, operated by the city of Jemez Springs. Elevation 6,200 ft. Open all year.

Natural mineral water flows out of a city-owned spring at 169° and is piped to a cooling tank and then to the bathhouse. There are four private rooms, each containing a one-person bathtub. Cool and hot mineral water are mixed to provide the desired water temperature. Tubs are drained and refilled after each use, so no chemical treatment of the water is necessary. Clothing is optional in the private rooms.

Massage and reflexology are available on the premises. No credit cards are accepted. It is one block to a store, cafe and service station. Phone for rates, reservations and directions.

▲ *Jemez Springs Bathhouse*: The city of Jemez Springs now operates this bathhouse in order to carry on a long therapeutic tradition.

▲ *Bodhi Mandala Zen Center Motel and Hot Springs*: This is one of the few locations where it is possible to find a cold river dip, a natural hot spring soak and a comfortable motel room within a few steps.

 Ten Thousand Waves: Despite the amount of snow on the deck, it is not necessary to cut away ice on the water to soak in this pool.

The creative use of wood and greenery creates a degree of primitive atmosphere around the private-space pools at Ten Thousand Waves.

---

907   TEN THOUSAND WAVES

P.O. Box 6138   (505) 982-9304
☐   Santa Fe, NM 87502   PR

An intriguing blend of American technology and Japanese hot-tub traditions, located on Ski Basin Rd., northeast of Santa Fe.

Eight pools in private, roofless enclosures are for rent to the public. The pools use gas-heated well water treated with ultraviolet light and hydrogen peroxide and maintained at 104-106°. A sauna is available in two of the enclosures. One enclosed communal wood tub is large enough for 14 people. Bathing suits are optional everywhere, except at the front desk.

Kimonos, sandals, shampoo and hair dryers are provided. Private lockers are available in the men's and women's dressing rooms. Massage, rolfing, herbal wraps, yoga, facials and a juice bar are available on the premises. Visa and MasterCard are accepted. Phone for rates, reservations and directions.

---

908   MONTEZUMA HOT SPRINGS

● **Northwest of the town of Las Vegas (NM)**

The once-abandoned ruins of a major turn-of-the-century hot-springs resort bathhouse. The indoor and outdoor soaking pools have been cleaned up with public cooperation and are open to the public without charge. Located at the mouth of a mountain canyon, just below the main buildings occupied by United World College, a project of the Armand Hammer Foundation. Elevation 7,700 ft. Open all year.

Natural mineral water flows out of several springs (94-113°) into nine old-fashioned, cement soaking pits (four outdoor, five in a bathhouse), resulting in a wide range of temperature choices. Continuous flow-through eliminates the need for chemical treatment of the water. Bathing suits are required.

There are no services available on the premises. It is six miles to a store, cafe, service station, etc.

Directions: From the town of Las Vegas, go six miles northwest on NM 65. The hot-spring area is on the right side of the road, below the group of large college buildings.

909   SPLASH

9800 Montgomery N.E., Ste. S   (505) 293-3008
☐   Albuquerque, NM 87111   PR

Modern, suburban rent-a-tub facility located in a commercial corner building north of downtown Albuquerque.

Private-space hot pools using gas-heated tap water treated with bromine are for rent to the public. There are fifteen indoor acrylic hydropools with water temperature maintained at 103-105°. Each room also contains a shower and private dressing area. Children under 12 are free when accompanied by parents.

Massage is available by appointment. Visa and MasterCard are accepted. Phone for rates, reservations and directions.

 Splash: The design of modern rent-a-tub establishments incorporates a large amount of tile because it is so easy to keep clean.

THE SPRINGS OF TRUTH OR CONSEQUENCES

There are eight natural mineral water establishments located in the hot springs area of Truth or Consequences (see adjoining map). Take either of two exits from I-25. The city is on the Rio Grande River below Elephant Butte Dam. Elevation 4,300 ft. Open all year. A cafe, store, service station, and RV hookups are within four blocks of every location.

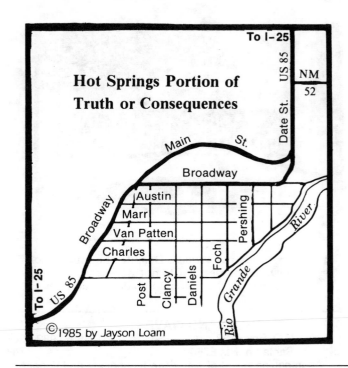

Hot Springs Portion of Truth or Consequences

©1985 by Jayson Loam

910A   ARTESIAN BATH HOUSE AND TRAILER PARK
■   312 Marr   (505) 894-2684
Truth or Consequences, NM 87901   PR+CRV
Older bathhouse and trailer park.
Nine private rooms, each containing a massage table and soaking pool. Six are single-size and three are double-size pools. Water temperature is controllable up to 110˚.
RV hookups are available on the premises. No credit cards are accepted.

910B   BLACKSTONE APARTMENT & BATH HOUSE
■   508 Austin   (505) 894-6303
Truth or Consequences, NM 87901   PR+MH
Older bathhouse and motel units converted to apartments, now rented by the week or month.
Four private rooms, each containing a sunken tub and massage table. Water temperature in tubs is controllable up to 110˚.
Massage and sweat wrap are available on the premises. No credit cards are accepted.

910C   CHARLES MOTEL AND BATH HOUSE
■   701 Broadway   (505) 894-7154
Truth or Consequences, NM 87901   PR+MH
Older bathhouse and motel with some new units.
Separate indoor men's and women's sections, each equipped with a sauna, steambath and four individual tubs with controllable water temperature up to 110˚.
Massage is available on the premises. Visa and MasterCard are accepted.

910D   DAVE'S CLOVERLEAF BATHS
■   207 S. Daniels   (505)894-6303
Truth or Consequences, NM 87901   PR
Primarily a therapy and health facility owned and operated by a physical therapist and naturopathic doctor.
Six private rooms, each containing a sunken pool and massage table. Temperature of pool controllable up to 108˚.
Massage, acupressure, reflexology, diathermy and corrective physical therapy are available on the premises. No credit cards are accepted.

910E   MARSHALL APARTMENTS AND BATHS
■   213 S. Pershing   (505) 894-3343
Truth or Consequences, NM 87901   PR+MH
Older bathhouse and motel units converted to apartments, now rented by the week or month.
Four private rooms with large pools, each with a gravel bottom and direct flow-through of unchlorinated hot mineral water. Temperatures range from 106-112˚.
Massage available on the premises. No credit cards are accepted.

910F   ROYCE BATHS
■   720 Broadway   (505) 894-3619
Truth or Consequences, NM 87901   PR+MH
Therapy-oriented bathhouse.
Three private rooms, each equipped with a sunken tub and massage table. Water temperature is controllable up to 110˚.
Massage and reflexology therapy are available on the premises, conducted by two doctors of naturopathy. Visa and MasterCard are accepted.

910G   OLE WEST LODGINGS
■   409 Broadway   (no phone)
Truth or Consequences, NM 87901   PR+MH
Older motel with bathhouse.
Three private rooms, each containing a sunken tub and massage table. Water temperature is controllable up to 110˚.
No credit cards are accepted.

910H   YUCCA GARDEN BATH HOUSE
■   316 Austin   (505) 894-3779
Truth or Consequences, NM 87901   PR
Historic bathhouse.
Two private rooms, each containing a large soaking pool in which temperatures are maintained between 105-108˚.
Massage and sweat wraps are available on the premises. No credit cards are accepted.

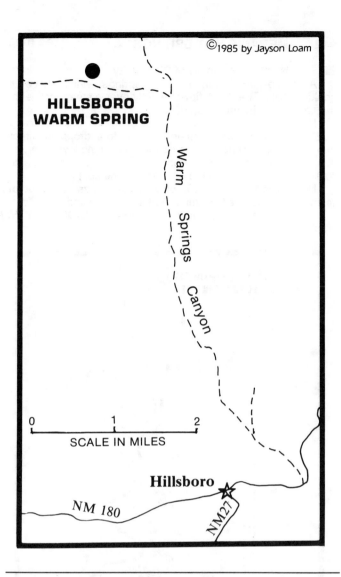

HILLSBORO
WARM SPRING

Warm Springs Canyon

0   1   2
SCALE IN MILES

Hillsboro

NM 180   NM 27

911   HILLSBORO WARM SPRING   (see map)

●   **North of the town of Hillsboro**

Primarily a cattle-watering tank frequently used by humans for soaking. Elevation 5,800 ft. Open all year. (Note: The BLM access road is open to the public. There are two closed but unlocked cattle gates which must be carefully reclosed after you drive through.)

Natural mineral water flows out of the ground at 94° directly into a ten-foot by fifteen-foot by four-foot deep concrete reservoir where the water temperature is approximately 88°. The reservoir is fenced to keep cattle from falling in, but there are plenty of cow pies and flies under the nearby cottonwood trees. The remote location indicates the probability of a clothing-optional custom, but that should be checked with anyone present when you arrive.

There are no services available, and it is four miles to a store, cafe, service station, etc. There is abundant level space on which overnight parking is not prohibited.

Source map: USGS *Hillsboro* (Note: The spring is marked "tank.")

Hillsboro Warm Spring: Fences do not always indicate private property. The rancher who leases this land from the BLM has the right to build fences to control his stock <u>and</u> the public also has access to this spring.

912   MELANIE HOT SPRINGS   (see map)

● **North of the town of Silver City**

A group of wilderness hot springs which have no soakingpools. The water flows directly over a steep incline into the Gila River. Elevation 5,200 ft.

Natural mineral water flows out of many rock fissures at 102° and runs across a steep slope before dropping directly into the river. Springs are accessible only during low water, and it is necessary to ford the river several times on unmaintained trails before climbing up the bank to find the springs.

Note: It is necessary to obtain a wilderness permit before taking the 1 1/2 mile trail out of Forks Campground.

Source maps: *Gila National Forest.* USGS *Gila Hot Springs.*

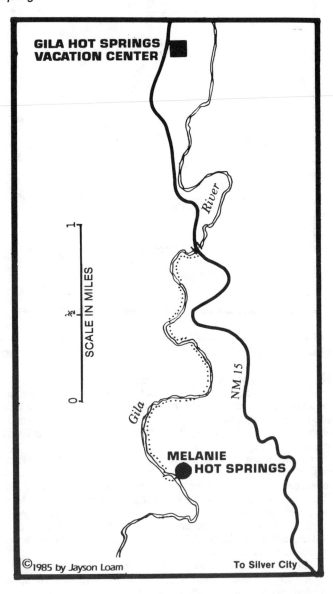

Melanie Hot Springs: The hike to and from this location would be a nice one-day trip with picnic lunch, if only a volunteer would build a nice soaking pool at the springs.

Gila Hot Springs Vacation Center: For those city dwellers who prefer all baths to be spic-and-span private, even in a wilderness area, this fully-fenced mineral water soaking pool will seem just like being back in town.

913   GILA HOT SPRINGS VACATION CENTER
(see map)

Gila Hot Springs, Rte. 11   (505) 534-9551
Silver City, NM 88061   MH+CRV

An all-year vacation resort located in the middle of the Gila National Forest. Elevation 5,000 ft. Open all year.

Natural mineral water flows out of springs on the east bank of the Gila River at 150° and is piped under the river to the Vacation Center, where it is used in an enclosed fiberglass hydropool available only to registered guests. Pool water temperature is maintained at 90° in the summer and 100° in the winter. Clothing is optional within the pool enclosure.

Store, snack bar, cabins, RV hookups, laundromat, showers, trailer rental, service station, campground and picnic area are available on the premises. No credit cards are accepted.

914A LIGHTFEATHER HOT SPRING (see map)

● **North of the Gila Visitors Center**

A primitive, rock-and-sand soaking pool on the Middle Fork of the Gila River, one-half mile from the Gila Visitors Center. Elevation 5,800 ft. Open all year, subject to high water in the river, which must be forded twice.

Natural mineral water flows out of the spring at 150° directly into a large rock-and-sand pool where the water gradually cools as it flows to the other end. Bathing suits are probably advisable during the daytime at this location.

There are no services available. It is four miles to a store, cafe, service station and RV hookups.

914B THE MEADOWS HOT SPRING (see map)

■ **Near the Gila Visitors Center**

A remote unimproved hot spring on a tree- and fern-covered hillside in the Gila Wilderness, on the Middle Fork on the Gila River. Elevation 6,200 ft. Accessible only during low water level in the river.

Natural mineral water flows out of a spring at 92° and cascades directly into a log- and rock-dammed pool large enough to hold ten people. The apparent local custom is clothing optional.

There are no services available. The nine-mile hike from Lightfeather Hot Spring requires fording the river 42 times, so come prepared to camp overnight. All services are south of Lightfeather Hot Spring.

Note: A wilderness permit is required before entering this area. While obtaining your permit from the ranger at the Gila Visitors Center, check on the adequacy of your provisions and on the level of the water in the river.

Source maps: Gila National Forest. USGS *Woodland Park*. (Note: This hot spring is not shown on either map.)

▲ *Lightfeather Hot Spring*: 150° water flowing out of the source spring in the foreground tends to stay near the surface as it spreads out. Therefore, it is occasionally necessary to stir up the cooler water to avoid being scalded by that hot surface layer.

3-27-96 THE POOL I OBSERVED DID NOT LOOK LIKE THIS. SMALL INDIVIDUAL POOL WITH SCUM LINED BOTTOMS. EASY HIKE ALONG THE RIVER, THE POOL ARE NOT WORTH THE WALK.

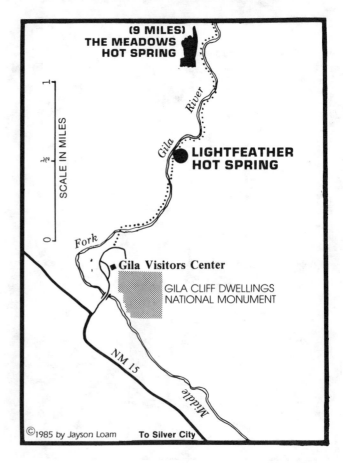

(9 MILES)
THE MEADOWS
HOT SPRING

Gila River

SCALE IN MILES

LIGHTFEATHER
HOT SPRING

Fork

Gila Visitors Center

GILA CLIFF DWELLINGS
NATIONAL MONUMENT

NM 15

Middle

©1985 by Jayson Loam   To Silver City

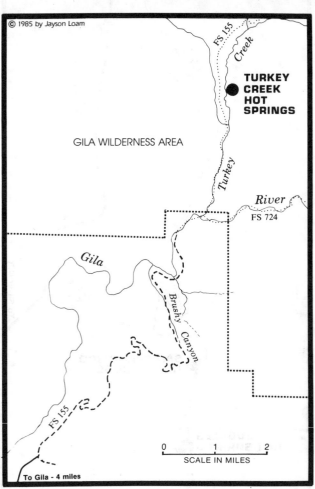

Turkey Creek Hot Springs: Experienced soakers can fine tune the water temperature in each pool by moving just a few of the rocks.

915   TURKEY CREEK HOT SPRINGS   (see map)

● **North of the town of Gila**

Several truly primitive hot springs accessible only via a challenging and rewarding hike into the Gila Wilderness. Elevation 5,200 ft. Not accessible during high water flow in the Gila River.

Natural mineral water (approximately 160°) flows out of many rock fractures along the bottom of Turkey Creek Canyon and combines with creek water in several volunteer-built soaking pools. Temperatures are regulated by controlling the relative amounts of hot and cold water entering a pool. The apparent local custom is clothing optional.

There are no services available, but there are a limited number of overnight camping spots near the hot springs. Visitors have done an excellent job of packing out all their trash; please do your part to maintain this tradition. All services are 17 miles away.

Directions: From the end of the jeep road, Wilderness Trail FS 724 crosses the Gila River several times before reaching a junction with Wilderness Trail FS 155, which starts up Turkey Creek Canyon. Approximately two miles from that junction, FS 155 begins to climb up onto a ridge separating Turkey Creek from Skeleton Canyon. Do not follow FS 155 up onto that ridge. Instead, stay in the bottom of Turkey Creek Canyon, even though there is often no visible trail. Another half-mile will bring you to the first of the springs.

Source maps: *Gila National Forest. Gila Wilderness* and *Black Range Primitive Area.* USGS *Canyon Hill.* (Note: Turkey Creek Hot Springs does not appear on any of these maps.)

916A   SAN FRANCISCO HOT SPRINGS   (see map)

● **South of the town of Pleasanton**

Several primitive hot springs along the east bank of the San Francisco River in the Gila National Forest. Elevation 4,600 ft. Open all year.

Natural mineral water flows out of the ground at 108° and flows into a series of volunteer-built, rock-and-mud pools on the riverbank. The parking area for this popular hot-spring site is only ten yards away, but the apparent local custom is clothing optional in the pools and adjoining river.

There are no services available, and overnight parking and camping are prohibited. It is five miles to a store, cafe, service station, etc., seven miles to a campground, and 52 miles to RV hookups.

Directions: Watch for San Francisco Hot Spring signs on US 180, two miles south of Pleasanton. Turn off onto gravel road leading to parking area.

916B   BUBBLES HOT SPRINGS   (see map)

● **South of the town of Pleasanton**

One of the truly great unimproved hot springs in terms of size, water temperature, location and scenery. Elevation 4,600 ft. Open all year, except during high water in the river.

Several years ago a major flood scoured out a 50- by 100-foot pool under a spectacular cliff, deposited a giant sand bar in front of the pool, and dropped the normal river flow into a channel 100 yards away. Natural mineral water now flows up through the sandy pool bottom at 106°, maintaining the entire five-foot-deep pool at 102°. The pool even skims and cleans itself by flowing out over a small volunteer-built dam. The apparent local custom is clothing optional.

There are no services available. See listing for San Francisco Hot Springs for the distance to services.

Directions: From the parking area at San Francisco Hot Springs, hike downstream approximately 1/2 mile, crossing the river three times.

Source map: USGS *Wilson Mountain.*

▲   *San Francisco Hot Springs*: These shallow pools are washed away every year when heavy run-off changes the banks of the Gila River.

3/11/99   Driving north on US180 to Pleasanton. Didn't see the San Francisco Hot springs sign. Apparently it has been removed.

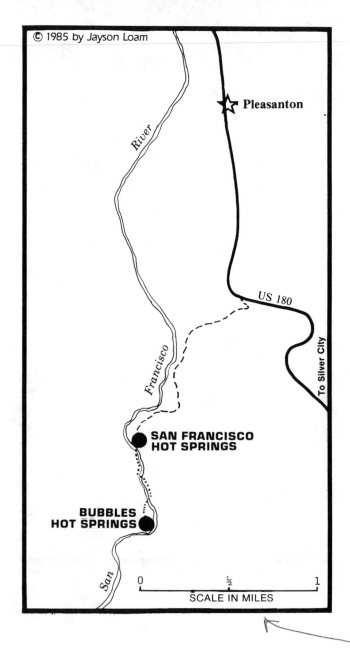

© 1985 by Jayson Loam

SCALE IN MILES

▼ *Bubbles Hot Springs*: The pool skims itself as the water flows over a rock dam to join the river channel on the far side of the canyon.

▲ *Bubbles Hot Springs*: This entire corner under a high cliff was scoured out by the Gila River during a record-setting flood season.

917   FRISCO BOX HOT SPRING

● **East of the town of Luna**

Shallow, concrete soaking pool in a scenic canyon at the end of a rough road and a rugged but beautiful 1 1/2 mile trail. Elevation 6,800 st. Open all year.

Natural mineral water flows out of a spring at 100° and is piped to a 4-foot by 8-foot by 20-inch deep concrete box. The apparent local custom is clothing optional.

There are no services available on the premises. There is a walkin camping area just north across the river from the hot spring. Overnight parking is permitted on level land just east of the private property gate. It is ten miles to groceries and gasoline, and 20 miles to all other services.

Directions: Start at the Luna Ranger Station to obtain current information on weather conditions, river level and a Gila National Forest Map. From US 180 in Luna drive north on FS 19 (signed *Bill Knight Gap Road*) and turn east on FS 210 (signed *Frisco Box Road*) to a private-property gate. Pass through the gate, carefully closing it after you, and continue east   until road becomes impassable. Park and hike an additional 1 1/2 miles east, fording the river six times. On the south bank look for a pipe and sign *Frisco Box Spring.* Follow a well worn, slightly uphill path 75 yards to the concrete box. Enjoy the spectacular view of the river and surrounding mountains.

Nov. 22, 1992   No Nude bathing at either hot springs. This area is patrolled by a county sheriff who will give you a ticket. I was lucky, I didn't get one because I was at Bubbles Hot springs - very nice, which is away from the parking area.   oops ← wrong page!

267

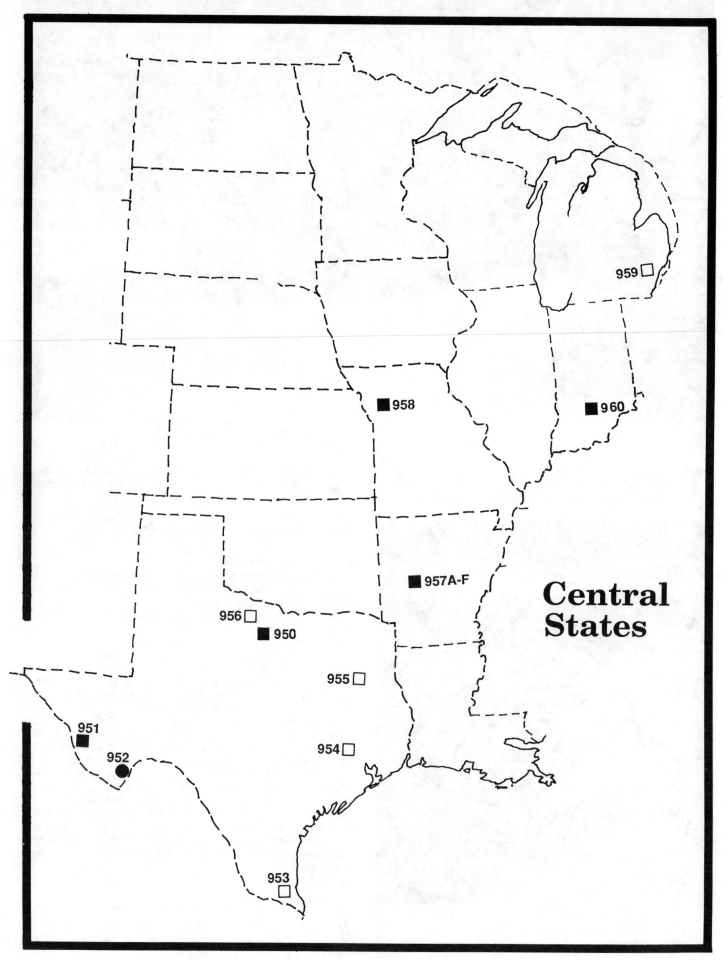

Central States

959 □

958 ■

960 ■

957A-F ■

956 □   950 ■

955 □

951 ■

952 ●

954 □

953 □

Kingston Hot Springs: At this location you can be sure of avoiding the kind of crowds found in typical vacation resort towns.

950   STOVALL HOT WELLS

PO Box 68   (817) 362-4423
South Bend, TX 76081   PR+MH+CRV

A healing-oriented residential resort in northern Texas which combines mineral water therapy with energy balancing and other therapies. Elevation 500 ft. Open all year.

Natural mineral water flows out of a well at 130º and is piped to separate men's and women's bathhouses, each containing two large bathing pools. Pool water temperatures are maintained at 101º on a continuous flow-through basis so no chemical treatment of the water is necessary. Bathing suits are not required in bathhouses. Day-use customers are welcome.

Facilities include guest rooms, cabins and spaces for campers and RV's. Reflexology, acupressure, mineral-water therapy, massage and energy-balancing are available on the premises. No credit cards are accepted. It is 12 miles to a store, restaurant, service station and other services.

Phone for rates, reservations and directions.

951   KINGSTON HOT SPRINGS

Box 22, Ruidosa Route   (915) 229-3416
Marfa, TX 79843   PR+MH+CRV

Older, commercial resort in a verdant canyon surrounded by miles of barren, rugged desert. Elevation 3,600 ft. Open all year.

Natural mineral water flows out of a spring at 118˚ and is piped to individual soaking tubs in four small, private rooms. Water temperature is adjusted by adding cold or hot water as desired. Tubs are drained and refilled after each use, so no chemical treatment of the water is needed.

Motel rooms and overnight camping are available on the premises. It is 15 miles to a service station and 45 miles to a restaurant and RV hookups.

Directions: From the town of Presidio, go 40 miles northwest on TX 170 to Ruidosa. Follow signs seven miles to Kingston Hot Springs.

269

▲ *Boquillas (Langford) Hot Spring:* The 105°
mineral water flowing into this soaking pool
does not need to be mixed with river water.

Cool, but not frigid, Rio Grand River water is a nice change of pace in between dips in the *Boquillas Hot Spring* soaking pool.

952   BOQUILLAS (LANGFORD) HOT SPRING

● **Near the town of Lajitas, Texas**

Historic masonry hot pool in the ruins of an old resort on the banks of the Rio Grande River. Located near the Rio Grande Village Campground in Big Bend National Park. Elevation 1,800 ft. Open all year.

Natural mineral water flows out of the ground at 105° into a large, shallow soaking pool a few feet above river level. Bathing suits are advisable in the daytime.

There are no services on the premises. It is six miles to a store, service station, overnight camping and RV hookups, 28 miles to a motel and restaurant.

Directions: From Big Bend National Park Headquarters, drive 16 miles toward Rio Grand Village Campground. Turn right at Hot Springs sign, then drive two miles on dirt road to the end and walk 1/4 mile downriver to hot spring.

Source map: *Big Bend National Park.*

953   SANDPIPERS HOLIDAY PARK

☐   Rte. 7, Box 309   (512) 383-7589
      Edinburg, TX 78539   PR+MH+CRV

North America's southernmost nudist park located on 21 acres, seven miles north of McAllen and 20 miles north of Mexico. Elevation 100 ft. Open all year.

The outdoor hydrojet spa is filled with gas-heated well water, treated with chlorine, and maintained at 103°. The outdoor Olympic-size swimming pool is filled with unheated well water in the summer and is gas-heated in the winter to maintain 75°. Clothing is prohibited in the spa and pool, optional elsewhere.

Facilities include rental units, tenting spaces, RV hook-ups, clubhouse, volleyball and shuffleboard courts. Meals are served on weekends. Visa and MasterCard are accepted. It is one mile to all other services.

Note: This is a membership organization not open to the public for drop-in visits, but prospective members and guests may be issued a guest pass by prior arrangement. Telephone or write for information.

954   LIVE OAK RESORT, INC.

☐   Rt. 1, Box 916   (409) 878-2216
      Washington, TX 77880   PR+MH+CRV

A well-maintained, family nudist park with 17 acres of mowed lawn, interspersed with shade-providing oak trees, nestled in rolling farm country near Houston. Elevation 525 ft. Open all year.

Gas-heated well water, chlorine-treated, is used in an outdoor hydropool maintained at 104°. The Olympic-size swimming pool using similar water is unheated but averages over 80° between June and September. Clothing is optional on the first visit, except in the pools, where it is prohibited at all times.

Cabins, a full-service restaurant, camping and RV hookups are available on the premises. Other facilities include a lighted, sand volleyball court and a clubhouse with pool table and ping pong. A children's playground with a waterslide is also available. It is four miles to a store and service station. No credit cards are accepted.

Note: This is a membership organization not open to the public for drop-in visits, but a guest pass may be issued by prior arrangement. Resort rules prohibit guns, drugs and erotic behavior. Phone for more information and directions.

955   PONDAROSA RANCH

☐   P.O. Box 133   (214) 873-3311
      Wills Point, TX 75169   PR+MH+CRV

Modern, residential nature park and health resort on 60 rolling acres, 55 miles east of Dallas. Elevation 2,000 ft. Open all year.

The outdoor hydrospa is filled with gas-heated well and tap water, treated with chlorine, and is maintained at 102°. The outdoor swimming pool is filled with unheated well and tap water and treated with chlorine. Clothing is prohibited in the spa, pool and sauna; optional elsewhere.

Other facilities include rental trailers, RV hook-ups, tenting spaces, a clubhouse, and volleyball, horseshoe and shuffleboard courts, plus a full service restaurant during the summer season. Visa and MasterCard are accepted. It is eight miles to all other services.

Note: This is a membership organization, but it is open to the public for drop-in visits. No reservations are required except for the rental trailers. Telephone or write for further information.

956   BLUEBONNET

☐   Rt. 1, Box 146   (817) 627-2313
      Alvord, TX 76225   PR+MH+CRV

Modern nudist resort on 66 acres of rolling hills, four miles north of Decatur in northern Texas. Elevation 500 ft. Open all year.

The indoor whirlpool spa is filled with gas-heated well water, treated with chlorine, and maintained at 103°. The indoor swimming pool is filled with gas-heated well water, treated with chlorine, and maintained at 80°. Clothing is prohibited in spa, pool and sauna; optional elsewhere.

Facilities include cabins, trailers, tenting spaces, RV hook-ups, tenting spaces, clubhouse, sauna, and volleyball, tennis and shuffleboard courts. Visa, MasterCard and American Express are accepted. It is four miles to all other services.

Note: This is a membership organization not open to the public for drop-in visits, but interested visitors may be issued a guest pass by prior arrangement. Telephone or write for information and directions.

The opportunity to "soak in peace" has drawn humankind to this Hot Spring Mountain for thousands of years. Hernando De Soto may or may not have been the first European on the scene, but today's Hot Springs National Park, and the surrounding community, have their roots in the 1803 Louisiana Purchase. President Thomas Jefferson sent an expedition to explore the springs in 1804, the resultant publicity greatly increased their usage, and also escalated the controversy over their ownership.

In 1832 Congress took the unprecedented step of establishing public ownership by setting aside four sections of land as a reservation. Unfortunately, no one adequately identified the exact boundaries of this reservation, so the mid 19th century was filled with conflicting claims and counterclaims to the springs and surrounding land.

By 1870 a system evolved that reserved the springs for the Federal Government and sold the developed land to the persons who had settled it. At the same time the government agreed to collect the 143º geothermal spring water into a central distribution system which carried it to private property establishments where baths were offered to the public. By 1877 all primitive soaking "pits" along Hot Springs Creek were eliminated when the creek was confined to a concrete channel, roofed over, and then paved to create what is now Central Avenue.

In 1921 the Federal Reservation became Hot Springs National Park, custodian of all the springs, and the exclusive contractual supplier of hot mineral water to those elaborate establishments which had become the famous Bathhouse Row. It is also the authority which approves every establishment's rates, equipment, personnel and services related to that water.

Until 1949 each bathhouse needed to have its own evaporation tower in order to cool the incoming hot mineral water to a tolerable temperature for human use. In that year the Park Service installed air-cooled radiators and tap-water-cooled heat exchangers to supply a new central "cool" mineral water reservoir. Now all thermal water customers receive their supply from the National Park through two pipes, "hot" at 143º and "cool" at 90º.

During the last four decades declining patronage has forced the closure of most of those historic temples for "taking the waters." However, resort hotels, motels and therapy centers in downtown Hot Springs have responded to increasing demands for thermal soaking, and some of the historic Bathhouse Row locations are being refurbished and reopened. For additional information write to the Hot Springs Chamber of Commerce, P.O. Box 1500, Hot Springs, AR 71902

Two of the hot springs in the Park have been left uncovered, for visitor observation only. There is a campground for tents and trailers, but it does not have electrical or water connections.

The BUCKSTAFF BATHHOUSE and the LIBBEY MEMORIAL PHYSICAL MEDICAL CENTER AND HOT SPRINGS HEALTH SPA are National Park Service concessioners located in the Park. All of the other locations described below operate in the city adjacent to the Park, under National Park regulations as a condition for receiving thermal water through the Park's distribution system. Each establishment has its own phone number for information, rates and reservations.

957A   BUCKSTAFF BATHS

■   (501) 623-2308
One of the historic Bathhouse Row establishments in continuous operation since 1912, located at the south end of the Row near the Visitor Center.

Separate men's and women's sections offer one-person soaking tubs which are individually temperature-controlled. They are drained and refilled after each use so no chemical treatment of the water is needed. Whirlpool baths and massage are available.

Facilities include a third-floor coed lounge with separate men's and women's sun decks at each end. No credit cards are accepted.

▲ *Hot Springs Health Spa*: These upstairs pools are designed for family recreation, separate from the physical therapy pools downstairs.

957B LIBBEY MEMORIAL (501) 321-1997
PHYSICAL MEDICINE CENTER AND
■ HOT SPRINGS HEALTH SPA

Downstairs, a modern, "Medicare-Approved, Federally Regulated" therapy facility and, upstairs, a modern spa with coed soaking tubs, located on Reserve Avenue, three blocks east of Central Avenue.

The Libbey Memorial coed thermal whirlpool (105°) and coed exercise pool (98°) are drained and refilled each day, so no chemical treatment of the water is necessary. Facilities include steam and vapor cabinets and electric hoists at therapy pools. Hot packs, massage and prescribed treatments such as Paraffin Immersion, Ultra Sound Therapy, and Electric Stimulation are also available. No credit cards are accepted.

The Health Spa's eight large coed soaking tubs are individually temperature-controlled as desired between 102° and 108°. All of them are drained and filled each day so that no chemical treatment of the water is necessary. Children are welcome. Massage, steam and vapor cabinets, sunbeds and exercise equipment are available. No credit cards are accepted.

 This alert organization is responding to public demand for both therapeutic use, and recreational use of mineral water by creating the *Libbey Memorial Physical Medicine Center and Hot Springs Health Spa.*

▲ The upper floor *Hot Springs Health Spa* offers a variety of soaking pool sizes and shapes.

 Arlington Resort Hotel & Spa: This historic hot springs resort has responded to public demand by adding this large communal pool.

957C ARLINGTON RESORT HOTEL & SPA

■   **1 (800) 643-1502**
                        Arkansas (501) 623-7771

A magnificent, luxurious resort in a dominant location overlooking Central Avenue and Bathhouse Row.

The in-hotel bathhouse with separate men's and women's sections is open to the public. Private soaking tubs are individually temperature-controlled and drained after each use so that no chemical treatment of the water is necessary. Massage, hot packs, saunas, sitz-baths and needle showers are available.

A hot-spring, mineral-water, redwood hot tub, two tap water swimming pools treated with chlorine, and a multi-level sundeck are reserved for registered guests. The hot tub is maintained at 104°, and the twin pools are maintained at 80° year round.

Facilities include several restaurants and lounges, beauty salon, exercise room, ballroom, conference and exhibit centers, VIP Club and shopping mall. Visa, MasterCard, American Express, Diners Club and Discover are accepted.

957D DOWNTOWNER MOTOR INN AND BATHS

■   **(501) 624-5521**

A modern motor lodge with a large second-floor bathhouse, located on Central Avenue north of Bathhouse Row.

A bathhouse with separate men's and women's sections is open to the public. One-person soaking tubs are individually temperature-controlled and drained after each use so that no chemical treatment of the water is necessary. Whirlpool baths, vapor treatments and massage are available.

An outdoor swimming pool filled with chlorine-treated tap water, is reserved for the use of registered guests.

Facilities include a beauty salon, sun decks and a restaurant. Visa, MasterCard, American Express and Diners Club are accepted.

 Hot Springs Hilton: This indoor-outdoor swimming pool is convenient in bad weather.

957E HOT SPRINGS HILTON

■   **1 (800) HILTONS**
                        Arkansas (501) 623-6600

Large, modern, resort hotel located next to the Hot Springs Convention Center, two blocks south of Bathhouse Row.

A bathhouse with separate men's and women's sections is open to the public. One-person soaking tubs are individually temperature-controlled and drained after each use so that no chemical treatment of the water is necessary. Massage is available.

An indoor whirlpool (108°) and an indoor-outdoor swimming pool filled with chlorine-treated tap water are reserved for the use of registered guests.

Facilities include restaurants, lounge, meeting rooms and banquet facilities. Visa, MasterCard, American Express, Diners Club and Discover are accepted.

957F MAJESTIC RESORT/SPA

■   **1 (800) 643-1504**
                        Arkansas (501) 623-5511

A unique combination of hotel, motel and health spa facilities located at the north end of Central Avenue.

A bathhouse with separate men's and women's sections is open to the public. Individual soaking tubs are temperature-controlled and drained after each use so that no chemical treatment of the water is necessary. Massage and nutritional counseling are available.

An outdoor swimming pool filled with chlorine-treated tap water and heated in the winter is reserved for the use of registered guests.

Facilities include deluxe rooms and tower suites, beauty salon, restaurant and lounge, dress shops, conference and banquet rooms. Visa, MasterCard, American Express and Discover are accepted.

958A EXCELSIOR SPRINGS MINERAL WATER SPA

Hall Of Waters (816) 637-0753
■ **Excelsior Springs, MO 64024** **PR**

A large, historic building originally constructed for health-oriented activities is now owned and operated on a limited scale by the city. Elevation 900 ft. Open weekdays only.

Cold (54˚) natural mineral water is pumped from wells (which used to be flowing springs) and piped to a bathhouse where it is gas-heated and used in four individual, private-space tubs. After each use they are drained and refilled so that no chemical treatment of the water is necessary. The bathhouse is for men only in the morning and women only in the afternoon. Steambaths and massage are available on the premises. The indoor swimming pool, using gas-heated, chlorine-treated tap water is maintained at approximately 75˚ and open only in the summer. Bathing suits are required in this coed pool.

Facilities include dressing rooms and a water bar, where mineral water is sold by the gallon. Visa and MasterCard are accepted. Phone for rates, reservations and directions.

958B THE ELMS RESORT HOTEL

Regent and Elms Blvd. (816) 637-2141
■ **Excelsior Springs, MO 64024** **PR+MH**

An historic luxury resort on 23 wooded acres, a half-hour northeast of Kansas City. Elevation 900 ft. Open all year.

Cold (54˚) natural mineral water is pumped from wells on the property and piped to the elaborate New Leaf Spa, where it is gas-heated to 100˚. In separate men's and women's sections there are individual soaking tubs which are drained and filled after each use so no chemical treatment of the water is necessary. There are also ten theme rooms, each containing environmental effects and a two-person soaking tub, using tap water, which is drained and filled after each use.

Chlorine-treated tap water is used in all other pools. The indoor European Swimming Track is maintained at 75˚, the three large, outdoor hot tub pools are maintained at 100˚, and the outdoor swimming pool is maintained at 75˚. The five large group hot tubs, including a waterfall hot tub, are maintained at 100˚. Bathing suits are required in these public-area coed pools. The New Leaf Spa is open to the public as well as to registered guests.

New Leaf Spa services include steambaths, jogging track, saunas, beauty shop, exercise room, herbal wrap and massage. Other facilities include rooms, suites, condos, restaurant, golf course and various sports courts. Visa, MasterCard, American Express and Diners Club are accepted. Phone for rates, reservations and directions.

959 WHISPERING OAKS

5864 Baldwin (313) 628-2676
❑ **Oxford, MI 48051** **PR+CRV**

A traditional nudist resort on 52 acres of beautiful rolling woodland with a private lake, 35 miles north of Detroit. Elevation 1,200 ft. Open from April to October.

The outdoor whirlpool spa is filled with propane-heated well water, treated with chlorine, and maintained at 105˚. The outdoor diving pool is filled with propane-heated well water, treated with chlorine, and maintained at 80˚. This is a nudist facility, so everyone is expected to be nude weather and health permitting.

Facilities include sauna, clubhouse, RV hook-ups, tenting spaces, and volleyball, tennis and shuffleboard courts. Visa and MasterCard are accepted. It is five miles to a service station, cafe and motel.

Note: This is a membership organization not open to the public for drop-in visits, but prospective members may be issued a guest pass by prior arrangement. Telephone or write for information and directions.

Elms Resort Hotel: Although mineral water is used only in the New Leaf Spa small tubs, there are many other hot water pools, including this one with its own waterfall.

960 FRENCH LICK SPRINGS RESORT

(812) 936-9300
■ **French Lick, IN 47432** **PR+MH**

The "Largest Most Complete Resort in the Midwest," located on 2600 wooded acres in southwest Indiana, 2 hours from Indianapolis. Elevation 600 ft. Open all year.

Natural mineral water flows from a spring at 50º and is piped to separate men's and women's bathhouses where it is heated by gas-generated steam, as needed, into one-person soaking tubs. Tubs are drained and filled after each use so no chemical treatment of the water is necessary. All other pools use steam-heated tap water treated with chlorine. The outdoor and indoor whirlpools are maintained at 104º, the dome pool ranges from 72º in the summer to 82º in the winter, and the Olympic swimming pool, for summer use only, is not heated. Bathing suits are required except in bathhouses.

Facilities include two 18-hole golf courses, indoor and outdoor tennis courts, equestrian stables and riding trails, guest rooms, nine restaurants and lounges, bowling alleys, conference center, exercise facility and beauty salon. Massage, body treatments, saunas, steambaths, reflexology, salt rubs, facials and manicures are available on the premises. Visa, MasterCard and American Express are accepted. It is three blocks to a service station, store and other services.

Phone for rates, reservations and directions.

275

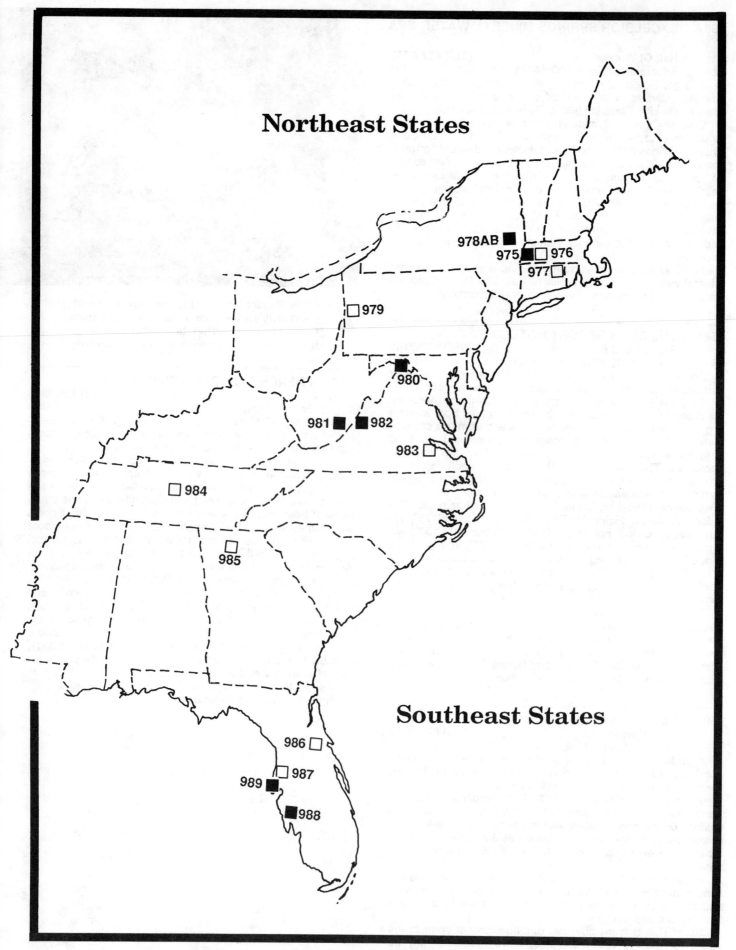

Northeast States

978AB

975 976

977

979

980

981 982

983

984

985

Southeast States

986

987

989

988

MAP AND DIRECTORY SYMBOLS

● Non-commercial mineral water pool

■ Commercial (fee) mineral water pool

□ Gas-heated tap or well water pool

〜〜〜 Paved highway

- - - - - Unpaved road

··∴···∴·· Hiking route

PR = Tubs or pools for rent by hour, day or treatment

MH = Rooms, cabins or dormitory spaces for rent by day, week or month

CRV = Camping or vehicle parking spaces, some with hookups,
for rent by day, week, month or year

975   SAND SPRINGS POOL

■ Sand Springs Road   (413) 458-5205
Williamstown, MA 01267   PR

An historic seasonal plunge located in the heart of the Berkshire Hills in northwestern Massachusetts. Elevation 900 ft. Open May to September.

Natural mineral water flows out of a spring at 74º and is piped to several pools where it is gas-heated and treated with chlorine. The whirlpool is maintained at a temperature of 102º. The swimming pool and toddler's pool are maintained at approximately 80º. Bathing suits are required.

Facilities include changing rooms, sundeck, exercise room, sauna, snack bar, dance floor, picnic tables and large lawn. A motel, service stations, restuarant and other services are available within 10 blocks. No credit cards are accepted.

Directions: From the Williamstown municipal building on US 7 drive north to Sand Springs Rd. Turn right and follow signs to pool.

 East Heaven Tub Co.: This establishment handles hot tub sales and service in addition to hourly rentals. Therefore, it offers different types and sizes of tubs for rent so that potential buyers can base their purchase decisions on direct personal experience.

976   EAST HEAVEN TUB CO.

33 West St.   (413) 586-6843
□ Northampton, MA 01060   PR

Beautiful, Japanese-motif rental facility located across from Smith College in the Connecticut Valley.

Private-space hot pools using gas-heated tap water treated with bromine are for rent to the public. There are four indoor tubs in private rooms and three outdoor tubs in private, roofless enclosures on the roof. All are maintained at a temperature of 104˚.

Sales of saunas, hot tubs and spas are conducted on the premises. No credit cards are accepted. Phone for rates, reservations and directions.

977   SOLAIR RECREATION LEAGUE

P.O. Box 187   (203) 928-9174
□ Southbridge, MA 01550   PR+MH+CRV

A family nudist campground with its own private lake, located on 350 hilly acres in northeast Connecticut. Elevation 600 ft. Open to visitors from April to November.

The hydrojet tub in the clubhouse uses gas-heated well water treated with bromine and is maintained at 104˚. Clothing is prohibited in the pool and beach area, optional elsewhere.

Facilities include hiking trails, a private lake for swimming and boating, a clubhouse with an electric sauna, a wood-fired sauna, a shower building, a large game room, dining hall, tennis and volleyball courts, horsehoe pits and children's playground. Rental cabins, RV hook-ups and tenting spaces are available on the premises. No credit cards are accepted. It is four miles to a store and service station.

Note: This is a membership organization not open to the public for drop-in visits, but interested visitors may be issued a guest pass by prior arrangement. Telephone or write for information and directions.

The Saratoga Springs area has a two-century-old tradition of providing natural beauty, health-giving geothermal water, and the gaiety of it's summer racetrack season. More than a dozen springs and hot wells discharge naturally-carbonated mineral water along the Saratoga Fault which is located in a low basin between Lake George and Albany.

In 1909, the State of New York created a Reservation Commission and acquired the land around Geyser Creek, which has now been designated as Saratoga Spa State Park. Some geothermal activities are still accessible for public viewing, such as the only spouting geyser east of the Mississippi.

Bathing in mineral water is available only at the Lincoln and Roosevelt bathhouses in the State Park, and at the Crystal Spa bathhouse, on South Broadway in the city of Saratoga Springs. All bathhouses have separate men's and women' sections using one-person tubs which are drained and filled after each use so that no chemical treatment of the water is necessary.

978A   ROOSEVELT BATHHOUSE
■   Saratoga Spa State Park   (518) 584-2011
     Saratoga Springs, NY 12866   PR

Large, traditional, state-owned bathhouse with nearby hotel and conference center operated by TW Services. Open all year.

Mineral water flows out of a spring at 52° and is piped to individual tubs in private rooms. Along the way it is heated to 99°, the maximum permitted in the state-owned bathhouse.

Hot packs and massage are also available on the premises.

Credit cards are not accepted. Phone for rates, reservations and directions.

978B   CRYSTAL SPA
■   92 S. Broadway   (518) 584-2556
     Saratoga Springs, NY 12866   PR

Newly constructed, privately-owned spa associated with the Grand Union Motel. Open all year.

Mineral water flows out of a spring at 52° and is piped to individual soaking tubs where it is mixed with 149° tap water as needed to obtain the desired soaking temperature.

Sauna and massage are also available on the premises. No credit cards are accepted. Phone for rates, reservations and directions.

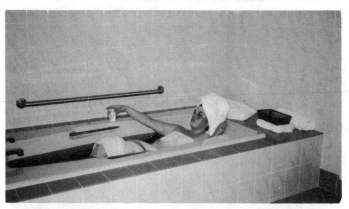

 Crystal Spa: In modern bathhouses, single-person tubs are acrylic trimmed in tile rather than claw-footed cast iron.

---

979   WHITE THORN LODGE
☐   RD #1, Box 242   (412) 846-5984
     Darlington, PA 16115   PR+MH+CRV

A 106-acre, member-owned nudist park located in western Pennsylvania near the Ohio state line, 50 miles from downtown Pittsburg. Elevation 1,000 ft. Open for visitors May through September.

The outdoor hot tub using electrically-heated well water treated with bromine is maintained at 105°. The swimming pool, using sun-heated well water treated with bromine, varies in temperature. Nudity is expected, weather permitting, everywhere on the grounds.

Facilities include hiking trails, rooms, RV hook-ups, camping spaces, clubhouse, sauna, weekend snackbar, tennis and volleyball courts, horseshoe pits, junior clubhouse and play area. No credit cards are accepted.

Note: This is a membership organization not open to the public for drop-in visits, but interested visitors may be issued a guest pass by prior arrangement. Telephone or write for information and directions.

▲ *Berkeley Springs State Park*: The mineral water at this location must be heated an extra 30° above ground temperature, but the Old Roman Bath House does have coed pools.

▼ Massage is one of the health services offered at this state-owned hot springs enterprise.

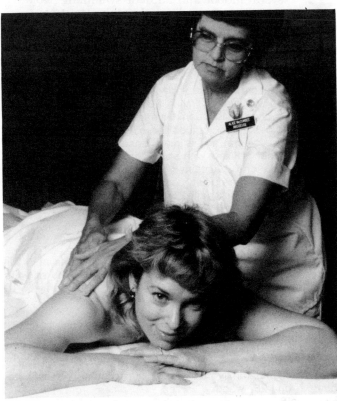

▲ *The Greenbrier* offers medical diagnostic services plus many recreation opportunities such as this elegant indoor pool.

980   BERKELEY SPRINGS STATE PARK
(304) 258-2711
■ Berkeley Springs, WV 25411   PR

Large, traditional bathhouse and plunge operated as a state park, located in a narrow valley in West Virginia's eastern panhandle. Elevation 620 ft. Open 362 days per year.

Two thousand gallons-per-minute of mineral water flow out of several springs at a temperature of 74.3°. A portion of this water is steam-heated to 102° and piped to private, one-person bathtubs in the main bathhouse and to private tiled baths in the Old Roman Bath House. All are drained and refilled after each use so that no chemical treatment of the water is necessary. The Old Roman Bath House is open weekends in May, daily from Memorial Day to Columbus Day, and weekends through October. Mineral spring water is also piped directly to the outdoor swimming pool which is treated with chlorine and is open from Memorial Day through Labor Day.

Facilities include steam cabinets and a health and fitness room. Massage, heat treatments and other health services are available on the premises. Visa and Mastercard are accepted. All other services are available in the adjoining town of Berkeley Springs. Phone for rates, reservations and directions.

981   THE GREENBRIER
(304) 536-1110
■ White Sulphur Springs, WV 24986   MH

A large, historic, health-oriented mineral spring resort occupying 6,500 acres in an upland valley of the Allegheny Mountains, near the Virginia border. Elevation 2,900 ft. Open all year.

Natural mineral water flows out of a sulphur spring at 58° and is piped to individual soaking tubs in separate men's and women's sections of the mineral-bath wing, where it is heated by electricity to the desired temperature. Tubs are drained and filled after each use, so no chemical treatment is needed. Water from a fresh-water spring is piped to an outdoor pool and the *Grand Indoor Pool*, where it is treated with chlorine and heated by steam to a temperature of 75°. Bathing suits are required.

Facilities include rooms and luxury suites, dining rooms and restaurants, a complete convention center, shops, service station, tennis courts, golf course, aerobics studio, exercise equipment, beauty salon and a complete diagnostic clinic. Services include fitness evaluations, massage, herbal wrap, facials, manicures and pedicures. The diagnostic clinic and shops are available to the public. All other facilities are for the use of registered guests only. Visa, MasterCard, American Express and Diners Club are accepted. Phone or write for rates, reservations and directions.

279

The Homestead: An abundance of hot mineral water enables this famous resort to offer several indoor and outdoor swimming pools in addition to traditional bathhouse tubs.

982   THE HOMESTEAD

Hot Springs, VA 24445   (703) 839-5500
     MH

A very large, very historic, luxurious resort on the west slope of the Alleghany Mountains near the West Virginia Border. Elevation 2,500 ft. Open all year.

The odorless mineral water used at the Homestead Spa flows from several springs at temperatures ranging from 102º to 106º. It is piped to individual, one-person bathtubs in separate men's and women's bathhouses, where it is mixed to provide an ideal temperature of 104º. Tubs are drained and refilled after each use so that no chemical treatment of the water is necessary. Mineral water from the same springs is used in an indoor swimming pool maintained at 84º and an outdoor swimmming pool maintained at 72º. Both pools receive a minimum of chlorine treatment. Use of the spa and all pools is restricted to registered guests only. Bathing suits are required except as indicated in the bathhouses.

Five miles away but still within the 15,000-acre Homestead property are the Warm Springs, which flow at 96º. The rate of discharge is so great that the two large Warms Springs pools, in separate men's and women's buildings, maintain a temperature of 96º on a flow-through basis requiring no chemical treatment of the water. These Warm Springs' pools are open only during the warm months and are open to the public. Bathing suits are optional.

The facilites include 600 bedrooms and parlors, restaurants, shops, conference center, bowling alley, movie theatre and tennis courts. Recreational activities available on the premises include golf, archery, fishing, hiking, riding, skeet and trap shooting and tennis, plus skiing and ice skating in the winter. There are many resort services available, some of which are included in the basic room rate. Phone or write for complete information. Visa, MasterCard and American Express are accepted.

983   WHITE TAIL PARK

P.O. Box 160   (804) 859-6123
Zuni, VA 23898   PR+MH+CRV

Large (47-acre), well-equipped family nudist park located in southeastern Virginia, 35 miles from I-95 and 45 miles from Norfolk. Elevation 39 ft. Open all year.

A large, indoor spa/hot tub filled with gas-heated well water, treated with bromine, and is maintained at 104˚. The outdoor swimming pool is filled with solar-heated well water, treated with Baquacil, and maintained in the low 80's from April to November. This is a nudist resort, so everyone is expected to be nude, weather and health permitting.

Facilities include nature trail, recreation hall, children's rec center, game courts, rooms, tenting spaces, RV hookups and seasonal snack bar. Visa and MasterCard are accepted. It is seven miles to all other services.

Note: This is a membership organization, but the park will accept drop-in, first-time visitors anytime. Telephone or write for information and directions.

984   ROCK HAVEN LODGE

P.O. Box 1291   (615) 896-3553
Murfreesboro, TN 37133   PR+MH+CRV

A traditional, family nudist park with a country atmosphere, located on 25 wooded acres, 40 miles from Nashville. Elevation 650 ft. Open for visitors April 1 to October 31.

One large, outdoor whirlpool spa using chlorine-treated well water is maintained at 103˚, and one outdoor unheated swimming pool using similar water averages over 70˚ in the summer. Clothing is prohibited in pools. This is a nudist park, not a clothing-optional resort, so members and guests are expected to be nude, weather permitting.

Facilities include rental cabins, RV hookups, camping area, clubhouse, volleyball, tennis and other sports courts. No credit cards are accepted. It is six miles to stores, restaurants and motels.

Note: This is a membership organization not open to the public for drop-in visits, but interested visitors may be issued a guest pass by prior arrangement. Telephone or write for information and directions.

985 HIDDEN VALLEY

Rt. 3, Box 3452
Dawsonville, GA 30534

(404) 476-8955
PR+MH+CRV

A secluded, heavily wooded nudist resort nestled in the scenic foothills of the North Georgia Mountains. Elevation 1,500 ft. Open mid-March through early December.

Gas-heated well water, treated with bromine and chlorine, is used in an enclosed outdoor hydropool which comfortably holds 12 and is maintained at 104°. A spacious cement-and-rock-lined pond, fed by a running mountain stream, maintains a temperature of 65°. Clothing is prohibited in both pools. This is a nudist club, not a clothing-optional resort, so nudity is generally expected everywhere, weather permitting.

Facilities include rental rooms and housekeeping units, RV spaces, camping area, seasonal snack bar, volleyball, tennis and shuffleboard courts. Visa and MasterCard are accepted. It is five miles to a store and restaurant.

This is a family-oriented club which accepts singles on a reservation basis only. Membership is not required to visit, and couples and families may visit without making reservations. Phone or write for further information and directions.

986 SUNNY SANDS RESORT

502 Central Blvd.
Pierson, FL 32080

(904) 749-2233
PR+MH+CRV

Fifty acres of rustic woods surrounding a private lake, located 20 miles north of Deland in Northeastern Florida. Elevation 20 ft. Open all year.

The outdoor hydrojet spa is filled with gas-heated well water, treated with bromine, and maintained at 103°. The swimming pool is filled with unheated well water, treated with chlorine, and varies in temperature with the seasons. Clothing is prohibited in the pools, and nudity is expected elsewhere, weather and health permitting.

Facilities include mobile-home rentals, RV hook-ups, tenting spaces, recreation hall, fishing, volleyball and shuffleboard courts, horseshoe pit and playground. No credit cards are accepted. It is 20 miles to Deland and all other services.

Note: This is a membership organization open for drop-in visits by couples or families. Telephone or write for more information and directions.

987 CITY RETREAT NUDIST PARK

13220 Houston Ave.
Hudson, FL 34667

(813) 868-1061
PR+MH+CRV

Forty acres of tree-shaded nudist tranquility in a grassy-sandy country setting, 45 miles north of Tampa. Elevation 30 ft. Open all year.

The outdoor hydrospa is filled with gas-heated well water treated with chlorine, and maintained at 101°. The outdoor pool is filled with unheated well water (pending the installation of a solar-heating system) and is treated with chlorine. Clothing is prohibited in the pool and spa area. This is a nudist club, not a clothing-optional resort.

Facilities include a club house, rooms, tenting spaces, RV hook-ups, snack bar, tennis court horseshoe pits, and shuffleboard courts. Visa and MasterCard are accepted. It is five miles to a shopping center.

Note: This is a membership club; however, those with a sincere interest in nudism are welcome for daily visits. Please call or write first for a brochure and further information.

988 RESORT AND SPA AT WARM MINERAL SPRINGS

San Servando Ave.
Warm Mineral Springs, FL 34287

(813) 426-9581
PR+MH

Modern spa, health studio and nearby apartment complex, with a nine-million-gallons-per-day mineral spring, located halfway between Ft. Meyers and Sarasota. Elevation 10 ft. Open all year.

Mineral water flows out of the ground at 87° into a two-acre private lake and is also piped to a health studio. The lake, which is used for swimming, does not need chlorination because of the volume of flow-through mineral water. The indoor soaking tubs and whirlpool baths are filled with 87° water. The tubs are drained and refilled after each use so that no chemical treatment is needed. Bathing suits are required except in private rooms.

Facilities include sauna, gift shop, post office, bakery and snack bar. Massage, hot pack, medical examinations and rental of nearby apartments are available on the premises. No credit cards are accepted. Phone for rates, reservations and directions.

989 SAFETY HARBOR SPA AND FITNESS CENTER

105 N. Bayshore Dr.
Safety Harbor, FL 34695

1-800-237-0155
PR+MH

An upscale historic spa, recently refurbished, specializing in fitness and beauty programs, located at the west end of Tampa Bay. Elevation 10ft. Open all year.

Natural mineral water flows from four springs at approximately 55º and is piped to several pools and to separate men's and women's bathhouses. Gas is used to heat the water as needed. The six individual soaking tubs in the men's bathhouse are drained and filled after each use so no chemical treatment of the water is necessary. All other pools are treated with chlorine. The courtyard swimming pool, the lap pool, the indoor exercise pool and the ladies pool are maintained at 85º. Two coed hydrojet pools are maintained at 99º and 101º. Bathing suits are not required in bathhouses.

Facilities include fitness center, tennis courts, golf driving range, guest rooms, dining room and conference center. Tennis and golf lessons, excercise classes, medical and nutritional consultation, massage, herbal wraps, Lancome skin care treatment and complete beauty salon services are available on the premises. All facilities and services are reserved for the use of registered guests only. Visa, MasterCard, American Express, and Diners Club are accepted.

Phone for rates, reservations and directions.

Alphabetical Master Index of Mineral Water Locations

This index is designed to help you locate a hot springs or resort listing when you start with the location name. You will find the locations described on the page given for that name.

Within the index the abbreviations listed below are used to identify the state or geographical area followed by the page number where the key map for that state or area will be found.

AB Alberta, Canada / 26
AZ Arizona / 242
BC British Columbia, Canada / 26
CCA Central California / 182
CO Colorado / 142
CS Central States / 268
ID Idaho / 74
MT Montana / 124
NCA Northern California / 168
NM New Mexico / 252
NS Northeast States / 276
NV Nevada / 234
OR Oregon / 52
SCA Southern California / 212
SS Southeast States / 276
UT Utah / 160
WA Washington / 42
WY Wyoming / 132

NUBP Not Usable By the Public
See Page 286

Not Usable By the Public

The index on the preceding pages contains several locations labeled NUBP, with no further information. This means that the location is not open for business, is not accessible to the public or is no longer in existence. Space does not permit including all NUBP locations in this index, but some examples have been listed to convey the fact that they were not simply overlooked. The photographs in this section illustrate the NUBP status of several such locations.

At the beginning of field research for this guidebook we attempted to determine why some of the once-popular commercial hot spring resorts went out of business, but many had been defunct for so long that nobody clearly remembered what happened. If we talked to four different local residents we got four different stories, none of which could be verified. Eventually we concluded that the only significant fact, for the purpose of this book, was that a specific site was no longer usable, regardless of the reason. We decided to let the historians speculate about what happened at those places where we *can't* go, and concentrated on what is presently happening at the places where we *can* go.

▲ When the Park Service took over *Huckleberry Hot Springs* campground from the Forest Service, they bulldozed this pool, leaving only a few small volunteer-built pools.

◆ Agua Caliente springs stopped flowing when new ranch wells began pumping hot water. Giving only traditional hot baths failed to keep *Steamboat Springs* economically viable.

▲ *Lidy Hot Springs* has not reopened since snow collapsed the roof over the swimming pool.

 New owners have trouble surviving when old buildings, such as *Boulder Hot Springs*, cannot meet health department standards.

Gold Fork Hot Spring: Volunteers built this pool on lumber company property. A new owner tore it out but has not built a replacement.